STRENGTHENING
THE WISCONSIN
LEGISLATURE

К

STRENGTHENING
THE WISCONSIN
LEGISLATURE

AN EAGLETON
STUDY AND REPORT

BY ALAN SETH CHARTOCK
and MAX BERKING

PUBLISHED FOR

THE EAGLETON INSTITUTE OF POLITICS

BY

RUTGERS UNIVERSITY PRESS
NEW BRUNSWICK, NEW JERSEY

PREFACE

For Eagleton, the task of proposing reform for the Wisconsin legislature was not an easy one. Wisconsin, with its long and progressive tradition of open government, has a record of self-scrutiny and already leads the nation in terms of governmental innovations. Problems that are confronting other governments in the fifty states have been met and solved in Wisconsin.

As part of its tradition of modernization, Wisconsin is fortunate to have leaders who know that the task of keeping pace with a fast-growing society is a continuous job. Wisconsin's legislature is far advanced, as compared to the legislatures in many other states.

Nevertheless, the legislature has not succeeded in keeping pace with the governor and with state agencies and departments in providing itself with resources most needed to do its job. Wherever the legislature has provided itself with internal resources, this has made a difference in the relationship of the two branches. One respondent for a major bureaucracy in Wisconsin pointed out that wherever the legislature has become more sophisticated, better informed, and better trained, the balance of power between the legislature and state agencies has changed. "As legislators become better in their jobs, there are many more conflicts; they ask better questions," he said. One newspaperman stated that the legislature has become the "stepchild" of the three branches, that its great power has become somewhat diluted. A leader of the minority party states that the situation has become extremely critical, because as a result of a burgeoning bureaucracy, the governor himself is losing control of his own executive family. The president pro tempore of the legislature has noted the increasing impact of policy-making by boards rather than by legislature in Wisconsin.

Legislative leaders in Wisconsin have had the foresight to strive continually to keep pace with governmental innovation. For this reason, this Eagleton study is just one of a number which have been commissioned by the legislature.

In order to conduct its most recent program of self-improvement, the legislature appropriated $120,000, which was matched by $120,000 from the Ford Foundation. This $240,000 was used to strengthen the Wisconsin legislature. In 1962, as part of this Ford program, Paul Mason, author of Mason's *Manual on Legislative Procedure,* was engaged to advise the Wisconsin legislature on its legislative organization and procedure. Mr. Mason's report led to "The Wisconsin Study: Report of the Committee on Legislative Organization and Procedure" (Madison: Legislative Council, January, 1964). Many of the reforms suggested by Mr. Mason led to revision of earlier legislative rules and statutes.

In 1963, Professor W. D. Knight was engaged as a consultant on problems relating to legislative fiscal review. Mr. Knight worked closely with the Committee of Twenty-Five which had been directed to evaluate state government programs and their financing. Professor Knight's findings were incorporated into *The Wisconsin Study: Second Report of the Committee on Legislative Organization and Procedure,* Phase I, Fiscal Review (Madison: Legislative Council, April, 1965). This report was in part responsible for the employment of Dale Cattanach to develop a program of increased fiscal review for the legislature. Subsequently, this group, headed by Mr. Cattanach, became the Legislative Fiscal Committee. In December of 1964 the Joint Organization Committee, as part

of Phase III of their legislative improvement project, authorized one caucus analyst for each of the four house caucuses.
These caucus analysts have proven most useful. As a result,
each caucus staff is much increased. A system of legislative
interns was also established by the legislature as part of
Phase III.

The Eagleton Institute was hired in November, 1966, to
take a further look at legislative improvement for Wisconsin.
Eagleton developed a comprehensive interview schedule which
was administered to a stratified probability sample of the
legislature. The interviewing was done by four doctoral can-
didates from the University of Wisconsin: Marilyn Wennel,
Thomas Fitzpatrick, Lynn Kelly, and David Burks. In all,
Eagleton conducted seventy-four interviews with Wisconsin's
legislators. In addition, Eagleton has viewed the problem from
several other perspectives. In-depth interviews with many
of those persons connected with the legislature were also
conducted. Included in this latter group were lobbyists, jour-
nalists, agency heads, members of the Department of Administration staff, and former legislators.

Eagleton's survey of the legislature showed that legislators
and legislative leaders alike believe that there is still substantial
room for improvement. For example, 70 percent of the members believed that the legislature was doing either only a fair
or poor job of overseeing the agencies of state government.
In addition, 80 percent of the legislators believed that the
legislature was doing less than an excellent job of formulating
new state programs.

By the spring of 1967, the legislature had Assembly Bill
1069 before it. This legislation dealing with legislative modernization, and prepared by Rupert Theobald of the Legislative
Reference Bureau, was an excellent piece of work and had
been developed over a number of years. Eagleton endorsed
the legislation and spelled out those areas it believed could

use some further clarification. The writers have relied on material developed in Assembly Bill 1069. This is because, basically, the bill contains ideas that are now correct for Wisconsin.

After the failure of Bill 1069 in December, 1967, the Joint Committee on Legislative Organization decided that a thorough look at each aspect of the bill was in order. For this reason, four subcommittees of the parent Legislative Organization Committee were appointed. These four bodies were the subcommittees on Permanent Legislative Agencies and Administration, chaired by Assemblyman David O. Martin; Legislative Sessions and Compensation, chaired by Assemblyman David Obey; Ethics and Conflict of Interest, chaired by Senate Assistant Minority Leader Taylor Benson; and Staffing and Committee Procedures, chaired by Senator Robert W. Warren.

Simultaneously, the Joint Committee on Legislative Organization asked Eagleton to work with each of the separate subcommittees. Eagleton agreed, and members of our staff attended most meetings of the subcommittees, presenting their ideas and proposals to the subcommittees as they met. Many of the Eagleton proposals, therefore, come as a result of discussions between the Eagleton staff and members of the committees. Often the reports of the subcommittees and the Eagleton report overlap considerably.

This report is divided into chapters corresponding to the responsibilities of the four subcommittees. The first three chapters on committees, we believe, are the most important. Until the legislature organizes its own elected manpower in the most economical and efficient way, it will have failed to capitalize on its greatest asset. Chapter IV deals with sessions and compensation and gives another suggestion for ways in which the legislature's resources may be more effectively used. Chapters V to VII are concerned with staff services in the

Wisconsin legislature. Chapter VIII deals with the sensitive area of legislative ethics.

In many cases, Eagleton has added supplementary ideas of its own, to broaden the recommendations of the four sub-committees. Nevertheless, the procedure followed by Eagleton in dealing with these four subcommittees represents a departure from former Eagleton studies. In the past Eagleton surveyed the legislature in much the same manner as it did in Wisconsin, but previously, Eagleton staff have not met with legislators regularly in what amounts to working sessions, devoted to specific problems of reform. This procedure was most helpful and has provided additional insights into the Wisconsin legislative process.

Eagleton has never believed that its role is to make recommendations that are not needed, new though they may be. The Wisconsin legislature is moving in the right direction. Certain areas need real strengthening, and Eagleton has addressed itself in depth to those.

One of the authors of this study, Alan Chartock, is responsible for Chapters I through IV, on legislative committees and scheduling. Dr. Chartock, who is Assistant Director of Eagleton's Center for Legislative Research and Service and Assistant Professor of Political Science, previously served as a staff member in the New York State Senate. His co-author, Max Berking, is responsible for Chapters V through VIII, on legislative services and ethics. Mr. Berking, who presently heads an advertising firm, also served in the New York State Senate.

The interview schedule and the research design for the Eagleton study were prepared by Alan Rosenthal, whose over-all direction and knowledge of American legislatures proved invaluable.

Of particular assistance to the authors were the six members of the Joint Committee on Legislative Organization. The two co-chairmen of the latter, Senator Robert Knowles and Speaker Harold Froehlich, were most helpful. We are also grateful for the aid given by the chairmen of the four subcommittees appointed to study legislative improvement—Assemblyman David Martin, Senator Taylor Benson, Senator Robert Warren, and Assemblyman David Obey. Many other members of the legislature and its staff were generous with their time and ideas. Of particular importance were Rupert Theobald, Director of the Legislative Reference Bureau; Earl Sachse, Secretary of the Legislative Council; and Dale Cattanach, Director of the Fiscal Research Bureau.

In addition, the authors wish to thank the entire Eagleton staff, under the direction of Professor Donald Herzberg, for their support. We wish, in particular, to thank Mrs. Edith Saks and Miss Christine Shaw for their coordination, typing, and morale-building during the entire study. We also gratefully acknowledge the support of Miss Karen Osowski, Mrs. Patricia deCandia, and Mrs. Bernice Charwin in the preparation of the manuscript.

It is our hope that this report has some merit and that it can be useful to the people of Wisconsin. The Eagleton Institute has gained immeasurably from this experience.

Alan Seth Chartock
Max Berking

New Brunswick, New Jersey
October, 1968

CONTENTS

PREFACE   v

I. A REORGANIZED COMMITTEE SYSTEM   3
    Parallel Standing Committees Meeting Jointly
    in the Interim, 6. Legislative Council, 7. The
    Case of Change, 9. The Legislative Council
    Board, 11. Advisory Committee, 14. The
    Administrative Subcommittee, 16. Subcom-
    mittees, 18.

II. COMMITTEE JURISDICTION   20
    Individual Committee Responsibilities, 24. As-
    sembly Governmental and Military Affairs,
    24. Assembly Judiciary Committee, 29.
    Senate Committee on Judiciary, Govern-
    mental, and Military Affairs, 29. Assembly
    Committee on Commerce, 29. Assembly
    Committee on Transportation, 30. Senate
    Committee on Commerce and Transporta-
    tion, 30. Assembly Committee on Agricul-
    ture and Consumer Services, 31. Assembly
    Committee on Natural Resources, 31. Sen-
    ate Committee on Agriculture, Consumer
    Services, and Natural Resources, 32. As-
    sembly and Senate Committees on Health
    and Social Services, 33. Assembly Commit-
    tee on Human Resources, 33. Assembly
    Committee on Education, 34. Senate Com-
    mittee on Education and Human Resources,
    34. Assembly and Senate Operations

Boards, 35. The Joint Committee on Finance, 36. Relationship Between Joint Committee on Finance and Other Standing Committees of the Legislature, 37. Subcommittees of the Joint Committee on Finance, 39. Single Committee Consideration of Legislation with Little or No Fiscal Impact, 40. Statutory Committees, 43. Joint Survey Committee on Tax Exemptions, 44. Joint Survey Committee on Retirement Systems, 44. State Building Commission, 45. Board on Government Operations, 46. Council for Home and Family, 46. Commission on Interstate Cooperation, 47. Menominee Indian Study Committee, 49. Committee to Visit State Properties, 49. Commission on Uniform State Laws, 49. The Use of Committees for Governmental Oversight, 50. Administrative Rules, 53.

III. INTERNAL COMMITTEE ORGANIZATION AND RULES   54

Appointment of Committees, 56. Committee Meetings, 57. Committee Hearings, 58. Committee Rules, 62. Discharge of a Committee, 66. Committee Reports, 67. Committee Staffing, 68. Permanent Committee Staff, 69.

IV. LEGISLATIVE SESSIONS AND COMPENSATION   72

Annual Sessions, 72. Biennial or Annual Budgets, 76. Organization of the Session, 78. Problems of Procedure, 85. Air Conditioning, 85. Organization of the Full House Meetings, 85. Proposal for Revised Order of Business, 87. Moving the Previous Question, 89. The Conference, 90. Submission

of Bills, 91. Deadlines, 92. The Consent
Calendar, 92. Legislative Compensation, 93.
Legislative Compensation Council, 97.

V. CENTRALIZATION AND CONTROL OF
    LEGISLATIVE SERVICES   98
Overview, 100. The Case for Centralization,
101. The Governing Boards, 107. The Secretary and the Administrator, 111. Secretary of the Legislature, 112. Administrator
of Services, 114. Division of Services, 117.
Senate and Assembly Divisions, 121. Employees of the Legislature, 123. Categories
of Staff, 124. Centralized Personnel Management, 127. Recruitment and Training of
Staff, 129.

VI. ORGANIZATIONS AND FUNCTIONS OF
     CENTRAL STAFF   132
The Legal Bureau, 132. Bill Drafting, 132.
Bill Analysis, 136. Legal Counseling, 137.
Serving as Parliamentarians, 140. Enrollment of Bills, 141. Reference and Library
Bureau, 141. Research Bureau, 146. Revisor of Statutes Bureau, 149. Fiscal Bureau,
151. Fiscal Review in Wisconsin, 152. Statutory Authority for the Fiscal Bureau, 154.
Assuming the Function of BOGO, 156.
Budget Analysis, 157. Final Budget Report,
160. Revenue Estimating, 160. Relations
with Other Agencies, 160. Looking Ahead,
161. Fiscal Notes, 163. Legislative Audit
Bureau, 169. Frequency of Audit, 171.
Staffing, 172. Direction for the Audit Bureau, 175. Performance Auditing: Definition
and Background, 179. The Problem of
Measurement, 183. Different Approaches to

Performance Auditing, 185. What Kind of
Audit for Wisconsin?, 186. Inter-Agency
Standards, 188. Electronic Data Processing,
188. Internal Audits, 189. Relations with
Fiscal Bureau, 189. An Audit Advisory
Committee, 191.

VII.   SPECIAL NEEDS AND ASSISTANCE   194
Administrative and Secretarial Aid for Legis-
lators, 194. Administrative Aides, 195. Secretarial Help, 196. Caucus Staffs, 198.
Legislative Interns, 200. An Orientation
Program for Legislators, 206. Timing, 208.
Location, 209. The Content of Meetings,
209. Field Trips, 211. A Buddy System,
212. Orientation Manuals, 212. Seminars,
213. Expenses, 213. Public Information,
214. A Transcript of Debate, 219. Committee Minutes, 225.

VIII.   ETHICS AND CONFLICTS OF INTEREST   227
Action in Other States, 231. Legislative Ethics
in Wisconsin, 231. The Benson Subcommit-
tee's Bill and Joint Resolution, 232. Accept-
ance of Gifts and Favors, 234. Special
Privileges, 237. Representation before State
Agencies, 238. Contracts with the State,
241. Use of Inside Information, 244. Inside
Lobbying, 245. A Joint Legislative Ethics
Committee (JLEC), 246. Procedures, 248.
Code of Ethics, 252.

IX.   SUMMARY OF RECOMMENDATIONS   258

STRENGTHENING
THE WISCONSIN
LEGISLATURE

CHAPTER I.

A REORGANIZED
COMMITTEE SYSTEM

The Wisconsin legislature is ready for an integrated system of standing and joint committees to assist it in performing its tasks. The legislature's membership, its leadership, and those who have observed it at close hand all agree on the need for major improvement in the committee system. Eagleton's work in Wisconsin has found evidence of this need at every turn. In the creation of a viable committee system, the Wisconsin legislature has an opportunity, once again, to be a leader in the modernization of state government.

Of the fifty state legislatures in the United States, only a few have anything approaching effective and responsible committee systems. If the membership of the legislature is to participate most effectively, there must be a fair division of labor by which members of both houses may specialize in different subject areas and then pass on their knowledge to other members of the legislature. The committee system constitutes the best way of achieving greater participation on the part of the legislators themselves. According to one majority senator: "At present, it's [the committee system] not as good as it should be because members do not give sincere and individual attention to the work on the committee."

Studies of state legislatures have pointed to the need for more effective committees. The American Assembly recommends "standing committees, few in number, with broad well-defined jurisdictions." The Assembly states that "committees should, as far as possible, reflect the major functions of state government." [1] Alan Rosenthal's Eagleton report, *Strengthening the Maryland Legislature*,[2] makes similar recommendations. Similar reports in Colorado, California, Illinois, Indiana, Louisiana, Massachusetts, Ohio, and other states have called for more effective committee systems.

It is crucial to revamp the committee system in order to rebalance what a Wisconsin legislative leader has termed "a near-critical situation." Legislators believe that there is room for improvement in the operation of standing committees in Wisconsin. Only two out of five of those legislators interviewed in our study believe the standing committees of the Senate and Assembly are very effective.

The Senate majority leader has maintained that the present committee system is not working. He mentioned that "it needs staff, a way to manage it, train it, and train members to use it." [3] One lobbyist has suggested that the single most important recommendation he could make for improving the legislature was for an "improved committee system." This is not surprising. Indeed, the average proportion of working time devoted to committee hearings, meetings, and caucuses reported by legislators is about two-fifths.[4] Despite the fact that committees do not perform as well as they might, there can be no question of the importance of committees, even under the present system. According to one committee chairman: "Unless it's a very controversial issue most senators rely on their [standing committees'] recommendations be-

[1] American Assembly, *Final Report of the 28th American Assembly* (New York: Columbia University Press, 1966), p. 8.

[2] See Alan Rosenthal, *Strengthening the Maryland Legislature* (New Brunswick, N.J.: Rutgers University Press, 1968).

[3] Wisconsin Joint Committee on Legislative Organization, "Minutes," December 11, 1967. (Xerox ed.)

[4] *Wisconsin Committee on Improved Expenditure Management, Report and Recommendations Regarding a Compensation Plan for Legislators* (Madison, August, 1966), p. 3.

cause they have to." Yet the committee system may be getting weaker. A former legislative leader states that "their [committees'] recommendations are no longer followed as they once were when the chairman was the person who knew most about a bill and explained it." Eagleton, of course, does not believe that the chairman should be the only person on the committee with intimate knowledge of the subject matter. Rather, full participation is the key to an effective committee system.

The Wisconsin legislature is a part of a partisan political system. Eagleton believes that this is healthy and provides motivation for both parties to excel. The committee structure should be built in such a way that both parties, majority and minority, have a chance to participate in, contribute to, and benefit from the system. One leader has pointed out that because of the weak committee system, too much time is spent in caucus, which often serves as the only place to get information on particular bills. Eagleton believes that caucus discussions are no substitute for strong standing committees. Committees must develop their ideas in an open manner, ever subject to public scrutiny. Party caucuses are, and should continue to be, closed meetings. As one lobbyist put it: "Things said in the caucus go unchallenged. On the floor, a committee chairman, interpreting a bill, must be responsible—he can be checked there."

The present committee system is unsatisfactory because of (1) overlapping committees; (2) lack of time to consider legislation in depth; (3) lack of pertinent information; (4) lack of staff to assist in committee deliberations; (5) lack of clarity of committee jurisdictions; (6) the unequal allocation of power and responsibility among committees; (7) the almost complete lack of committee oversight of administrative agencies; (8) the lack of fair representation on many committees;

(9) the uneconomical and disorganized ways in which committees hold public hearings and report out bills; and (10) the ineffective use of committee members.

In order to meet the problems of Wisconsin's committee structure, Eagleton believes that there are definite directions in which to proceed. The number of committees must be reduced and made parallel where possible in both houses. They should be given specific jurisdiction and committees should continue on a year-round basis.

PARALLEL STANDING COMMITTEES MEETING JOINTLY IN THE INTERIM

In the fifty states today, only a few state legislatures have adopted a system of standing committees which continues to operate after the legislature itself has adjourned its session. Instead, approximately two-thirds of the states have a legislative council or some similar mechanism which is responsible for the conduct of interim studies. The Wisconsin legislature has reached the point where the legislative council is no longer a satisfactory device for the organization and management of work between legislative sessions. Changes need to be made, although a number of the important features of the council system should be retained.

This may be demonstrated by the fact that, according to Eagleton's survey data, legislators are more critical of Wisconsin's Legislative Council than they are of other legislative institutions. Whereas only from one-fifth to one-third of the members criticized the effectiveness of party leaders and party caucuses and the Legislative Fiscal Bureau and Legislative Reference Bureau, as many as 56 percent questioned the effectiveness of the Legislative Council, and, despite the fact that legislators are critical of the job being done by standing committees, they are virtually unanimous in their belief that standing committees should be doing interim work. In fact, over two-thirds believe that standing committees of the legislature should take over the investigative job now being performed by committees of the Legislative Council.

LEGISLATIVE COUNCIL

Although the staff work of the Legislative Council is treated at length elsewhere in this report, we will deal here with the Council membership as it has operated in the interim session. The Council was created in 1947. It was designed to give careful study and consideration to problems facing the citizens of Wisconsin.

The Legislative Council was to operate during the interim and report results of its studies to the legislature. This arrangement has compared favorably with the previous arrangement whereby ad hoc committees, consisting of legislative and public members, were appointed to study different problems. The principal failing of that arrangement was the lack of coordination of interim studies. Each time a new study committee was appointed, it had to start from the beginning. In addressing itself to this problem, the Council attempted to coordinate all interim legislative studies. Problems, as they arose, have been referred to the Council by joint resolution or by the passage of a law. In many instances, the Legislative Council has sponsored legislation itself. Council committees have been established in different areas, such as mental health, education, and insurance law revision. After submission of committee reports, the full Council has decided whether to approve or reject the finished product. Those which have been approved are submitted to the legislature in bill form. In addition, Legislative Council committees may ask the Legislative Council for permission to study a matter. The secretary of the Council has reported that such permission is "invariably granted." He states that in the past, 95 percent of the assignments to Council committees have come directly from the legislature and the remaining 5 percent from the Council itself.

The membership of the Council has grown over the years. Initially, the Council was composed of twelve members. Subsequently, the membership was increased to fifteen legislators. In 1966 the legislature increased the number to nineteen. Of these members, eleven are ex officio and eight are appointed from the membership of the legislature. The ex-officio members include six members of the Joint Committee on Legislative Organization, the speaker pro tempore of the Assembly, the two co-chairmen of the Joint Committee on Finance, and the ranking minority member from each house on the Joint Committee on Finance. Of the eight additional legislators who are appointed, five are assemblymen and three are senators. The Council is organized in such a way that each of the ten congressional districts in Wisconsin has at least one representative on the Legislative Council. In order to perform its duties, the Council appoints a series of substantive committees which consist of senators, assemblymen, and public members.

In the past, one of the major tasks of the Council's committees and staff has been in a particular subject area, that of the preparation of major revision and recodification of bills. Revision, in this sense, is the making of substantive policy changes. The staff of the Legislative Council reports that there has been a high percentage of legislative success for major recodification and revisions. According to the Council secretary, there has been very little change on the floor when these recodifications have been introduced. Respondents have cited the revision of the children's code and the criminal code as examples of the excellent recodification work performed by the Legislative Council committees.

Legislative Council committees have been bipartisan in composition. In the past, each Legislative Council committee has been assisted by public members, composed of experts and interested individuals. Public members have had the same vote within the committee as legislative members. Sometimes the outcome of the legislation submitted by the committee has been defeat, because of a difference in philosophy of government between the members of the committee and the total legislature. The argument has been made, and Eagleton agrees, that the majority party should have control of interim committees as they do of standing committees. The majority has been elected to office and is responsible to the electorate for legislative actions during its incumbency. It should therefore have the tools it needs to achieve its program. In Eagleton's opinion, this change will strengthen responsible party government.

THE CASE FOR CHANGE

Despite the fact that the Legislative Council has made countless contributions to Wisconsin government, the time has come for change. In the first place, the interim period during which legislative committees have been operating has been steadily decreasing. Wisconsin is one of seven states which has split the regular sessions into alternate sittings and recesses. Since 1959 every Wisconsin legislature has had at least four session periods. The result of this change in sessions has been the decrease in interim time during which the Legislative Council's committees operate.

Another major problem concerns continuity between the interim Legislative Council committees and the standing committees. Because membership often differs, present interim committees may not have much influence in the next legislative session. Recognizing this fact, in 1967 sixty-seven cosigners of Assembly Resolution 22 proposed the establishment of standing committees operating on a continuing basis. If the Assembly were to adopt such a proposal, Legislative Council committees probably would not survive. With the demise of the Legislative Council, the task of conducting in-depths studies, investigation, and policy reviews will fall to the standing committees, joined together in the interim.

Eagleton believes that joint committees, composed of members of both houses, operating in the interim, will be more satisfactory than separate standing committees of the Assembly and Senate operating independently of each other. As in the case of the Legislative Council, assemblymen and senators will be able to serve together, both houses will be able to pool their staff and advisory committee resources for greatest efficiency, and committee manpower can be channeled into subcommittees in order to accomplish in-depth research. In order to allow the committees of both houses to form joint interim committees it will be essential that parallel committees in both houses be established.

The standing committees themselves will concentrate on reviewing the legislation which the previous interim committee has proposed and which is proposed by individual members of either house. They will recommend major studies growing out of the submission of legislation to their committee. In addition, by operating on a year-round basis, the members of each committee should develop expertise in their subject areas.

A citizen who wishes to initiate legislative research in a particular area could get in touch with either a specific joint committee chairman or the Legislative Council Board. This gives the citizen two opportunities to request a study, whereas in the past if the Legislative Council denied a request, there were few other alternatives. Therefore, Eagleton recommends that:

(1) *The Legislative Council, as presently constituted, be abolished, and the functions of Council committees be taken over by parallel standing committees which operate jointly during interim periods.*

THE LEGISLATIVE COUNCIL BOARD

If the legislature adopts a series of standing committees operating jointly in the interim, there must be a coordinating mechanism to replace the Legislative Council. With a series of standing committees operating during and between actual sessions of the full legislature, there will be a need for a strong continuing agency which will oversee the legislature's managerial and policy-making operations. The coordinating mechanism for each house will be the Assembly and Senate Operations Boards. It will be the responsibility of these boards to oversee the work of committees within their respective houses. It will fall to the Legislative Council Board, composed of the members of the Operations Boards, to coordinate the work of the full legislature including the work of the proposed joint interim committees.

It is essential that the task of coordinating the work of the legislature not be divided between different bodies. For this reason, certain committees which have been operating up to this time, such as the committees on contingent expenditures, should be abolished and their powers vested in the Assembly and Senate Operations Boards and the Legislative Council Board.

There are dangers in establishing interim committees: some may be more diligent than others; some committee chairmen will delegate responsibility to other members; some committees will act as spokesmen for their parallel executive agency; some committees may undertake witch hunts; some committees may seek headlines; and some committees may prove arbitrary and vindictive. These abuses can be avoided.

If this is to be the case, there must be an agency of the legislature which will help to prevent abuse. This agency should be composed of the legislative leadership and should be ready and able to exercise control whenever necessary. It is on this leadership committee's shoulders that the success or failure of the new system will depend.

The Legislative Council Board should be composed of ten members. These will include the speaker of the Assembly, the president pro tempore of the Senate, the Senate majority leader, the Senate minority leader, the Assembly majority leader, the Assembly minority leader, the Senate assistant majority leader, the Assembly assistant majority leader, the Senate assistant minority leader, and the Assembly assistant minority leader.

This structure differs from the present ex-officio membership of the Joint Legislative Council in that members of the Finance Committee are excluded, while the assistant leaders of both houses are included. Eagleton, as well as many legislators and most leaders, believes that this board should be composed of the leadership elected by both houses.

Senator Robert Knowles, in his efforts to upgrade the Wisconsin legislature, has consistently called for the implementation of a planning arm for research and development problems of the legislature. The Legislative Council Board will assume the important role of a "policy-planning arm" of the legislative leadership. This is because there will be a need or certainly a use for a function of long-range planning, long-range research, or long-range policy formulation that should be carried out by the joint leadership. It will be the responsibility of the leadership to rule on the jurisdiction of each committee, in such a way as to define the subject matter and to determine the scope of inquiry by each committee. Furthermore, it will be the responsibility of the Legislative Council Board, in the case of interim committees, and of the Senate and Assembly Operations Boards, in the case of standing committees, to assign studies which the individual committee leadership requests, or which the Board itself believes the committee should undertake. Therefore, Eagleton recommends that:

(2) *A ten-member Legislative Council Board be created, composed of the speaker of the Assembly, the president pro tempore of the Senate, the Senate majority leader, the Senate minority leader, the Assembly majority leader, the Assembly minority leader, the Senate assistant majority leader, the Assembly assistant majority leader, the Senate assistant minority leader, and the Assembly assistant minority leader;*

(3) *The Legislative Council Board be responsible for the supervision of joint legislative services, the coordination of studies and investigations of joint legislative committees, and the development every two years of a long-range plan for the legislature which will spell out specific priorities for the legislature during that period;* and

(4) *It be the responsibility of the Assembly and Senate Operations Boards to coordinate the activities of the standing committees of each house.*

In order to facilitate interim committee coordination by the Legislative Council Board, Eagleton recommends that:

(5) *Each joint committee present separate budgets for its regular expenses and for special study, expenses to be approved by the Legislative Council Board, and each standing committee follow the same procedure in its relationship with the house Operations Board to whom it reports;*

(6) Each standing committee be required to go before the Operations Board of its house for allocations of staff, monies, and the necessary jurisdiction required for each new study. When a joint committee, operating mainly in interim, between sessions, undertakes a study, it should be up to the Legislative Council Board to supply these resources. In order to co-ordinate staff resources between the two houses, each house's Operations Board should act in its capacity as a subcommittee of the Legislative Council Board; and

(7) Each standing committee supply to its Operations Board a report every month of its activity and planned agenda. Interim committees should do the same with respect to the Legislative Council Board.

ADVISORY COMMITTEE

Perhaps the most valuable aspect of the Legislative Council, since its inception, has been its ability to recruit top-notch citizen members and experts to serve on its committees as public members. It can be demonstrated that millions of dollars of free expertise have been supplied to the legislature in this manner. This system also has given organized interest groups a channel in which to operate in areas of concern, quite different from the subterfuge into which lobbyists in other states are often forced.

Most important, public membership has afforded the opportunity for constructive participation by citizens in legislative affairs. This has contributed greatly to citizen understanding of the legislative process, as well as to legislative proposals for solving state problems. It is important that standing committees of both houses utilize the knowledge of the advisory committees. For this reason, advisory committees should be appointed to serve each joint committee during the interim and the parallel standing committees of the two houses during the actual legislative session.

Members of advisory committees should be appointed on the recommendation of the administrative subcommittee of each joint committee. As was the custom of the Legislative Council, the advisory committee membership should be composed of the most informed people in a particular area. If particular problems arise which require the attention of specialized ad hoc or advisory groups, the Legislative Council Board should, on the advice of the administrative subcommittees, or particular interim committees, appoint special advisory groups to help these committees with problems, legislation, and investigations.

Advisory committees on a particular problem should report to the subcommittee or to the particular committee to whom it was appointed. The full legislative committee should consider the report of the advisory committee and then draft its own report for the Legislative Council Board in the case of interim committees, or for the individual house in the case of standing committees. In fact, one complaint voiced to Eagleton's staff by public participants on Legislative Council committees is that the advisory committees tend to formulate proposals without sufficient political advice. Under a standing committee system, it is quite likely that political factors will combine with the technical and expert formulation of proposals at an earlier stage, and proposals advanced by the advisory committees will, therefore, have a better chance of realization.

Citizen members should be allowed to participate in committee matters related to subjects which they are considering. Otherwise, there might be a tendency to relegate advisory committees to a "window-dressing" status. Advisory committee members should vote on whether or not to submit legislative proposals to the full standing committee for consideration.

Eagleton disagrees with the provision of the 1967 Assembly Bill 1069 which makes mandatory the assignment of at least one member of the parent committee to the advisory committee. In cases in which interim committees and standing committees have invited advisory members to participate in a particular matter, the members of the advisory committees may participate in the proceedings of the parent committee.

In summary, Eagleton recommends that:

(8) *The Legislative Council Board be responsible for appointing a five-member advisory committee for each legislative committee, to serve during the term of the legislature;*

(9) *Advisory committees to interim committees also serve as advisory committees to component Assembly and Senate committees;*

(10) *Legislative members not formally be members of the advisory committee itself, since it is assumed that the members of the committee and the advisory committee will work with the legislative members throughout the life of the advisory committee; and*

(11) *Advisory groups be permitted to vote on whether or not to recommend a proposal to their parent committees, but have no power to vote with legislative committee members on whether or not to introduce bills to the legislature.*

THE ADMINISTRATIVE SUBCOMMITTEE

Eagleton agrees with proposals for an administrative subcommittee on each standing committee, composed of the chairman, vice-chairman, and ranking minority member. As in the past, the chairman's views should be highly regarded on all matters brought before the committee. Because of the party control of both the full committee and its administrative subcommittee this will continue to be the case. One major responsibility of the chairman should be for recommending majority appointments to subcommittees of the full committee. Similarly, the views of the ranking minority member of the committee should be considered in the selection of members of the minority for service on different subcommittees. This will prepare the ranking minority members on committees for the responsibility of leadership in the event that the minority is transformed into the majority.

Eagleton believes that if the administrative subcommittee is to function effectively it must have specific duties. Although the chairman of each committee will quite obviously play the major role in the direction of each committee, the administrative subcommittee should, by majority vote, ratify all decisions relating to scheduling of bills, hearings, research and investigations undertaken by the committee. This arrangement, we feel, will encourage maximum participation by all members of standing and joint committees.

Eagleton recommends that:

(12) *An administrative subcommittee be organized for every standing and interim committee;* and

(13) *The administrative subcommittee plan, schedule, and facilitate the work load of joint and standing committees; select and request staff in conjunction with the Legislative Council Board; and be responsible for the appointment of subcommittees, and in the case of minority members, the views of the ranking minority member should be weighed heavily.*

SUBCOMMITTEES

If committees are to utilize the membership of the legislature in an effective and economical manner, subcommittees of each standing and joint committee should be established. This arrangement has worked well in the United States Congress. Subcommittees have been given major responsibilities and have proved themselves time and again through hearings, investigations, and the preparation of major legislation. In addition, the creation of subcommittees will provide more opportunities for leadership by individual members than presently exist.

Subcommittees should report to the full committee. In order to best utilize valuable hearing time, subcommittees of both houses considering similar legislation should hold joint hearings whenever possible. Although Eagleton has recommended that the administrative subcommittee of each full committee appoint subcommittee members, it is our feeling that a transitional arrangement would be helpful. During the transition (one or two legislative sessions), the two house Operations Boards should be asked to appoint the members of specified subcommittees of standing committees. The Legislative Council Board would serve the same function for the joint interim committees.

The chairman of each committee, standing or joint, should serve as an ex-officio member of each subcommittee. This will strengthen the concept of the chairman as coordinator of subcommittee activities. It will assist the chairman in his planning, connected with each of the subcommittees of the full committee. It is also important that the chairman of each subcommittee be free from other committee assignments.

Eagleton recommends that:

(14) *Each of the standing committees in the two houses be encouraged to establish subcommittees, which would be responsible for subject areas selected by the administrative subcommittee of the full committee;*

(15) *The chairman of the full committee be an ex-officio member of all subcommittees;*

(16) *Subcommittees be authorized, with the approval of the administrative subcommittee, to hold hearings and write reports for the consideration of the full committee;* and

(17) *Because of the demands which will be made on the subcommittee chairman, no person serving as a subcommittee chairman be assigned to more than one subcommittee.*

CHAPTER II.

COMMITTEE JURISDICTION

If the committee system is to function effectively, there must be a limited number of committees which can be staffed, manned, and funded with the resources available to the Wisconsin legislature.

According to an American Assembly report: "State legislatures should not permit the unhealthy proliferation of standing committees. The optimum number of committees is somewhere between ten and fifteen, and serious efforts should be exerted to keep down the number of committee assignments each legislator is asked to shoulder." [1] In Wisconsin the number of standing committees has declined over the past two decades. Still, there are presently twenty-five standing committees in the Assembly and thirteen in the Senate, as is indicated in Table 1. This is approximately twice the number that is necessary. Eagleton recommends that:

(18) *There be established eleven standing committees in the Assembly and seven standing committees in the Senate.*

Once committees are established, legislation, studies, and investigations should be assigned to them and a firm rule should be established that special committees functioning on an ad hoc basis should not be appointed. The committee system that is suggested can cover all contingencies. Once proliferation of committees occurs, the system becomes diffused and weakened. Any progress achieved by the reduction of

[1] American Assembly, "Our State Legislature: Prospects and Prob-

TABLE 1. EXISTING STANDING COMMITTEES OF THE ASSEMBLY AND SENATE

Assembly	Senate
Agriculture	Agriculture
Assembly Organization	Committee on Committees
Commerce and Manufacturers	Conservation
Conservation	Education
Contingent Expenditures	Finance, Joint Committee on
Education	Governmental and Veterans'
Elections	Affairs
Engrossed Bills	Highways
Enrolled Bills	Interstate Cooperation
Excise and Fees	Judiciary
Finance, Joint Committee on	Labor, Taxation, Insurance,
Highways	and Banking
Insurance and Banking	Legislative Procedure
Judiciary	Public Welfare
Labor	Senate Organization
Municipalities	
Printing	
Public Welfare	
Revision	
Rules	
State Affairs	
Taxation	
Third Reading	
Transportation	
Veterans' and Military Affairs	

SOURCE: *The Assembly Manual of the Wisconsin Legislature* (Madison, 1967), pp. 1–40, 22.

committees might collapse. If emphasis is need to dramatize a particular problem, the leadership may always exercise the option of appointing an advisory committee to a standing or interim committee.

Eagleton believes that there should be an over-all scheme for establishing committee jurisdiction. Once that scheme is

lems" (paper delivered at an American Asssembly Conference held at Tulane University, Baton Rouge, La., on January 26–29, 1967), p. 12.

established, it ought to be adhered to wherever possible by the leadership and by the members of the legislature. Eagleton recommends that:

(19) *Major legislation, affecting a particular program, be sent by the presiding officers in each house, first to the legislative committee, under whose jurisdiction the legislation properly falls and then, if necessary, to the Finance Committee; each piece of legislation be accompanied by a recommendation of the standing committee to which it was first referred; and the Finance Committee take the recommendation of the substantive committee into consideration.*

In the case of the Wisconsin legislature, a clear rationale for committee organization presently exists. As a result of the report by the Kellett Committee (Temporary Reorganization Committee), the state government during the past year has been reorganized on a thoughtful and functional basis. If the legislature is to oversee state government adequately, it should establish a similar pattern of jurisdiction. This would mean that departments will fall within the purview of a single committee. Consequently, committee members will have the opportunity to get a total picture of the plans and programs of a particular department or agency. This would fit in with the program budget and performance audit plans upon which Wisconsin has already embarked. Support for this proposal comes from all elements of legislative staff and membership. Therefore, Eagleton recommends that:

(20) *In the Assembly there be established, in addition to the Operations Board, standing committees on: (1) Finance; (2) Governmental and Military Affairs; (3) Judiciary; (4) Commerce; (5) Transportation; (6) Agriculture and Consumer Services; (7) Natural Resources; (8) Health and Social*

Services; (9) Human Resources; and (10) Education; and in the Senate there be established, in addition to the Operations Board, standing committees on: (1) Finance; (2) Judiciary, Governmental, and Military Affairs; (3) Commerce and Transportation; (4) Agriculture, Consumer Services, and Natural Resources; (5) Health and Social Services; and (6) Education and Human Resources.

The proposed arrangement of the two systems, seen on Table 2, is structured in such a way that one or more Assembly committees will mirror one Senate committee. The Senate committee name will also be the name of the joint interim committee. Table 3 shows the joint interim committees proposed for the Wisconsin legislature and in Table 4 the jurisdictions of each of the proposed committees are spelled out.

TABLE 2.   PROPOSED STANDING COMMITTEES
OF ASSEMBLY AND SENATE

Assembly	Senate
Finance	Finance
Governmental and Military Affairs / Judiciary	Judiciary, Governmental, and Military Affairs
Commerce / Transportation	Commerce and Transportation
Agriculture and Consumer Services / Natural Resources	Agriculture, Consumer Services, and Natural Resources
Health and Social Services	Health and Social Services
Human Resources / Education	Education and Human Resources
Assembly Operations Board	Senate Operations Board

TABLE 3. PROPOSED JOINT INTERIM COMMITTEES

Finance
Judiciary, Governmental, and Military Affairs
Commerce and Transportation
Education and Human Resources
Agriculture, Consumer Services, Natural Resources
Health and Social Services
Legislative Council Board

INDIVIDUAL COMMITTEE RESPONSIBILITIES [2]

The Finance Committee has traditionally been the most important committee in both houses. It has considered nearly all legislation of major importance. It has had an overpowering relationship with the other committees of the Senate and Assembly. The responsibilities of the Finance Committee over the past reorganization will, therefore, be discussed after we have examined the other committees.

Assembly Governmental and Military Affairs

This committee should concern itself with two main areas. The first of these is intragovernmental and intergovernmental legislation. In addition, it should be responsible for legislation relating to veterans' affairs. In its responsibilities for governmental activities, the committee should have jurisdiction over legislation affecting urban affairs, local and regional planning, economic development, tourism, annexation, plan review, emergency government, and exposition activities. The committee should also be responsible for overseeing all grant-in-aid programs which are offered by the federal and state governments and for acting as a coordinator between the federal government and the individual substantive committees with

[2] In formulating the following sections, we have relied heavily on the recommendations proposed by the Temporary Reorganization Committee (referred to in the future as the Kellett Committee) of the Wisconsin Legislature, January, 1967. (Xeroxed.)

TABLE 4. JURISDICTION OF PROPOSED STANDING COMMITTEES AS THEY WILL CORRESPOND TO STATE GOVERNMENTAL UNITS

Assembly	Unit	Senate
FINANCE	(1) Dept. of Administration (2) Dept. of Revenue	*FINANCE*
GOVERNMENTAL AND MILITARY AFFAIRS	(1) Dept. of Employment Trust Fund (2) Dept. of Local Affairs and Development (3) Dept. of Military Affairs (4) Dept. of Veterans' Affairs (5) Great Lakes Compact Commission (6) Minnesota–Wisconsin Boundary Area Commission (7) Mississippi River Parkway Planning Commission	*JUDICIARY, GOVERNMENTAL, AND MILITARY AFFAIRS*
JUDICIARY	(8) Dept. of Justice (9) Bd. of State Bar Commissioners (10) Court Administrator	

TABLE 4 (continued)

Assembly	Unit	Senate
	(11) Judicial Council	
	(12) State Law Library	
	(13) Public Defender	
	(14) Supreme Court	
COMMERCE	(1) Office of the Commissioner of Banking	COMMERCE AND TRANS- PORTATION
	(2) Grain and Warehouse Commission	
	(3) Investment Board	
	(4) Office of the Commissioner of Insurance	
	(5) Office of the Commissioner of Savings and Loan	
	(6) Office of the Commissioner of Securities	
TRANSPORTATION	(7) Dept. of Transportation	
AGRICULTURE AND CONSUMER SERVICES	(1) Dept. of Agriculture	AGRICULTURE, CONSUMER SERVICES, AND NATURAL RESOURCES
	(2) Dept. of Regulation and Licensing	
NATURAL RESOURCES	(3) Dept. of Natural Resources	

TABLE 4 (continued)

Assembly	Unit	Senate
HEALTH AND SOCIAL SERVICES	(1) Dept. of Health and Social Services	*HEALTH AND SOCIAL SERVICES*
HUMAN RESOURCES	(1) Dept. of Industry, Labor, and Human Relations	*EDUCATION AND HUMAN RESOURCES*
	(2) Employment Relations Commission	
EDUCATION	(3) Dept. of Public Instruction	
	(4) Higher Educational Aids Boards	
	(5) Coordinating Committee for Higher Education	
	(6) Historical Society	
	(7) Board of Regents of State Universities	
	(8) University of Wisconsin	
	(9) Board of Vocational, Technical and Adult Education	
ASSEMBLY OPERATIONS BOARDS		*SENATE OPERATIONS BOARDS*

responsibility for a particular grant-in-aid program. For example, in the Assembly notice of an education program passed by the Congress would be sent to the Education Committee by the Governmental and Military Affairs Committee after it had received notice of such a program. The Education Committee would then assume responsibility for the program. Eagleton makes recommendation elsewhere in this report for a federal liaison office in Washington, which is funded either completely by Wisconsin or whose funding or financing is shared with other states. It will report to the Governmental and Military Affairs Committee in the Assembly and to the Judiciary Committee in the Senate. Eagleton recommends that:

(21) *A subcommittee of the Assembly Governmental and Military Affairs Committee, known as the Governmental Subcommittee, be established, and that members of this subcommittee be among the legislative members of the newly named Commission on Intergovernmental Relations.*

Continuity from the committees of both houses to the commission will be assured by having the membership overlap between the committees and the commission. Eagleton recommends that:

(22) *A second subcommittee of the full Governmental and Military Affairs Committee be established. We recommend that it be known as the Military Affairs Subcommittee. It will be the responsibility of this committee to oversee the Departments of Military Affairs and Veterans' Affairs. This subcommittee shall be responsible for legislation relating to national guard units, air defense, state armories, operation of veteran homes, housing loans to veterans, rehabilitation loans*

to veterans, education grants to veterans, and advisor service to veterans.

Assembly Judiciary Committee

The Assembly Judiciary Committee, traditionally one of the major committees of the legislature, will continue to concern itself with those subjects which have traditionally come under its purview. These include the legislation pertaining to the attorney general, courts, impeachment, legal services, criminal investigation, beverage and gambling, and law enforcement. Eagleton recommends that:

(23) *The establishment of subcommittees of the Assembly Judiciary Committee on the courts and on law enforcement.*

Senate Committee on Judiciary, Governmental, and Military Affairs

This committee will have the responsibility for that subject matter within the purview of the Governmental and Military Affairs Committee and of the Judiciary Committee in the Assembly. Eagleton recommends that:

(24) *There be two subcommittees of the Senate Committee on Judiciary, Governmental, and Military affairs—one known as the Judiciary Subcommittee and one known as the Governmental and Military Affairs Subcommittee.*

Assembly Committee on Commerce

This committee will be responsible for those problems relating to industry, labor, banking, insurance, securities, fraternal benefit societies, gas, electric, water, telephone company (except taxes, which go to Finance), and all matters related to alcoholic beverages (except for fees and taxes, which remain with Finance, and alcoholism, which will remain with the Committee on Health and Social Services). Eagleton recommends that:

(25) *The Assembly Committee on Commerce be divided into two subcommittees: one on insurance, banking, and business and the other on labor.*

Assembly Committee on Transportation

The Assembly Committee on Transportation should have within its jurisdiction matters relating to highway and bridge construction and maintenance, highway aids, vehicle registration, driver licensing, traffic safety, motor vehicle enforcement, airport development, motor carrier and railroad regulation. The committee will oversee the activities of the Department of Transportation. Eagleton recommends that:

(26) *The Assembly Committee on Transportation be divided into two subcommittees: one on highway and motor vehicles and the other on public transportation, which will include other modes of transportation outside of motor vehicles.*

Senate Committee on Commerce and Transportation

This committee will have jurisdiction over those matters covered by the Assembly Committees on Commerce and Transportation. Eagleton recommends that:

(27) *The Senate Committee on Commerce and Transportation establish two subcommittees: one on transportation and the other on commerce.*

Assembly Committee on Agriculture and Consumer Services

Most of the services relating to consumers in the state of Wisconsin are presently within the jurisdiction of the Department of Agriculture. Although there is some thought that this function should be kept entirely with the attorney general, Eagleton believes until such time as the legislature decides to do so by law, there should be a single committee on agriculture and consumer services. This committee will have jurisdiction over consumer protection, meat and poultry inspection, animal disease and plant pest eradication, economic and consumer services, dairy plan security, food and drink regulation. The committee shall also have responsibility for over-all program review over the Department of Regulation and Licensing. However, insofar as possible, standing committees with responsibilities for particular functional areas of government should oversee licensing in their jurisdictional areas. Eagleton recommends that:

(28) *There be two subcommittees of the Assembly Committee on Agriculture and Consumer Services; the Agriculture Subcommittee and the Consumer Affairs Subcommittee.*

The Consumer Affairs Subcommittee would have jurisdiction over those matters relating to the Department of Regulation and Licensing, except for those licensing functions relating to chiropractors, dentists, doctors, nurses, optometrists, pharmacists, and veterinarians, which should come under the scope of the Health and Social Services Committee.

Assembly Committee on Natural Resources

This committee would deal with those matters in the sphere of the Department of Conservation and Natural Resources. Subjects included in its jurisdiction would be parks and outdoor recreation, wild life management, forest protection and management, water management and regulation, air pollution control, land management, conservation youth camps, natural beauty, and law enforcement as it relates to conservation and natural resources. Eagleton recommends:

(29) *The establishment of two subcommittees of the full Assembly Committee on Natural Resources: one dealing with conservation and the other with natural resources.*

Senate Committee on Agriculture, Consumer Services, and Natural Resources

Eagleton recommends that:

(30) *The Senate Committee on Agriculture, Consumer Services, and Natural Resources be divided into three subcommittees: Agriculture, Consumer Services, and Natural Resources.*

The Agriculture Subcommittee would consider those agricultural matters already described in the previous section detailing the duties of the Assembly Committee on Agriculture and Consumer Services.

The Subcommittee on Consumer Services would have responsibility for those matters within the jurisdiction of the Department of Agriculture which related to consumer services, and the Subcommittee on Conservation and Natural Resources would be responsible for the matters which are presently within the jurisdiction of the Department of Natural Resources and which are detailed with the duties on the Assembly Committee on Natural Resources.

Assembly and Senate Committees on Health and Social Services

These committees would have responsibility for public health services, corrections, mental health, family services, children and youth, vocational rehabilitation, social services for the blind, deaf, and aging, community social services, and public assistance. Eagleton recommends that:

(31) *The Assembly and Senate Committees on Health and Social Services be divided into three subcommittees: Health, Mental Health, and Social Services.*

The Health Subcommittee will have responsibility for environmental sanitation, preventive medicine, community health services, and those activities undertaken by the Division of Health.

The Subcommittee on Mental Health will have jurisdiction over those matters relating to the activities of the Division of Mental Hygiene and over the activities of those agencies dealing with children and youth, corrections, and vocational rehabilitation.

The Subcommittee on Social Services would deal with social services for the blind, deaf, and aging, community social services, public assistance, and family services.

Assembly Committee on Human Resources

This committee would deal with problems of labor and human relations and all matters falling within the purview of the Department of Labor and Human Relations. Eagleton recommends that:

(32) *The Assembly Committee on Human Resources be divided into a Subcommittee on Labor which would have*

*jurisdiction over matters related to industrial safety, building
plan review, workmen's compensation, apprenticeship program, fair labor standards, employment service, and unemployment compensation; and a Subcommittee on Human
Relations dealing with problems of equal opportunities and
human rights throughout the state structure.*

Assembly Committee on Education

Eagleton recommends that:

(33) *The Assembly Committee on Education be divided
into a Subcommittee on Higher Education and a Subcommittee on Elementary, Secondary, and Special Education.*

The Subcommittee on Higher Education should consider
matters relating to post-high-school education and vocational, technical, and adult education. The Subcommittee on
Elementary, Secondary, and Special Education would deal
with matters relating to public instruction. These would include supervision, school aids (in conjunction with the Finance Committee), library services, school for the blind,
deaf, and handicapped children, and teacher certification.

Senate Committee on Education and Human Resources

Eagleton recommends that:

(34) *The Senate Committee on Education and Human
Resources be divided into two subcommittees: one on education and one on human resources.*

The Education Subcommittee would deal with the functions already delegated to the Assembly Subcommittees on
Higher Education and Elementary, Secondary, and Special

Education. The Human Resources Subcommittee would assume the duties already enumerated for the Assembly Subcommittees on Labor and Human Relations.

Assembly and Senate Operations Boards

Eagleton believes that leadership is a full-time job. For this reason, all leadership functions relating to the operation of both houses should be centralized in the Senate and Assembly Operations Boards. In the Assembly, the Operations Board should consist of the speaker, the majority and minority leaders, and the assistant leaders of both parties. In the Senate, the Operations Board should consist of the president pro tempore and the majority and minority leaders. The inclusion of the assistant leaders on the Operations Boards would provide more members and therefore more deliberations on specific issues and might discourage hastily arrived at decisions. In addition, the inclusion of the assistant leader on the Board should allow for a broader-based representation of both houses.

In the past, the Assembly has had a number of committees performing what Eagleton considers to be leadership functions (Committees on Contingent Expenditures, Engrossed Bills, Enrolled Bills, Printing, Revision, Rules, and Third Reading). Eagleton believes these functions should be combined into the Operations Boards in both houses. To a great extent, this has been done previously in the Senate. It is time the change occurred in the Assembly. Eagleton recommends that:

(35) *The Assembly Operations Board consist of the speaker, the majority and minority leaders, and the assistant leaders of both parties; and the Senate Operations Board consist of the president pro tempore, the majority and minority leaders, and the assistant leaders of both parties;* and

(36) *As a leadership committee, the Assembly Operations Board should assume the functions of the committees on contingent expenditures, engrossed bills, enrolled bills, printing, revision, rules, and third reading.*

THE JOINT COMMITTEE ON FINANCE

The Joint Committee on Finance is the most important committee in the legislature. In the view of most members we surveyed, the Joint Committee on Finance is now performing very effectively. In relation to the present standing committees of the legislature, it is overpowering. The need for such a finance committee is obvious. There must be a coordinating structure for the financing of that legislation which has been proposed by the substantive standing committee.

Eagleton believes that the Joint Committee on Finance could be strengthened still further and perform even more effectively as a legislative coordinating mechanism. For this reason, we endorse the intent of Assembly Bill 1069 to transfer certain duties of the Board of Government Operations to the Joint Committee on Finance.

The Joint Committee on Finance presently has the responsibility for formulating revenue and expenditure programs for the state and of reviewing the executive budget. The problem that occurs is that its very existence detracts from the meaning of standing committees, since almost all legislation has implications for finance. The Joint Committee on Finance, in effect, makes all legislative decisions. If other committees are to survive, there must be a more adequate division of responsibility between the substantive standing committees and the Joint Committee on Finance.

Relationship Between the Joint Committee on Finance and Other Standing Committees of the Legislature

The United States Congress, with its authorization and appropriations committees presents one of the most effective models for state legislatures. The authorizing and appropriating committees of Congress, with specialized staff and research facilities, have been able to initiate legislation and investigate executive performance. Thus, the federal bureaucracy and the President have become more and more aware of the existence and oversight of the Congress. Eagleton does not believe that Wisconsin should imitate the Congress to the letter in strengthening its committee system. Nevertheless, a method should be devised whereby standing committees, as well as the finance committees, have the opportunity to explore legislation thoroughly as it relates to state programs.

One problem of greatest concern to members and leaders of the legislature is the consideration of the budget by the legislature. In the course of Eagleton's interviewing in the Wisconsin legislature, many members in the Senate and Assembly expressed the opinion that a more broad-based understanding of the budget by all legislators has to be achieved.

Many legislators indicated that there was room for improvement in the way in which the legislature funds state programs. According to one former legislative leader: "Most legislators never open the budget volume or bill—they don't have time." There was strong sentiment that not enough men in the legislature actually participate in the budgetary process. Since the budget is the central policy-making vehicle within the legislature, the lack of members' participation constitutes an over-all weakening of the legislative process. In order to achieve this participation, Senate Minority Leader Fred A. Risser has called for more use of the Committee of the Whole in passing key budgetary measures. He believes this would increase the information and knowledge of the entire membership, rather than only that of the Joint Committee on Finance. It is his contention that more legislators must be exposed to information of this kind. If standing committees are to develop, they must be prepared to assume increased responsibility. Since the most important item for the legislature during the first six months of the legislative session, as it is now constituted, is the passage of the budget, the opportunity for each legislator to become acquainted with the budget should be enlarged. The revised committee system provides a chance for such participation.

Positive movement in the direction of greater information for all legislators, concerning the budget, has already begun. In 1967 the Bureau of Management, for the first time, put out a publication listing the fifty major policy decisions of the governor which were included in the budget document. Each standing committee should have the responsibility for examining that section of the budget with which it is concerned. It should make programmatic and, to some extent, fiscal decisions concerning the section of the budget which accrues to the department or departments under its jurisdiction.

Each standing committee should be responsible for understanding the fiscal impact of the program put forward by the department(s) within its jurisdiction. The committees should question additional monies requested for the departments with particular attention paid to each request's effect on the total state budget. In many cases, the Legislative Fiscal Bureau has information related to particular programs which should be brought to the attention of the standing committee membership and staff. Specialists within the Legislative Fiscal Bureau who are concerned with specific substantive areas, such as mental health, education, and transportation, should be responsible for transmitting this information to the appro-

priate standing committees under the supervision of the director of the Legislative Fiscal Bureau.

Subcommittees of the Joint Committee on Finance

In order to facilitate the transmission of the reports of the
standing committees to the Joint Committee on Finance,
Eagleton believes that four subcommittees of the Joint Committee on Finance should be appointed to facilitate transmittal. It would be the job of each of these subcommittees to
meet with the corresponding standing committee's chairman
and discuss the recommendations put forward by the standing
committees. In this way, by the time the budget hearings occur, there will be members of the Joint Committee on Finance who are aware of the policy positions of each of the
standing committees. Committee consideration of its section
of the budget should take place within thirty days of the receipt of the budget document. This will in no way hinder consideration of the budget by the Joint Committee on Finance.

Members of the substantive, as well as of the Joint Committee on Finance, should be invited to the governor's budget
hearings in order that they may gain greater insights into requests and problems put forward by agencies within their jurisdictions. In order to do this, for informational purposes, but
not participation, committee members would have to be appointed just after the November election so that they could
attend the governor's budget hearings, which occur no later
than November 20 of each biennial session.[3] The governor
has stated that he is in favor of such legislative participation.

Also, in order to integrate the work of the standing and
Finance committees, Eagleton believes that the budget should
be analyzed (but not voted on), section by section, on the
floor of each house. This will increase accountability of each

[3] Wisconsin Statutes, 1965, Sec. 16.43.

agency and will allow the committee specialists to disseminate their accumulated knowledge on a particular section of the budget.

Single Committee Consideration of Legislation with Little or No Fiscal Impact

In order to increase the responsibility and prestige of each standing committee, Eagleton believes that it should not be necessary to send minor pieces of legislation to the Joint Committee on Finance after consideration by the proper standing committee. Major programs should not be included in this category. It would be up to the presiding officer in each house to determine whether each piece of legislation would have major fiscal impact. An upward limit of $25,000 should be placed on all such pieces of legislation which may be considered by standing committees, without consideration by the Joint Committee on Finance.

In 1967, of approximately seventeen hundred bills introduced in the Wisconsin legislature, only 10 percent fell into the category we are considering. Many of these bills were never even reported out by substantive committees and consequently, did not reach Joint Committee on Finance. In other words, Joint Committee on Finance action on these minor bills not only consumed valuable time, but also failed to have a major impact on the state budget. Therefore, it is not justifiable to claim that a policy of permitting substantive committees to handle these minor bills would be fiscally irresponsible. The difference would be slight, for as the Legislative Fiscal Bureau states, "by and large, the bills with a full biennial impact of $25,000 or less, are insignificant when compared to state finances as a whole."

Eagleton believes that bills with a full biennial impact of less than $25,000 might well receive closer scrutiny in the standing committees than in the Joint Committee on Finance, which spends most of its time considering the budget. This proposal would undoubtedly take some of the load off the Joint Committee on Finance. According to the Legislative Fiscal Bureau, "since a limited number of the bills do receive a public hearing, it follows that there would be some time-saving if the bills with the fiscal impact of $25,000 bypassed the committee."

An argument, with which Eagleton disagrees, is that, although bills with an impact of $25,000 or less are insignificant in terms of expenditures for the biennium in which they are introduced, they may cost a great deal more in future bienniums and establish precedent which could have significant fiscal impact in the future. It is our belief that it is up to the presiding officers in both houses, in referring their legislation, to determine future financial effect of such legislation. If there is any question, the presiding officer could call on the Legislative Fiscal Bureau for advice on that particular matter.

Eagleton has given some consideration to the possibility of establishing separate taxation and revenue committees. We do not believe that this is in the best interests of the Wisconsin legislature at this time. It would be difficult to recruit members for such a committee, whose membership would have to assume the onus of voting for taxation legislation without having the opportunity to vote for spending measures. Another reason for maintaining the present arrangement is that coordination of the taxation and revenue functions is necessary. Unless agreements concerning revenue and spending can be worked out in the same committee, the need for more time and energy in this reconciliation will be multiplied.

An argument in favor of the present structure is that responsibility in the spending areas will be increased if the members of the committee know that they have to raise the necessary revenue. Although the proposal for separate taxation and finance committees has the merit of dividing up the legislative work load, Eagleton believes that at this time the process of strengthening the legislature will be more hurt than helped if these functions are separated.

In summary, Eagleton recommends that:

(37) *As soon as the budget document has been distributed, each standing committee of the legislature review that part of the executive budget document that affects the area of state government for which it is responsible, and a written committee report, based on this program review, be made to the Joint Committee on Finance and to the legislature no later than thirty days after the receipt of the budget document;*

(38) *The Joint Committee on Finance not consider any changes in the executive budget until receipt of the program report from the standing committee responsible for the areas of state government that the change affects or until thirty days after the receipt of the executive budget document;*

(39) *All bills introduced in either house of the legislature for the appropriation of money, providing for revenue, or relating to taxation, which have a full biennial impact in excess of $25,000 be referred to the Joint Committee on Finance before being passed;*

(40) *Standing committees utilize the services of the Legislative Fiscal Bureau, both when considering the budget and when working in areas related to new legislation;*

(41) *Representatives of the Joint Committee on Finance and the substantive committees with responsibilities for different sections of the budget be permitted and encouraged to attend the governors budgetary hearings;*

(42) *The Joint Committee on Finance invite each relevant committee to the joint budget hearings when a department's budget, which has previously been considered by the standing committee, is discussed by the Joint Committee on Finance;*

(43) *The Joint Committee on Finance appoint subject area subcommittees for the purpose of studying the reports of the standing committees of both houses which have considered particular sections of the budget;*

(44) *Four subcommittees of the Joint Committee on Finance be established. These subcommittees on education, health and social services, governmental affairs, and a general subcommittee (catchall) should be established to achieve integration between all standing committees and the Joint Committee on Finance;* and

(45) *Legislation with a fiscal note of less than $25,000 need not be referred to the Joint Committee on Finance.*

STATUTORY COMMITTEES

Besides the standing committees and Legislative Council committees, there also exist a number of statutory committees which are composed of legislative and non-legislative members. These committees are: the Committee to Visit State Properties; the State Building Commission; the Joint Survey Committee on Retirement Systems; the Retirement Research Committee; the Joint Survey Committee on Tax Exemptions; the Council for Home and Family; the Commission on Interstate Cooperation; the Commission on Uniform State Laws; the Committee for the Review of Administrative Rules; the Joint Legislative Council; the Permanent Committees of the Legislative Council, including the Menominee Indian Study Committee; the Joint Committee on Legislative Organization; and the Board on Government Operations. Eagleton recommends that:

(46) *The statutes authorizing each of the statutory committees be carefully reviewed, and where it is possible to include the statutory committees in the standing-joint committee structure, this should be done.*

Joint Survey Committee on Tax Exemptions

It is the job of the Joint Survey Committee on Tax Exemptions to provide the legislature with "a considered opinion of the legality of the proposal of the fiscal effect upon the state and its subdivisions and of the desirability as a matter of public policy of each legislative proposal which would modify existing laws or create new laws relating to the exemptions of property or persons from any state or local taxes or special assessments." [4] This committee with its legislative, executive, and public members has provided a worthwhile service to the people of Wisconsin. We think that the work of this committee is essentially a staff function. For this reason Eagleton recommends that:

(47) *The staff of the Joint Survey Committee on Tax Exemptions continue to operate as it has up until this time, minus the legislative members of the committee, and the staff be under the general supervision of the administrator of services.*

Joint Survey Committee on Retirement Systems

The Joint Survey Committee on Retirement Systems investigates amendments to legislation, which modify any retire-

---

[4] Wisconsin Statutes, 1965, as amended by the 1967 Acts, Section 13.52.

ment system of public officers or employees. Such legislation cannot be acted upon until this Survey Committee has submitted a report on the bill.[5] Like the Joint Survey Committee on Tax Exemptions, this committee performs well and should be maintained. As in the case of the Joint Survey Committee on Tax Exemptions, Eagleton recommends that:

(48) *The staff of the Joint Survey Committee on Retirement Systems continue to function and report to the administrator of services, but no legislative members be on the committee.*

State Building Commission

The State Building Commission was established by Chapter 563, Laws of 1949. The Commission was given authority (Chapter 604, Laws of 1949) to organize a non-profit sharing corporation (The Wisconsin State Public Building Corporation) to construct public buildings. In 1961, Chapter 267 authorized the creation of a non-profit corporation to finance public welfare buildings (The Wisconsin State Agencies Building Corporation). All of this came about because of a section of the Wisconsin constitution which says that the state may not contract public debts which in the aggregate exceed $100,000. The Building Commission and the resulting corporations were devices designed to circumnavigate this restriction. Eagleton believes that Wisconsin should amend its constitution in order to allow the state to borrow money openly. In the meantime, Eagleton recommends that:

(49) *In order to broaden the Building Commission's responsibility to the legislature and better integrate it into the budgetary process, the State Building Commission retain its*

[5] Wisconsin Statutes, 1965, as amended by the 1967 Acts, Section 13.52.

powers, but become advisory to the Joint Committee on Finance.

Board on Government Operations

The Board on Government Operations was created in 1959 for the purpose of approving the granting of emergency appropriations to departments. The Board itself is composed of the chairmen of the Senate and Assembly standing committees on finance, and, in addition, two senators and three assemblymen. The secretary of administration or his representative, is ex-officio secretary of the Board.

With the establishment of committees which operate in the interim, and with the proposed annual sessions, Eagleton believes that the Joint Committee on Finance, which has the responsibility of coordinating the state's financial program, should absorb the responsibilities of the Board on Government Operations. Eagleton recommends that:

(50) *The Board on Government Operations be abolished and the Joint Committee on Finance assume the Board's operational responsibilities.*

Council for Home and Family

The functions of the Council for Home and Family are to study and make recommendations for action to prevent family breakdowns and divorce, to study marital and child support laws, and to coordinate and stimulate the activities of country family life councils and other public and private organizations. The Council is composed of seventeen members. Four of these members are the chairmen of the Judiciary and Public Welfare Committees in the two houses of the legislature. The other thirteen members have up to now been appointed by the Legislative Council for two-year terms. The membership of this group includes three family court judges, three clergymen, two attorneys, one sociologist and college professor, one family court commissioner, one county welfare director, one county corporation counsel, and one voluntary social welfare agency representative. Eagleton has heard, and generally agrees with, arguments which state that this group does not properly belong in the legislative branch of government. The Council has operating responsibilities which should place it in the Department of Health and Social Services. Indeed, it is interesting that the very arguments used to abolish the old Mental Health Advisory Committee have not led to the abolition of the Council for Home and Family. Nevertheless, on the basis of Eagleton interviews, it has been established that the Council definitely will not be abolished and will remain in the legislature. As long as this is the case, Eagleton recommends that:

(51) *The Council for Home and Family retain its present form and become an advisory committee to the Joint Committee on Health and Social Services, and with the approval of the latter committee, reports of the Council for Home and Family be sent to the Judiciary, Governmental and Military Affairs Committee for consideration.*

Commission on Interstate Cooperation

This body, established in an effort to help achieve cooperation among the states, should be one of the most important groups in the legislature. Eagleton believes that certain action should be taken to strengthen it.

Presently, the Commission consists of seventeen members. Among these are the members of the present Joint Committee on Legislative Organization, three senators and three assemblymen appointed by their leadership, the chief of the Legislative Reference Bureau, the governor, and three state officials appointed by the governor. In addition, the executive secretary of the Legislative Council serves as a non-voting secretary. The Commission participates as a member of the Council of State Governments and involves itself in studies of interstate compacts.

The whole question of intergovernmental relations is an extremely salient one. Recently, the Executive Committee of the National Conference of State Legislative Leaders adopted a resolution which would ask each state legislature to establish a standing committee on intergovernmental relations. It was the intention of this resolution that each legislature should have a coordinating committee. For this reason, Eagleton recommends that:

(52) *A separate Joint Committee on Judiciary, Governmental, and Military Affairs coordinate grant-in-aid programs and supervise the legislature's office in Washington, D.C.;*

(53) *The name of the Committee on Interstate Cooperation be changed to Intergovernmental Relations Commission and that the duties of the Commission be expanded to include state-local and inter-local relations. The Intergovernmental Relations Commission should consist of the governor's council on intergovernmental relations and the advisory committee on intergovernmental relations of the Joint Committee on Judiciary, Governmental, and Military Affairs. This advisory committee shall serve as an integrating mechanism for the entire legislature.*

This latter recommendation would mean that if an interstate conference on agriculture were being held, members of the Agriculture Committee would be appointed to represent the legislature.

Menominee Indian Study Committee

This committee, in operation since 1955 and formerly attached to the Legislative Council, has as its goal the development of specific recommendations and legislative proposals relating to the transition of the Menominee Indian reservation from federal to state and local controls. Eagleton recommends that:

(54) *The Menominee Indians Study Committee continue as an advisory committee to the Joint Committee on Judiciary, Governmental, and Military Affairs and, specifically, the Subcommittee on Governmental Affairs.*

Committee to Visit State Properties

The committee, composed of Senate and Assembly members, is contrary to the philosophy of strengthened standing committees. Each standing committee should be made responsible for inspection of facilities which fall within its jurisdiction, and make recommendations concerning them. Staff should schedule such visits periodically. Eagleton recommends that:

(55) *The Committee to Visit State Properties be abolished.*

Commission on Uniform State Laws

The Commission on Uniform State Laws consists of two members of the Wisconsin Bar, appointed by the governor for four-year terms, and three ex-officio members who are the executive secretaries of the Legislative Council, the chief of the Legislative Reference Bureau, and the Revisor of Statutes. It is the function of the legislature to examine subjects on which uniformity of state legislation is desirable and to cooperate with commissions in other states in preparing such uniform acts. This commission provides valuable assistance to the legislature and should continue. Therefore, Eagleton recommends that:

(56) *The Commission on Uniform State Laws continue functioning in its present form, although in an advisory capacity to the Joint Committee on Judiciary, Governmental, and Military Affairs.*

THE USE OF COMMITTEES FOR GOVERNMENTAL OVERSIGHT

In the introduction to this report, one function of the legislature was identified as oversight over administrative agencies of government. In this, the legislature has, at least partially, failed. Only one out of four of those legislators questioned in our survey believed the legislature was doing either an excellent or a good job in overseeing state government. In its report, the Kellett Committee stated: "The existence of a large number of agencies, boards, and commissions not only makes state government difficult to administer, but also makes the legislature's policy-making and policy-review responsibilities cumbersome." [6]

One main reason for organizing committees along the same lines as state agencies is so that oversight may be facilitated. Suggestions for the alignment of standing committees have all followed the departmental lines suggested by the newly adopted proposals of the Kellett Temporary Reorganization Committee, established by the Wisconsin legislature in 1965. Indeed, that committee set the stage for this reorganization of standing and interim committees along functional lines. The

[6] The Kellett Committee, "Government Reorganization in Wisconsin, Senate Bill 55 and Assembly Bill 100" (Madison: The Temporary Reorganization Committee, January, 1967), p. 11.

Kellett Committee has maintained that the "policy review" of government is a primary function of the legislature. According to the Committee:

> This is the legislature's primary function. Through functional consolidation, the legislature will be better able to define and understand the relationships between state programs. The legislature's role in the budget process will also be strengthened because the priorities for spending in related programs can more clearly be evaluated. Further, because agencies will be able to do a better job of program planning the legislature will be in a better position to audit related policy issues and deal with them on a comprehensive basis.[7]

The complex question of oversight is one which needs some analysis. The powers of the bureaucracy have multiplied because of the technical and detailed nature of today's programs. Federal programs such as Medicare, the Community Health Facilities and Staffing Acts of 1963–1965, the Water Pollution Act, the Highways Act, Federal Aid to Education, Aid to Families with Dependent Children, and the Poverty Program make legislative oversight infinitely more complex each year. The state has to react, often with matching grants to federal programs. Often, the bureaucracy is in the position of having the only sufficient expertise to do this. If legislators are to act as true representatives, they must at least know what is contained in legislation proposed by the bureaucracy and what the key assumptions of such legislation are. Legislators must also know which new federal programs are vital to the citizens of the state. The legislature must be informed if state agencies are failing to implement federal programs efficiently and effectively.

The governor has the Department of Administration to coordinate state agencies. This is as it should be. Nevertheless,

---

[7] *Ibid.*

according to Section 16.50, it becomes clear that responsibility is placed on the Bureau of Management to insure that legislative intent is carried out by departments and agencies. The legislature must supply itself with similar resources.

The legislature not only must exercise negative control on the state's executive agencies but also must be in a position to present alternative policies to those of operating departments. If, for example, a "chargeback" program for county patients in state mental health facilities is not working in the way the legislature was told it would, corrective measures must be taken and suitable alternatives found. There is no better way of doing this than through the activities of standing committees. We have already proposed that standing committees review the budget in their particular areas of interest, prior to consideration by the Joint Committee on Finance.

Another proposal is for the standing committee to become more aware of the different programs a department is carrying on, and to ascertain the direction in which these programs are moving. The activities of the legislature should be conducted similar to those of business. Committees should know what departments plan for expansion and development of programs—at least four to six years in advance. If the information is available to the department, there is no reason the legislature should not have it. For this reason, Eagleton recommends that:

(57) *Departments, at the first available time in the session, make presentation of their policy goals to the appropriate standing committees of the legislature, and that standing committees make every effort to inform themselves in a comprehensive manner about the several programs operated by the departments and agencies (when possible, this should be done in joint meetings of corresponding committees of both houses)*; and

(58) *The departments, officers, and employees of Wisconsin state government, and the governing bodies of the political subdivisions of this state, assist legislative committees in the completion of their task; provide legislative committees with ready access to any books, records, or other information relating to such tasks; and upon request by a legislative committee, and within the limits of existing appropriations, supply such specialized staff assistance as a legislative committee may require.*

With standing committees meeting all year-round, legislators will be in a better position to keep an eye on what agencies are doing. This should be viewed as an advantage by agencies. According to the administrator of one agency: "As an agency head, I would like them to take part in drafting my bills, to be familiar with them before the session comes and they have to act on the bills."

ADMINISTRATIVE RULES

Up to now, in the Wisconsin legislature there has existed a single committee whose responsibility it is to review administrative rules promulgated by departments and agencies. Eagleton believes that each joint committee should assume responsibility for overseeing the development of administrative rules for the departments and agencies within its jurisdiction. One problem here will be that the several committees have different criteria for reviewing rules of the various agencies. It should be the job of the secretary of the legislature to develop certain criteria for the different committees. Eagleton recommends that:

(59) *Each standing committee of the legislature review all administrative rules for the area of state government that is the responsibility of that standing committee.*

CHAPTER III

INTERNAL COMMITTEE ORGANIZATION AND RULES

Eagleton has recommended reducing the number of committees in order to strengthen the legislature. Another proposal which goes hand in hand with that one is to limit severely the number of committees on which a legislator serves. Ideally, no member of the Senate or Assembly should serve on more than one major committee. If committees are to become specialized, each member, already burdened with constituency demands, should not have to divide his committee work and energies any more than is absolutely necessary. According to one legislator, the present system, with multiple assignments, has serious defects. "I'm going from one crisis to another crisis," he said. "There never seems to be time to get everything done." Experience in the Senate, for example, has shown that competing committee meetings and competing committee hearings have presented great attendance problems. In order to strengthen committees, legislators should serve on one committee only. This would give the members serving on a committee an opportunity to develop their expertise in a particular subject area and should alleviate the problems of attendance at meetings and proliferation of responsibility. Eagleton recognizes that in some cases this may not be possible because the majority may not have enough members to control all committees without duplication. For this reason, Eagleton recommends that:

(60) *Wherever possible, legislators should serve on only*

one committee and in no case should serve on more than two committees.

Obviously the leadership should retain some flexibility in establishing the number of members on a committee. However, the ratio of Republicans to Democrats in each committee should be determined by the political composition of both houses. This would leave the leadership free to deal with political contingencies as they arise. Where possible, the spirit of "one man—one assignment" should prevail. We also suggest that the flexibility allowed the leaders in determining committee composition should have its limits.

For many years, the Senate has provided that standing committees should all have five members. The Assembly does not have any definite rules as to the number of members on a committee and this has led to controversy. Eagleton believes that a middle course is advantageous and recommends that:

(61) *In the Senate, the number of members on each committee be determined by the appointing authority, but be not less than three nor more than nine;*

(62) *In the Assembly, the number of members be determined by the appointing authority, but should be not less than five nor more than thirteen;* and

(63) *Each committee reflect, as closely as possible, and with fractions resolved in favor of the majority party, the political composition of the house in which it is located, but each member serve on at least one committee.*

The membership of interim committees will consist of the combined standing committees. Because the Assembly will have greater numbers of members on the committees, a compromise has to be worked out. Eagleton recommends that:

(64) *The Senate chairman will preside in meetings of joint committees, but members of the committee, as a committee, will vote as individuals.*

Standing committees will, however, continue to vote as separate houses during the actual legislative session. Therefore, any recommendation made by the joint committee will not necessarily have to be adopted by either house. This helps to preserve the integrity of each house. Since the Senate chairman will serve as chairman of the joint committee, the problem of which Assembly committee chairman (in case two Assembly chairmen are members of the joint committee) will serve will be averted.

APPOINTMENT OF COMMITTEES

Closely aligned with the subject of the number of members serving on committees is the politically sensitive question of how committees will be appointed. Presently, this is done by a Senate Committee on Committees and by the speaker of the Assembly. This is as it should be. The Senate is a small enough group to assign members by utilizing a Committee on Committees. The speaker, however, needs all the political powers he can get in order to effectively control his house, which is three times as large as the Senate. Committee assignment constitutes an important resource at the disposal of party leadership. The members of his party expect him, as the elected leader of the majority, to wield that control.

In the Senate, a tradition has developed whereby minority members are appointed by the minority leadership. In the Assembly, this is not the case. Eagleton prefers the Senate system. The speaker should have the power to control his own party on standing and joint committees. By leaving the size of committees somewhat flexible, this control can be assured. Nevertheless, when the majority has control over minority appointments to committees several problems arise. For instance, it has occurred that legislators who would be most effective on particular committees, because of experience and commitment, do not get a chance to serve where they would prove most useful. In some cases, this is because the leadership of the majority party has chosen to weaken the minority by a policy of assigning non-specialists from the minority to inappropriate committees.

Eagleton believes that in a two-party system, such as Wisconsin's, both parties should be allowed to develop their manpower resources in such a way as to prepare them for leadership responsibilities. By developing this type of "shadow government," either party will be in a position to assume leadership. Problems of organization, at such a time, would be minimized, presumably with present minority experts on committees becoming chairmen in the future.

Eagleton is not concerned with the exact method by which this is accomplished. It has worked well without being included in the rules of the Senate. It can work just as well on an informal basis in the Assembly. For this reason, Eagleton recommends that:

(65) *The minority members of each committee be selected by the minority leadership of each house.*

COMMITTEE MEETINGS

Presently, Senate committees have separate meeting rooms. This is not true in the Assembly. Eagleton believes such a situation to be desirable. It would be helpful to have each legislator aware that a specific committee would always meet in the same room at a specific hour. Research information and committee staff should be accessible in the committee room. Furthermore, in case a chairman calls a special meeting of his committee, all members should be notified. To assure that each member has been contacted, Eagleton believes that a notification slip should be distributed among and initialed by each committee member. Therefore, Eagleton recommends that:

66) *Where possible, each committee have a constant meeting room and these rooms adjoin the offices of the committee chairman*; and

(67) *The members of a committee initial a notification slip at the time notice of a hearing or meeting is received and that such notification slips be returned to the committee chairman.*

COMMITTEE HEARINGS

If the legislature is to acquire the information it needs to develop its programs properly, it will have to improve its system of committee hearings. With the combining of committees during the interim, it will be possible for different committees to develop continuity between the hearings of the standing committees and of the interim committees.

Ideally, the standing committees or subcommittees of both houses, which have particular bills within their jurisdictions, will hold joint hearings. This will save valuable agency and legislative time and will permit legislators on both sides to acquire a feeling for the thinking of the other house. In addition, if a bill is considered by a committee, meeting jointly for hearings will help to avoid the problem of its getting full treatment in one house and "rush" treatment at the end of the session in another. Although committees of both houses may hold joint hearings, their deliberations should continue to be separate. This joint hearing procedure may well result in less conflict on conference committees. Whenever possible, standing committees hold hearings on a single bill or series of bills. In this way, all legislation pertaining to a single subject might be considered together, giving legislators more of an overview. The legislature should make itself more accessible to the citizens of the state by holding more hearings in different parts of the state.

The joint interim committees should also make use of hearings related to their more in-depth research. When a joint committee assigns or undertakes a study, open hearings relating to the research should be fully utilized. Eagleton recommends that:

(68) *Committees and subcommittees travel as much as necessary and hold hearings in different parts of the state*; and

(69) *Whenever possible, committees hold hearings on related bills.*

As is presently the case, the chairman of each standing committee should, before Wednesday noon of each week, file with the chief clerk a list of public hearings conducted by his committee which will be held during the following week. These are printed in the *Hearing Bulletins*. When possible, greater notice than that should be given. In some cases, an extra week's notice has been given in the *Hearing Bulletins* in past sessions. Under present circumstances, it is relatively hard to mobilize support for or against a bill in less than a week. Presently, some committee chairmen have been very cooperative in giving adequate notice on particular measures. Eagleton believes that hearings should be held in the afternoon, allowing the morning for travel of participants from other parts of the state.

One problem currently existing with hearings is that when bills are passed, information which is acquired during the hearings is not absorbed by the committee members. Partly, this is because representatives of organizations wishing to testify, appear with long, verbose typewritten statements which they read to the committee. It is not surprising that committee members, under such circumstances, often have a way of disappearing at these times. It would be in the best interest of witnesses and committee members to have the text of a witness's testimony in advance. The witness should limit himself to a short summary of his proposed testimony and to responding to questions of committee members.

In order to make hearings more interesting, opportunities to question witnesses should alternate between majority and minority committee members. Eagleton recommends that:

(70) *When a public hearing is scheduled, legislative representatives submit their testimony, in writing, to the chairman of the committee, as far in advance as possible; copies be distributed to all committee members; and oral remarks to the committee be in the nature of a summary, not lasting longer than five minutes;*

(71) *Public hearings be scheduled in the afternoon, whenever possible;*

(72) *Committee members may question witnesses only when they have been recognized by the chairman for that purpose and only for a five-minute period, a time which can be extended only with unanimous consent of members present;*

(73) *Questioning of witnesses at full and subcommittee hearings be initiated by the chairman, and opportunities be alternated between majority and minority members*; and

(74) *The administrative subcommittee set a definite period of time for hearings on each bill.*

Standing committees presently have subpoena power. Although it has not been used to a very large extent, it should be retained. Legal questions related to subpoena power should be routed through the legal staff assigned to the legislature. In addition, Eagleton recommends that:

(75) *Whenever possible, a verbatim or summary transcript of remarks at a hearing be kept.*

To allow relevant information to escape unrecorded would be a blow to legislative effectiveness. It has also been suggested, and Eagleton agrees, that whenever possible, committees should go into executive session immediately after committee hearings. Legislators often forget information which has been brought out at hearings. These executive sessions should provide some opportunity for discussion of what has transpired during the hearing. In order to further assist the legislator in his consideration of committee bills, Eagleton recommends that:

(76) *After a hearing on a bill is completed, each legislator be provided with a brief committee report deposited in his bill folder relating to each bill, which includes a list of those persons or organizations who appeared either in favor of or against a bill.*

COMMITTEE RULES

When and if Wisconsin adopts a strengthened committee system, certain basic rules will have to be implemented in order to assure an effective committee system. If abuses which have occurred on the committees of other legislatures are to be avoided in Wisconsin, such rules are the best way of achieving this objective.

What follows is a list of recommended rules. The Assembly presently has an excellent set of uniform committee rules. There is no reason why each committee should not have the same rules. This will be beneficial in cases in which a member goes from one committee to another and will avoid prolonged discussions of the rules at the beginning of each session. Uniform committee rules will also assist in the operation of joint committees. Although Eagleton has made recommendations for certain rules and procedures in the section on committee hearings, we include them, for the sake of clarity, in the list that follows. Those rules which are in italics are added to the existing Assembly rules; the rules set in roman type already exist. In constructing this list, Eagleton has relied heavily on other sources, particularly the rules of congressional committees and subcommittees.

Eagleton recommends that:

(77) *Committee rules include provision for the following*:

(a) *The rules of each house, as far as applicable, shall be the rules of the committee, and procedure in the committee, where not otherwise herein provided, shall follow the procedure of the house.*

(b) A majority of any committee shall constitute a quorum for the transaction of business.

(c) *A committee will not open a meeting without a quorum present.*

(d)   All committee meetings, except those designated as "executive session," should be open to the public.

(e)   In the absence of the chairman and the vice-chairman, the several members shall succeed to the position of presiding chairman in the order in which named to the committee.

(f)   *Each committee shall have an administrative subcommittee consisting of the chairman, the vice-chairman, and the ranking minority member. This committee will constitute the decision-making body of each committee. Priorities and schedules shall be set by it.*

(g)   In addition to meetings scheduled by the administrative subcommittee, meetings may be set by a written petition of a majority of a committee, filed with the chairman of the committee.

(h)   *The deadline for scheduling bills for a weekday meeting will be on the preceding Tuesday night.*

(i)   *A majority of the committee membership is required to pass a bill from committee. A simple majority of those present and voting is sufficient to adopt committee amendments.*

(j)   *A motion to "table" shall be put to the committee without discussion and require an affirmative vote by an absolute majority of the committee.*

(k)   *A motion to lift a tabled bill shall require an affirmative vote by an absolute majority of the committee.*

(l)   *The administrative subcommittee shall, immediately after the assignment of a study, investigation, or review to its committee develop and submit to the Legislative Council Board for its approval and review an operating budget setting forth the anticipated costs of the proposed study, investigation, or review. If required by the progress of the study, investigation, or review, the administrative subcommittee may submit to the Legislative Council Board at a later date an amended budget for the Council's review and approval. No committee shall, in the conduct of any study, investigation, or review, exceed the budget au-*

thorized for this purpose by the Legislative Council Board.

(*m*) Subcommittees may be appointed to consider subjects specified by the committee and report to the regular committee.

(*n*) The various committees shall meet as determined by the chairman within the times and places assigned by the Senate and Assembly Operations Boards. If anticipated public attendance so warrants, arrangements may be made through the Sergeant-at-Arms to hold public hearings in different quarters than the regularly assigned committee room.

(*o*) *Regular meetings of the committee on ———— shall be held on ———— [name of day—each week].*

(*p*) A committee shall act only when together, and all votes shall be taken in the presence of the committee. A member shall not be recorded as voting unless he was actually present in the committee when he voted.

(*q*) *Upon the written request of a committee member who has attended a portion of the committee meeting but who must leave temporarily, a roll call will be held open until the committee adjourns or until the member who has made the request has returned and been given an opportunity to vote on that issue only. The roll shall be held open only for the member who has made the written request.*

(*r*) Any vote in an executive session may be held open until the adjournment of that committee session to permit an absent member to vote; but such a vote shall only be recorded if the member votes in the presence of the committee in session.

(*s*) The members of the committee shall vote in sequence in the order in which named to the committee.

(*t*) Prior to a proposal being reported to the Assembly or Senate, the committee may reconsider its previous action.

(*u*) Public hearings may be held on any proposal referred to the committee for consideration.

(v) When special meetings of a committee are to be held, the chairman is responsible for notifying the members of such meetings. *Members should initial a notification form where possible.*

(w) *The day, hour, and place of a hearing before any committee shall be posted on the bulletin board of each house, and such notice shall specify the number, author, and title of the proposals to be considered.*

(x) *The chairman of each standing committee shall on or before Wednesday noon of each week file with the chief clerk a list of the public hearings on proposals before his committee which will be held during the following week. These lists shall be printed in advance in the weekly bulletin of committee hearings.*

(y) *No hearing on bills, joint resolutions, or simple resolutions, and the amendments thereto, shall be held until copies of the measures scheduled are available to the public.*

(z) *Secretaries to committees shall give notice of hearings on bills to those requesting them.*

(aa) *At any time prior to reporting a matter back to the Assembly, a committee may reconsider its previous actions relating to such matter.*

(bb) Every effort should be made to extend courtesy to legislators. Priority should be given to: (1) assemblymen, (2) senators present at the meeting but not members of the committee, (3) assemblymen who are members of the committee, and (4) representatives of assemblymen or senators who are not members of the committee.

(cc) *Committee members may question witnesses only when they have been recognized by the chairmen for that purpose, and only for a five-minute period. The five-minute period for questioning a witness by any one member can be extended only with the unanimous consent of all members present. The questioning of witnesses in both full and subcommittee hearings shall be initiated by the chairman, followed by*

> *the ranking minority member and all other members alternating between the majority and the minority.*

(*dd*)   *The proceedings of the committee shall be recorded in a journal which shall, among other things, show those present at each meeting and include a record of the votes of any question on which a record vote is demanded. All record votes shall be public information. A record vote may be demanded by one-fifth of the members present.*

If there is a serious backlog, it is the task of the leadership to confer with the chairman about ways of alleviating the problem. In addition, Eagleton recommends that:

(78) *All proposals should be considered as soon as possible, and the chairman of each committee should regularly report to the speaker and the president pro tempore of the Senate the number of proposals in the possession of his committee.*

DISCHARGE OF A COMMITTEE

There is presently a mechanical difference between the two houses in how bills can be recalled from committees. In the Senate, a bill can be recalled from a committee by a majority vote, but if a majority fails to recall a bill on a vote, subsequent attempts to discharge the committee must be by two-thirds vote. In the Assembly, a committee has sole jurisdiction for twenty-one days, except by a two-thirds vote, which can dislodge a bill from committee within those twenty-one days. After this time, however, a majority of members of the Assembly may recall a bill from committee.

Eagleton believes that each method can be defended with some justification. We do, however, prefer the assured consideration of legislation by a house for a specified period of time and, therefore, prefer the Assembly method.

COMMITTEE REPORTS

Theoretically, one of the most important aspects of committee work is the committee report. It is here that the committee transfers the knowledge, information, and expertise which it has acquired to other members of the legislature. Further, it is here that the division of labor either works or does not. Presently, the Assembly and Senate rules provide for reports from committees. But, with the exception of Legislative Council committees, it is infrequent that standing committee reports include more than a brief summary of committee opinion and those who appear for or against a piece of legislation. With the coming of the strengthened committee and committee staff, reports should contain more information and be more analytical. Eagleton recommends that:

(79) *Each committee report present major issues related to a bill with arguments both pro and con synopsized by the committee staff for the benefit of the members; in unusual circumstances relating to a piece of legislation in which a committee has devoted a large amount of time and energy, an oral report be made to the entire house, meeting as the Committee of the Whole, by the standing committee; and every bill submitted by a legislative committee (both standing and joint) have a negative or positive report attached to it by the committee;*

(80) *All proposals, in the form of bills, resolutions, petitions, and motions, which are referred to a committee, be acted upon as soon as practicable;*

(81) *Bills be arranged in committee journals, by subject, for reference by future legislators who may wish to consult a committee journal from a previous year; and*

(82) *Each joint committee which conducts an interim study be required to prepare an in-depth report dealing with the committee's findings and recommendations, including suggested legislation, and these reports be submitted to the legislature at the start of each new legislative session.*

COMMITTEE STAFFING

Implicit in the strengthening of the Wisconsin committee system is the staffing of standing and joint committees. The major problem which will be faced by the new committees will be the orientation of committee chairmen in the use of staff. In its study of the Wisconsin legislature, Eagleton has heard many predictions of failure because "chairmen will not know what to do with staff." Eagleton believes these predictions to be both degrading and insulting. If committees do not know presently how to use staff, they will have to learn. One way this problem may be alleviated is by establishing orientation sessions for staff and committees. These sessions would be one of the responsibilities of the secretary of the legislature.

Again, quality control and supervision over committee staff would be the responsibility of the administrator of services and ultimately the Legislative Council Board. Some of those who object to committee staffing have suggested that committee members will be less inclined to do their own work if staff does it for them. We disagree. It is obvious that a great deal of work, which should be done by someone, is not now done by anyone. We do feel, however, that it is the job of committee staff to present their report in such a precise manner as to allow busy legislators to absorb their findings with a minimum of time and effort.

PERMANENT COMMITTEE STAFF

The concept that each committee should have its own staff finds favor in the legislature. Fifty-eight percent of those responding to a question inquiring about the best method for staffing committees believed that each committee should have its own staff. According to one long-time legislative observer: "A man from a staff pool would be a jack-of-all trades, and master of none." The congressional experience provides a valuable model for the value of a semipermanent staff to a committee. Such a staff provides continuity and knowledge of issues which have developed over long periods of time. In the long run, Eagleton favors the development of permanent committee staff. It would make little sense to rotate staff positions on committees. Ideally, this staff should serve standing committees during the legislative session and joint committees during the interim.

Committee staff should be recruited from several disciplines. Staff should not be limited to those persons with legal training. The legislature requires experts with substantive training if it is to initiate new legislation and respond to proposals from the departments and agencies.

The full staffing of legislative committees might be accomplished on an experimental basis, by phases, with certain committees being staffed first. We believe that the Judiciary, Education, and Health and Social Service Committees would be an appropriate place to initiate full-time staffing.

In the past, when the Judiciary Committees have been staffed, the results have been excellent. By staffing the Education and Health and Social Services Committees, the usefulness of expert legislative staff recruited from substantive fields could be demonstrated.

Eagleton believes that the Wisconsin legislature is not yet

ready for full-time minority staff on standing and joint committees. Staff should be non-partisan and should be responsible to the entire committee, but primarily to the administrative subcommittee of the full committee. It is our opinion that such staff will be desirable in the future.

Eagleton believes that it is preferable to develop staff and informational resources that can continually serve the legislature. Nevertheless, there will be times when the legislature should hire, on a temporary or project basis, outside consultants.

In summary, Eagleton recommends that:

(83) *Staff be assigned to standing committees by the administrator of services, and this staff work with a combined joint committee operating in the interim;*

(84) *When staff, either permanent or temporary, is supplied by the Division of Services from a research pool, such personnel be assigned to a committee only upon approval of the administrative subcommittee of the committee;*

(85) *The Judiciary, Education, and Health and Social Services Committees in both houses be staffed on a full-time basis;*

(86) *Quality control over committee staff be the function of the administrator of services;*

(87) *In addition to the orientation session for new legislators, the secretary of the legislature hold an orientation session with each committee and its newly provided staff and explain all the ways in which staff may be used and the resources open to the committee and staff in the legislature;*

(88) *A legislative handbook be prepared by the secretary of the legislature, incorporating, among other things, an inventory of legislative services and setting forth committee procedures;*

(89) *The administrative subcommittee be responsible for staff assignment and no committee staff member be used for any task other than the work of the committee; and*

(90) *In cases where outside consultants are deemed necessary, a committee chairman request from either the Legislative Council Board, in the case of the joint committees, or the Assembly or Senate Operations Boards, in the case of standing committees, such authorization to employ these consultants.*

CHAPTER IV

LEGISLATIVE SESSIONS AND COMPENSATION

The way in which the legislature organizes its time will affect legislative efficiency in much the same way as a business' organization of its time affects its success or failure. The Wisconsin legislature is quickly arriving at another juncture, when it must decide whether legislators should lean more to full-time or part-time status. Furthermore, the legislature must decide whether there should be annual or biennial sessions and budgets. The members of the legislature are in favor of a more active role. A survey of the Wisconsin legislature indicated that the members themselves believe that more time and not less should be spent in session.

Paul Mason reports that since 1883, considering days in session only and excluding special sessions, the Assembly was in session about one hundred and three days from 1889 to 1920, an average of one hundred and seventeen days from 1921 to 1949, and an average of one hundred and twenty-two from 1950 to 1962. During this period, the Senate averaged a few days less in session than the Assembly.[1] In the 1967–68 biennium the Senate sat for one hundred and twenty days and the Assembly for one hundred and twenty-six days.

ANNUAL SESSIONS

The voters also appear to favor the concept of a more active legislature. On April 2, 1968, an overwhelming majority of the voters (670,757 to 267,979) decided that legislators

[1] Paul Mason, *Wisconsin Study; Report of the Committee on Legislative Organization and Procedure* (Madison: January, 1964), p. 6–1.

should set up their own meeting schedule. The amendment provided that "Section 11 [of the Wisconsin constitution] be amended to permit the legislature to meet in regular session oftener than once in two years." Since the issue in that referendum was the question of annual or biennial sessions, it appears that there is a mandate from the people that the legislature meet more than once every two years.

Legislators clearly favor the concept of an unlimited annual session. Furthermore, a questionnaire distributed to all Wisconsin assemblymen and senators by the Wisconsin Committee on Improved Expenditure Management indicates that four out of five legislators favor some sort of annual session.[2] Eagleton interviewers have also discovered a marked preference for this arrangement. If formal annual sessions were adopted, there is no need for more time to be spent in any single session. In making this point Senator Dorman has stated that: "If the legislature is in session for approximately six months, with three-day sessions each week, the first year, and in session approximately four months, the second year, the total number of days spent in session would be one hundred and seventeen days, or approximately the same number that was spent in the 1965 [biennial] session." Along the same lines, one research analyst in the Wisconsin Legislative Reference Bureau has pointed out that the Wisconsin legislature presently sits for longer periods than do most annual session legislatures:

> From 1959 to the present, every elected legislature had at least four session periods. The average length of the sessions was 34.6 weeks. Thus, Wisconsin, with its biennial sessions, spends more time sitting than the average annual legislature.[3]

[2] Wisconsin Committee on Improved Expenditure Management, *Report and Recommendations Regarding a Compensation Plan for Legislators* (Madison: August, 1966).

[3] *Milwaukee Journal,* June 12, 1968.

Eagleton agrees that Wisconsin should have annual sessions. The argument is overwhelming. The impact of government on the individual has never been greater. For this reason, the people's representatives ought to be in as much control of government as is possible. As has already been mentioned, annual sessions do not mean more time spent by legislators, but rather that nearly the same amount of time which is presently spent in Madison, during a biennial session, be divided into two annual sessions. Annual sessions will also mean that interim work can be more meaningful. By holding a first session devoted primarily to an intensive examination of the budget and a second devoted to implementing recommendations of joint study committees and to further budgetary activity the legislature will be improved. The interim sessions will be utilized to assist standing committees in policy research. These same legislators will then have the responsibility for seeing the findings of their committees introduced and enacted as legislation.

Eagleton does not accept the argument of critics of annual sessions that there is sufficient flexibility in Wisconsin's present procedure for calling legislative sessions. Section 11 of the Wisconsin constitution presently provides that a special session may be called only by the governor and must be limited to the special purposes for which it is convened. We think the legislature has to have more control over its own scheduling. We are not alone in this belief.

The concept of non-limited sessions finds support in the reports of the American Assembly, the Committee for Economic Development, and the Council of State Governments. This will allow the leadership sufficient flexibility should contingencies arise. This latter point is reinforced by Chairman Obey of the Subcommittee of Legislative Sessions and Compensation who has noted: "Everyone who has appeared before the subcommittee or who has worked in an advisory capacity has suggested that no definite period of time be set for when the legislature should be in session."

Scheduling of legislative matters is the business of the legislature. It should not be the exclusive province of the governor. With the advent of annual sessions, the legislature will meet regularly to consider the ever-growing agenda of state business. In addition, annual sessions justify to a greater degree than otherwise the employment of full-time staff for the legislature and its standing and joint committees.

Therefore, Eagleton recommends that:

(91) *The Wisconsin legislature authorize annual sessions, the length of which will be determined by the legislature.*

During the first session, preparation and passage of the budget should occur. Also, during this first session, committees should prepare and propose major legislation. The first session should run from January to July of odd-numbered years. At the end of the session, from June to the following March, interim work by joint standing committees and subsequently by standing committees should occur. Hearings and studies should take place.

The following March, in even-numbered years, the second session should commence. Ideally, this session should be shorter than the previous one and should continue for four or five months.

It is our belief that the legislature should not reconvene until March of even-numbered years. This would allow joint and standing committees approximately seven or eight months to complete in-depth research on topics assigned to them by the Legislative Council Board. Since one main rationale for annual sessions is the opportunity for interim research, the latter should be given sufficient opportunity to flourish. Since interim work conducted after the second session will face competition from the pressures of campaigning and elections, it stands to reason that the use of interim time between the first and second years should be maximized. In this way the legislators who do research on particular problems will also have responsibility for implementing bills that emanate from such research.

BIENNIAL OR ANNUAL BUDGETS

The question of annual or biennial budgets is a difficult one. There are excellent arguments offered both for and against annual budgets.

Some executive departments are opposed to an annual budget because of the extra time that will be involved in its preparation. On the other hand, the director of at least one of Wisconsin's major commissions believes the annual budget to be helpful in guiding his agency and believes that added staff would not be needed to prepare an annual budget. Another argument presented in favor of annual budgets is that an annual budget would lessen or eliminate the problem of supplementary appropriations requests. One argument for a budget every year is that it takes up to two years to plan a budget. Thus, by adding an additional year, as is the case of the biennial budget, there is a thirty-six-month gestation period for a budget. The argument continues that this thirty-six-month period could be lowered to twenty-four months by having annual budgets. Still another argument, presented by those in favor of annual budgets, is that when a budget reaches the size of the Wisconsin document, it should be revised annually because even small estimates in projections can have staggering effects.

There are telling arguments, on the other hand, for improvements of the present biennial system. It is suggested that by having biennial budgets, the first year of a two-year budget would be devoted to enacting a budget and the second year, for reviewing it in detail. According to the Speaker: "There is a great deal of support for such a plan." This plan makes a good deal of sense, considering that the budget, in recent years, has been passed in late May and published near the end of June.

A variation of this theme would be to maintain a biennial budget but divide it into two separate sections. Part A would be the first year's budget, Part B would contain the second year's budget. Part A would be passed the first year and Part B the second. In this way, the legislature could check the first year's estimates against actual expenditures. The agencies would then have to appear for a second time the following year. The Department of Administration would still have to prepare a single budget once every two years.

The legislature could concentrate on specific policy areas the second year, which appeared to be problems during the first. Such a compromise would have the advantage of allowing budget preparation once every two years and at the same time of making state agencies more responsible to the legislature. We agree that at this time there is no need to go through the entire budget cycle each year. The Joint Committee on Finance should hold its major hearings during the first year and another set of hearings the second year.

Eagleton believes that while separate annual budgets may be desirable, legislators do not know enough about the budget at this time. The legislature, through the revised committee procedures, should do a better job with the biennial budget. When this has been accomplished, then we believe there will be sufficient time to move on to an annual budget.

Therefore, Eagleton recommends that:

(92) *For the present, Wisconsin continue with a biennial budget, which permits the legislature, at its discretion, to make modifications and revisions in the second year.*

After some experience with annual sessions and rigorous study by joint committees operating in the interim, the legislature could consider adopting an annual budget plan.

ORGANIZATION OF THE SESSION

The legislature should also consider whether it would benefit from a new scheduling procedure. Although Eagleton does not see the immediate need for more time to be spent in the legislature, we do recognize the need for a better allocation of the legislature's time and for a better organization of the legislative session. In our survey of legislators, considerably more than half mentioned some dissatisfaction with the ways in which they had to spend their time. In fact, more than one-third mentioned that there should be some rearrangement in the use of time by the legislature.

Once the Wisconsin legislature has decided to go forward with annual sessions, concurrent responsibility to organize its sessions effectively and efficiently will have to be met. In order to achieve these ends, Eagleton has formulated a possible schedule for future sessions of the Wisconsin legislature.

At the beginning of the legislative session, the leadership should inform both houses as to goals for ending the session.

In order to assure a quick start for the legislature, the members should meet informally after elections, probably early December, and select leaders and assign committees. In this way the politics implicit in the choosing of leadership will not hold up the progress of legislative business.

To accomplish this, Eagleton recommends that:

(93) *Shortly after the election of the legislature, caucuses of both houses should meet and informally organize, so that on the first Monday in January they are ready to formalize the election of leadership;* and

(94) *Committee chairmen and committees be decided upon and the staff of the legislative services division meet with the newly designated standing committees and begin orientation sessions.*

In odd-numbered years, the legislature convenes for the first time on the first Monday in January. This is the same time that it meets for the governor's inauguration. At this time, committees will have already been organized and committee assignments will have been made. The legislature should then recess for five or six weeks. During these first weeks, bills would be presented and sent to committees and standing committee meetings, research, hearings, and investigations would commence. At this time, the individual house Operations Boards and Legislative Council Boards would be making staff allocations and assigning study topics to standing, and in some cases, joint committees. (Usually, joint committee assignments would be made at the end of the first year of a two-year cycle.)

Assembly Speaker Harold Froehlich has already taken steps to assure a quicker start of the session. He has written to the heads of state agencies asking them to submit proposed legislation to committee chairmen by November 1. This surely would mean that during the first weeks of the session, spokesmen for state agencies would be presenting their proposals at committee meetings.

After this initial five- or six-week recess, the legislature should reconvene. At that time the legislature should meet three days a week with priority still devoted to work in committee. This would mean that either three afternoons or one full day (Wednesday) should be devoted to committee work. Once the budget has cleared the Joint Committee on Finance, the legislature should meet for four or five days a week.

Again, committees should meet in the afternoon. Where possible, this schedule should be adhered to in order that legislators may know the days that they will be free to pursue their private careers and occupations.

On or about February 15, the legislators actually receive copies of the governor's budget, which has formally been presented to the legislature on or about February 1. At that time, standing committees and the Joint Committee on Finance will continue their policy and fiscal research, which has actually been going on since early January. Now, however, they will have the budget document with which to work. As Eagleton has already recommended, standing committees will now have thirty days in which to report their recommendations on their respective portions of the budget to the Joint Committee on Finance.

The bifurcated session (in which the legislature adjourns for Finance Committee hearings) has worked well for the Wisconsin legislature and for the Joint Committee on Finance. It should work well for standing committees. It gives needed time for the consideration of policy implications and issues. According to Senator Walter G. Hollander, Joint Committee on Finance co-chairman, the early recess has been quite helpful to the committee and has allowed the group to complete its work sooner. During the first two months of the odd-numbered years, Eagleton believes that the Joint Committee on Finance should be occupied with consideration of the sections of the budget devoted to the Department of Administration and to the Department of Revenue, both of which fall under its original jurisdiction. The Joint Committee on Finance will also be receiving and digesting reports submitted to it from its staff. Furthermore, the Joint Committee on Finance will be able to schedule hearings on sections of the budget which have been covered by substantive standing committees, after the first two weeks of the above mentioned thirty-day period. The Joint Committee on Finance staff would then analyze and digest the reports of the standing committees.

On March 1, the Joint Committee on Finance will convene its own hearings, attended by members of the affected agencies. In addition, members of the substantive committees, which first considered the particular section of the budget under consideration, should be invited to testify or attend.

According to many respondents questioned by Eagleton, the Joint Committee on Finance hearings have served their purpose. According to the legislative representative of the University of Wisconsin, "there were more and better hearings on the budget this year (1967) than ever before, and the budget is the most important job the legislature does."

After these staggered budget hearings are finished and after Joint Committee on Finance deliberation, the budget will be reported to one of the houses for consideration. It is at this point that both houses should make more frequent use of the rule allowing organization of the full houses into Committees of the Whole, to hear explanations of particularly controversial or technical information which has been deliberated by both the standing and Finance committees. At this time technical programs such as the 1967 "chargeback" concerning county payments for patients in state mental hospitals should be explained by the appropriate committee to their colleagues. To achieve improved floor consideration of the budget, Eagleton recommends that:

(95) *The legislature make more frequent use of the rule allowing organization of the full houses into Committees of the Whole, to hear explanations by standing committees of particularly controversial or technical legislation.*

Anywhere from the first of June through the end of the session the legislature should be considering other legislation reported out by the standing and Finance committees.

When the legislature adjourns after the first session, the Legislative Council Board will make study assignments to the joint committees.

In the second session, in even-numbered years, the legislature will commence in March and joint committee reports should then be offered to the legislature.

Separate standing committees should have met at this time and bills resulting from the work of the joint committees should have been prepared for consideration by both houses of the legislature. Also at this time, it should be possible for committee chairmen to make presentations to each house sitting as a Committee of the Whole concerning the results of their research.

In this way, individual legislators will benefit from the work accomplished by the joint committees. This procedure should encourage excellence for several reasons. Among these are that committee members will seek the approval of their colleagues and their constituents. In addition, the individual legislators will have been exposed to material presented verbally which they might not otherwise have considered. It is our belief that the remarks of the committee to the full houses will elicit questions and a healthy intellectual exchange leading to better understanding of the issues which have been studied by different committees.

Starting on the first of March, standing committees of both houses should be meeting to consider reports of the full joint committees and of other material which may have been submitted by advisory panels. Major bills resulting from joint and standing committee research should also be considered at this time. Other bills which were not considered in the first session of the legislature, because of the time allocated to the passage of the budget, should be considered during this period. Finally, the standing committees should be comparing agency projections for the preceding year with actual expenditures.

On or around May 15 of the second year, reports relating to the budget should be submitted by standing committees to the Joint Committee on Finance, which should commence its second set of hearings on the budget, or supplementary budget. This new budget should include the cost of new legislation developed by the several standing committees. From the time the budget adjustments have been made, to the end of the session, there should be time allocated for the consideration of legislation which is still pending. The entire two-year cycle suggested by Eagleton follows.

A PROPOSED LEGISLATIVE CALENDAR

FIRST YEAR SESSION (*odd years*)

Approx. December 1 (of even years)	Organization of leadership and committees. Orientation of new members begins. Prefiling of bills by legislators.
First Monday in January	Legislature meets for governor's inauguration. Committees officially organized and committee assignments made. Legislature recesses; bills presented and sent to committees; staff is allocated to committees by Division of Services; committee hearings and investigations commence. Agencies make presentations to appropriate standing committees.
February 1	Governor submits budget to Joint Committee on Finance.
Approx. February 15	Copies of the Executive Budget are delivered to the legislature.

	Standing committees begin deliberations on the particular sections of the budgets for which they are responsible; some begin reporting to the Finance Committee.
Approx. March 15	All standing committees have reported to the Finance Committee on respective portions of budget document.
March 1	Finance Committee convenes its own budget hearings.
May 1	Finance Committee finishes budget hearing.
May 15–June 1	Finance Committee meets to consider budget. Consideration of budget on floor.
June 1 until end of session	Pressing non-budgetary legislation is passed. Assignment of studies to interim joint committees. Legislature adjourns.
SECOND YEAR	
March 1	Legislature convenes. Consideration of pending bills. Standing committees of both houses consider implementation of their research. Standing committees develop legislation and consider revised fiscal estimates supplied by Department of Administration.
May 15	Standing committees submit developed legislative proposals to Finance Committee. Finance Committee commences second round of hearings for second annual or supplementary budget. Legislature considers new legislation.

End of Session	Legislative Council Board assigns new studies to joint committees. Legislature adjourns.

PROBLEMS OF PROCEDURE

Air Conditioning

In addition to the schedule already suggested, certain peripheral matters will have to be attended to. For example, if the legislature is to meet through July, Eagleton recommends that:

(96) *Air conditioning be installed in the capitol building.*

There is no reason for the legislature, or any good business, to operate under less than optimal conditions. Legislative observers have noted that tempers rise proportionately with the thermometer, as does the urge to return home. Undoubtedly, legislation has been passed or rejected because of the hot weather.

Organization of the Full House Meetings

The way in which the legislature does business on the floor of both houses can be improved. This contention is supported by numerous legislators and the chief clerks of both houses. What follows is a plan for implementing common orders of procedure in both houses.

Following is the Regular Order of Business for both houses of the legislature as it now stands.

EXISTING REGULAR ORDER OF BUSINESS

Assembly	*Senate*
(1) Call of the roll	(1) Prayer
(2) Amendments may be offered	(2) Roll call
(3) Motions may be offered	(3) Introduction of amendments
(4) Introduction and reference of resolutions	(4) Introduction and reference of resolutions
(5) Introduction, first reading and reference of bills	(5) Introduction, first reading and reference of bills
(6) Petitions and communications	(6) Petitions and communications
(7) Reports of standing committees	(7) Reports of standing committees
(8) Reports of special committees	(8) Reports of special committees
(9) Executive communications	(9) Executive communications
(10) Messages from the Senate and action thereon	(10) Messages from Assembly
(11) Consideration of motions	(11) Introduction and consideration of motions
(12) Consideration of resolutions	(12) Consideration of resolutions
(13) Second reading and amendment of Assembly bills	(13) Second reading and amendment of Senate bills and resolutions
(14) Second reading and amendment of Senate bills	(14) Second reading and amendment of Assembly bills and resolutions
(15) Third reading of Assembly bills	(15) Third reading of bills and resolutions
(16) Third reading of Senate bills	(16) Special orders
(17) Announcements	(17) Announcements
(18) Adjournment	(18) Adjournment

The major change recommended for the Assembly is to move the Third Order of Business until after the Assembly daily "housekeeping" functions have been disposed of. Since this "housekeeping," which includes calling the roll, introducing bills and resolutions, petitions, and communications, and accepting reports of standing committees, takes only a few minutes each day, it should not be interrupted. The Third Order of Business in the Assembly in which "motions may be offered" disrupts the "housekeeping" procedure. This change will contribute to an understanding of the legislative process on the part of the legislators, the press, and the public, with the concurrence of the clerks of both houses of the legislature.

As we recommended in our section on committees, Eagleton believes it would be advantageous to consider all bills pertaining to a single subject on the floor at the same time. This change would affect scheduling under the Ninth to Fourteenth Orders of Business. Eagleton therefore recommends:

(97) *Moving what previously constituted the Third Order of Business to the Fourteenth Order of Business in the new schedule. Inasmuch as amendments are automatically recorded in the journals, it is not necessary to "read them." This change is reflected in the new schedule. Under the new "Orders of Business" both houses will operate under similar procedures. In addition, bills relating to similar subject matter should be considered together.*

PROPOSAL FOR REVISED ORDER OF BUSINESS

Assembly	*Senate*
(1) Call of roll	(1) Call of roll
(2) Recording of amendments	(2) Recording of amendments
(3) Introduction and referral of resolution	(3) Introduction and referral of resolutions
(4) Introduction, first reading and referral of bills	(4) Introduction, first reading and referral of bills
(5) Petitions and communications	(5) Petitions and communications

PROPOSAL FOR REVISED ORDER OF BUSINESS

Assembly	*Senate*
(6) Committee reports	(6) Committee reports
(7) Executive communications	(7) Executive Communications
(8) Messages from the Senate and action thereon	(8) Messages from the Assembly and action thereon
(9) Special order of business	(9) Special order of business
(10) Consideration of motions and resolutions	(10) Consideration of motions and resolutions
(11) Second reading of Assembly bills	(11) Second reading of Senate bills
(12) Second reading of Senate bills	(12) Second reading of Assembly bills
(13) Third reading of Assembly and Senate bills	(13) Third reading of Senate and Assembly bills
(14) Motion may be offered	(14) Motion may be offered
(15) Announcements and Adjournment	(15) Announcements and Adjournment

The following considerations of changes proposed above should be noted. The Prayer (formerly Item 1 in the Senate) should not be an Order of Business. It may be provided for by resolution. In the Second Order in the revised schedule, it should be remembered that amendments may be offered at any time. However, Eagleton recommends that:

(98) *Only one person, the chief record clerk, be designated responsible for receiving amendments.*

This applies mainly to the Assembly, where a number of persons now have the authority to receive amendments.

In the proposed Tenth Order of Business, under the proposed revised Order of Business, Eagleton recommends that:

(99) *Special orders be taken in sequence and receive priority over regular Orders of Business on the calendar.*

Moving the Previous Question

Eagleton believes that although unlimited debate is ideal, there ought to be ways in which debate may, upon occasion, be limited in a one-hundred member assembly. Presently, there is a rule for moving the "previous question," thereby shutting off debate. Nevertheless, this procedure is seldom employed, and many members complain that debate too often is desultory. It is up to the leadership of the Assembly to make the "previous question" motion work.

In the Senate, a change is called for in the rules. Although the Senate has a rule (Senate Rule 76) for moving the previous question, it does not use it. The reason for this situation is that when the previous question is moved in the Senate, the rule automatically cuts out debate for the whole bill rather than on a particular question. The "previous question" should be changed so that debate on a *particular* question may be halted.

Mr. Nugent, the chief clerk of the Senate, has supplied such language and Eagleton believes it would be wise to adopt this with dispatch in order that the use of "previous question" may become more viable. The new language appears directly below.

(1) *When any matter is under consideration any member being in order and having the floor may move the "question" or that the "question be put." Such motion is undebatable and if carried by a majority the particular question then pending before the Senate shall be put without debate.*

(2) *A motion to establish the amount of time to be given a particular matter may be made in the same manner as provided in para. (1), except that this motion shall*

> *be subject to one amendment, which also shall be de-
> cided without debate.*

The Conference

Joint Rule 2 of the Senate and Assembly discusses the way
in which the conference committees of both houses work out
disagreements and arrive at a final bill, when Senate and Assembly versions have differed. Again, Mr. Nugent has proposed new language which simplifies the description of the
procedure. Eagleton recommends the adoption of this new
language, so that:

(100) *Joint Rule 2, "Committees of Conference," be
changed to read*:

> *When the house of origin fails to concur in amendments
> of the second house, it* may *request a committee of con-
> ference. The house offering the amendments may recede
> from its position, or if it adheres to its position it* shall
> *appoint a committee of conference and notify the house
> of origin.*

> *The committee of conference shall consist of three mem-
> bers from each house who shall have supported and
> voted for the positions of their respective house. The ap-
> pointment of such committee shall be made by the pre-
> siding officer, but Senate members shall be confirmed by
> the Senate.*

> *The report of the committee shall be presented to the
> second house (house offering amendments). It shall be
> approved by at least two members of each house.*

> *If the conference report is approved by a vote sufficient
> to constitute final passage of the proposal by both houses,
> it is final action thereof.*

If the committee of conference reports failure to reach an agreement or if either house rejects the report another conference committee may be requested by either house.

Submission of Bills

Another way in which Wisconsin can improve its schedule relates to the submission of bills. The session should get off to a swifter start. After November, or before January, legislators should make every attempt to develop their bill proposals, using the excellent staff drafting services available to them.

Wisconsin Statute has provided authority to the clerks of both houses for prefiling. Preprinting actually constitutes prefiling, since nothing can be done formally before the legislature is organized. In the decade from 1955 through 1965, over eight thousand bills were introduced in the Senate and Assembly. Of these, however, only one hundred and twenty-seven or less than 1.5 percent were prefiled.

Once bills are prefiled, they should be formally assigned by the chief clerk and the presiding officer to committees so that on the first day of the session, committees have material to work with, and the legislative machinery is ready to roll. As has already been mentioned, the same is true of bills introduced on behalf of departments and agencies. Departmental proposals, many of which have been drafted for months, should be similarly introduced directly after the November elections.

There were 8,186 requests for bill drafts in the 1967 session submitted to the Legislative Reference Bureau. These requests were handled by six draftsmen (five hundred bills each). Since a good deal of work goes into each bill draft, it is extremely important that the work be distributed over the session and that, where possible, legislation be drafted and introduced before the session actually begins.

Deadlines

Eagleton believes that rigid deadlines can help some states, but hurt others. Wisconsin, at this stage, is in the latter category. A clear majority of those legislators responding to the Eagleton survey believed that there should be no imposition of further legislative deadlines. There presently exists a deadline on the introduction of bills. Drafting instructions have to be submitted to the Legislative Reference Bureau by the fifty-first day of the legislative session to preserve for an individual member the right to introduce his proposal. Drafts requested after the deadline may still be introduced with the permission of the Assembly Rules Committee, the Senate Committee on Legislative Procedure, the Joint Committee on Finance, or by unanimous consent.

The chief of the Legislative Reference Bureau has argued for this elimination, since the rule is abused as a matter of course and since several methods of avoiding it have been ingeniously and studiously worked out.

The other alternative which Eagleton would recommend, is that the proposed Organization Committee of each house, in case the deadline is maintained, should not allow this abuse of the rules and should insist that there be no new legislation, other than that submitted by the leadership in urgent matters, after the cutoff date. In effect, the "spirit" of the rule must not be abused. The practice of instructing bill draftsmen in such a way as to reserve the right to introduce legislation at any time during the session constitutes an impediment to the legislative process.

The Consent Calendar

The Consent Calendar is one way of facilitating the passage of non-controversial bills during the session and may well assist in preventing the late session log jam. Senate Rule 26 and Assembly Rule 18A both provide for committee chairmen to construct a list of non-controversial bills. In the case that such a consent calendar were devised, the bills would be read and if there were objections by a number of members to a particular bill, it would be automatically removed from the consent calendar. On the other hand, if there were no objections, the presiding officer would announce that: "The bill was ordered to be engrossed and read a third time, was read the third time and passed, and a motion to reconsider was rejected." Although the legislature has made provision for a consent calendar (called a "special calendar"), it has not been very much used. Eagleton therefore recommends that:

(101) *The Wisconsin legislature make greater use of the existing procedure and make it more understandable by renaming the "special calendars" consent calendars.*

LEGISLATIVE COMPENSATION

Wisconsin legislators are underpaid. In fact, most state legislators are. This last fact helps the argument raised by certain individuals that legislators in a particular state should not be paid more because the state ranks seventh or eighth highest in the country for legislative compensation.

According to Larry Margolis, Executive Director of the Citizens Conference on State Legislatures, there is no legislature in the United States which, in his opinion, pays its legislators adequately. In addition, the almost non-existent pay differential between leadership and rank-and-file members makes no sense in Wisconsin. Legislators deserve an executive salary, considering that they are elected by the people of the state to make the most important decisions relating to the state. Also, the job of the legislator is an extremely high-risk activity. The people should compensate the legislator who may be removed from office at any time.

The Committee on Economic Development has stated that legislators should be paid at the rate of $25,000 per year in large states, and at least $15,000 in the other states.[4] Wisconsin legislators presently make $8,400 per year. A number of writers have disposed of the ill-considered argument that legislators are part time and should be paid as such. Responsibilities outside the capitol, relating to constituents and preparation for the legislative session, make the job of a legislator extremely demanding.

Even if legislators were to say that they spend 70 percent of their time on their legislative work, there is no guarantee that they would have enough energy or opportunity to find employment for the remaining 30 percent of their time. Wisconsin is progressing in the area of legislative compensation, but it does not pay its legislators nearly as adequately as New York, Pennsylvania, or California—all of whose legislators' salaries range upward of $15,000 per year. One wonders whether decisions are less important in Wisconsin than in these other states. A legislator must be allowed a decent standard of living, rather than having continually to face the dilemma of whether particular "outside" work constitutes a "conflict of interest." For these reasons, Eagleton believes that the $500 legislative pay raise urged by the six-member Legislative Compensation Council is not adequate. Therefore, Eagleton recommends that:

(102) *Legislative salaries be raised to: $12,000 per year for rank-and-file legislators; $17,000 per year for the president*

[4] Committee for Economic Development, *Modernizing State Government* (New York: The Committee, July, 1967), p. 39.

pro tempore of the Senate and the speaker of the Assembly; $16,000 per year for the majority and minority leaders of the Senate; $15,000 per year for the co-chairmen and ranking minority members of the Joint Committee on Finance and assistant floor leaders; and $14,000 per year for chairmen of the party caucuses.

There can be no question that the job of the legislative leaders is full time. The Legislative Compensation Council's recommendation, of $2,250 raise per year for the Assembly speaker and the president pro tempore of the Senate, and for a raise of $1,335 per year for the majority and minority leaders in both legislative houses and for the co-chairmen of the Joint Committee on Finance, is also considerably less than what it should be. The argument presented by this Council that an increase of about 6 percent in legislative pay appeared fair in terms of raises given to state employees and those in private industry is based on the fallacy that existing legislative compensation is established at a level bearing some relation to the responsibility of the job.

Another argument advanced by the Special Taxpayers Committee on the State Budget, which Eagleton believes to be weak, is that legislators should not serve because of monetary reward, but because of a desire for public service and their interest in government. Eagleton believes that there is no excuse for penalizing the public-spirited. According to a study put out by the Citizens' Conference on State Legislatures and the study of the Wisconsin Committee on Improved Expenditure Management, legislative pay compares unfavorably with the pay of other public officials taking into consideration the time spent on the job. This study demonstrated that the median annual salary of state legislators was well below that of congressmen, city aldermen, and other state government officials.[5] Governors make $25,000; lieutenant-governors, $9,750; attorneys-general, $19,500; secretaries of state, $16,000; executive secretaries to governors, $16,000; finance or administrative secretaries $20,000; revenue or taxation secretaries, $17,500; and health department heads, $23,000. In addition, the president of the University of Wisconsin is paid a salary of $47,000 a year. When the University makes its budget request for higher salary, it makes the argument that higher wages are needed to keep top professionals. We wonder if the legislature is any different? Legislators have a considerable way to go before they will be making salaries commensurate with their duties and responsibilities.

In addition, Eagleton believes the existing per diem allowance for legislators is not sufficient, and recommends that:

(103) *The present per diem allowance of $15 for residence in Madison during legislative sessions be increased to $25. On the basis of rates in adequate hotels and motels in Wisconsin and on the basis of food prices which legislators must pay in even moderately priced restaurants, where they dine with their colleagues and constituents, $25 per day is not at all unreasonable;* and

(104) *This rate of reimbursement apply for all interim and joint committee meetings.*

We do, however, agree with the conclusions of the Wisconsin Committee on Improved Expenditure Management, that no extra compensation should be provided for attending interim study committee meetings.[6]

[5] *Report and Recommendations Regarding a Compensation Plan for Legislators.*
[6] *Ibid.,* p. 6.

Legislative Compensation Council

Wisconsin has initiated a plan by which compensation for legislators is determined by a Legislative Compensation Council. This six-member citizen group reports its recommendations to the state personnel board, which makes its recommendations to the Joint Committee on Finance. The argument has been advanced by many students of state legislatures that devices such as compensation councils serve as a way of decreasing resentment among the members of the public over legislative pay raises. This may be true. But the practice of shifting the burden may be dangerously extended. When the legislature starts finding ways out of politically risky situations, it may abdicate its responsibility. The legislature is, after all, a decision-making body. What if this principle were to be extended to taxation or to education formulas? Furthermore, Eagleton believes that when legislators are correct, they can mobilize public opinion and professional resources in such a way as to present their case effectively. Therefore, Eagleton recommends that:

(105) *The Legislative Compensation Council be abolished or, at the very least, the legislature rather than the governor be responsible for appointments of the Council's members.*

CHAPTER V.

CENTRALIZATION AND CONTROL OF LEGISLATIVE SERVICES

Improving legislative services has long been part of Wisconsin's tradition of sustained effort to improve its state government. Several of Wisconsin's innovative contributions to the art of government—the Legislative Reference Bureau and the Revisor's Office—are legislative services. These efforts for improvement have accelerated in recent years.

Following a nationwide trend to bring legislative service agencies entirely under the control of their respective legislatures, Wisconsin, in 1963, put the Legislative Reference Library and the Revisor of Statutes, for the first time, under the control of the legislature. In the same year, the legislature established a Committee on Organization in each house to handle employees, printing, and other duties and a Joint Committee on Legislative Organization (JCLO) to coordinate the work of the houses and recommend legislative improvement.

Major changes were also made to provide legislative fiscal services. The Budget Staff (now the Legislative Fiscal Bureau) was established in 1963 as part of a $240,000 grant from the Ford Foundation for studies and for pilot programs demonstrating the use of legislative interns, caucus staff, and fiscal analysts. And in 1965, the State Auditor's office was brought under legislative control as the Legislative Audit Bureau.

In May, 1965, a proposal was made to combine nearly all legislative services into a Legislative Services Department, and, in 1966, the JCLO sponsored a proposal to group all fiscal research services.

None of these attempts was successful, and the effort to strengthen and realign legislative services carried over to the next session and to 1967 Assembly Bill 1069 (AB 1069), which sought "to provide for a streamlined structure of legislative services integrated into a department of the legislature."

AB 1069 followed the main thrust of its predecessors. In brief, it proposed:

> the creation of a Legislative Council Board to oversee a Department of the Legislature and three operating bodies, embracing all legislative employees: a Senate Division, an Assembly Division, and a Division of Services;

> the integration of all services not inherently part of either house (i.e., chief clerk and sergeant-at-arms functions) into a Division of Services; and

> the consolidation of these services so that one administrator would be responsible for that division and thereby for the staffs of the Legislative Reference Bureau, Legislative Council, Fiscal Bureau, Audit Bureau, and Statutory Revision Bureau.

This bill was not passed during 1967, but its subject matter was distributed among four subcommittees of the JCLO for further study. Service and staffing went to the Subcommittee on Permanent Legislative Agencies and Administration. The subcommittee met in the capitol nine times between its first meeting on March 19, 1968, and its final report meeting of September 19, 1968. Eagleton was privileged to attend and participate in all its discussions.

OVERVIEW

Wisconsin's investment in its legislative service agencies currently runs a little over $1 million a year, with an additional $2 million needed annually to finance salaries of members and staff, and upkeep for the Senate and Assembly.

Comparing Wisconsin's legislative services budget against those of other states is, of course, difficult. So, too, is a comparison of Wisconsin's own expenditures year by year. Many services, such as the Legislative Audit and Statutory Revision Bureaus, have not been included in the legislative budget prior to recent years. And in a comparison between states, it is equally difficult to sort out what is and is not included in any given legislature's expenditures.

Our concern in this chapter is primarily with reorganization of service agencies. There is little need to describe them in detail at this point. All are covered in the Wisconsin *Blue Book* and in a recent bulletin of the Legislative Reference Bureau.[1]

It is important, however, when studying reorganization, to have a clear picture of how these services fit into the legislature and how they relate to each other and to the committees that oversee their activity. These relationships are shown in Table 5.

The functions covered by the legislature's service agencies are also of interest. Those required in a state legislature have been described by the National Legislative Conference and arranged by the Legislative Reference Bureau in the following breakdown.

---

[1] For an excellent description of legislative services in Wisconsin see LRB Bulletin No. 68–4, "Legislative Staffing and Services." Both the chart and the checklist of functions shown on the following pages are taken from it.

Administrative Services	*Research Services*
Administrative and clerical staff	Information
	Policy assistance
Recording and indexing legislative developments	Substantive law revision
	Review of government operations
Assistance to legislative leaders, individual members, and standing committees	Review of administrative rules and regulations
	Orientation Conferences for Legislators
Fiscal Services	*Other Services*
Budget review and fiscal analysis	Legislative printing
Post-audit	Legislative manuals and handbooks
Fiscal notes	Public information
Legal Services	Legislative internships
Statutory and code revision	
Bill drafting	
Bill analysis	
Legislative legal counseling	
Summarizing legislative session developments	

It is worth noting that Wisconsin's legislature provides all these services to at least some degree. It does not yet have administrative aides for every member. Legal counseling for legislators has been available, but only on an informal basis.

The problem, in brief, is not a lack of any critical service, or a failure of the legislature to appropriate sufficient monies. It lies, instead, in strengthening certain services, eliminating duplication and overlap, encouraging clear lines of responsibility, and realigning all of them to gain maximum efficiency and effectiveness for the future.

THE CASE FOR CENTRALIZATION

As we have pointed out in discussing committees, there is no reason for the same members of the legislature's leadership to meet as four or more separate committees for different

TABLE 5. THE PRESENT ORGANIZATION OF LEGISLATIVE STAFFING AND SERVICES

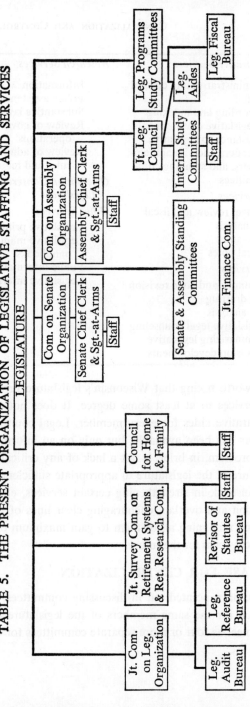

purposes. Similarly, there is no reason for the staff of the legislature to be reporting to some eight different legislative committees. At the present time, the following committees are responsible for the following legislative staffs:

Committee	Service
Joint Committee on Legislative Organization	Legislative Reference Bureau Audit Bureau Revisor of Statutes JCLO Staff
Joint Legislative Council	Legislative Council Staff
Joint Survey Committee on Retirement Systems	Own Staff
Council for Home and Family	Own Staff
Committee on Senate Organization	Senate Staff
Committee on Assembly Organization	Assembly Staff
Joint Finance Committee	Legislative Fiscal Bureau
Legislative Programs Study Committee	Legislative Aides

Under the proposed reorganization, the staff for all the above functions would be organized into three divisions of the Department of the Legislature: an Assembly and a Senate Division, for those functions attached to each of the separate houses, and a Division of Services, under a single administrator, for all joint legislative services and staff. The joint services would be organized into a unified command, as shown in Table 6.

We shall discuss in detail the role of each of these service units later, together with various units and staff *not* shown here. These include the secretary of the legislature, the specialized units (such as retirement and tax exemption), and the Senate and Assembly divisions. The important thing to note at the moment is the logic and simplicity of this proposed organization. The confusing hodgepodge of the present

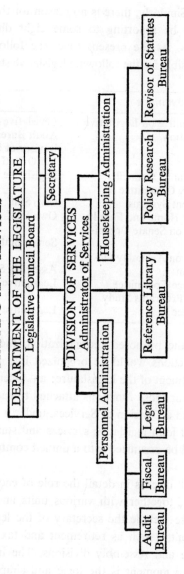

TABLE 6. THE PROPOSED ORGANIZATION OF JOINT LEGISLATIVE STAFFING AND SERVICES

DEPARTMENT OF THE LEGISLATURE
Legislative Council Board

Secretary

DIVISION OF SERVICES
Administrator of Services

Personnel Administration

Housekeeping Administration

Audit Bureau

Fiscal Bureau

Legal Bureau

Reference Library Bureau

Policy Research Bureau

Revisor of Statutes Bureau

structure has been eliminated. All policy flows down directly from the legislature and the Legislative Council Board. Problems and suggestions flow up from the operating bureaus, through appropriate channels. Although the new setup appears to be a sweeping reorganization, only minor changes will be felt in day-to-day operations of the bureaus.

The case for such centralization of joint services can easily be summarized in terms of:

(1) clear-cut lines of responsibility;

(2) a coordinated use of personnel;

(3) greater assurance of non-partisan staffing;

(4) greater flexibility;

(5) centralized data collection and coordination;

(6) a broader perspective of the relative merits of different areas of consideration.[2]

We doubt that centralized staffing could make Wisconsin's legislative services much more non-partisan than they are already. But all of the other advantages would seem to apply.

Clear-cut Lines of Responsibility. Although some lines of responsibility are clear on the organization chart of the present structure, they have been rather murky in practice. During the early existence of the Budget Staff its employees found themselves working for one committee (Joint Finance), controlled by another (The Ford Committee), and paid by another (Legislative Council). In the past, a resignation occurred because of the delays in adjusting wage scale inequities—presumed or real. Another resignation was threatened on the caucus staff. Legislative interns complained about the lack of clear lines of authority.

Similarly, with staff reporting to the JCLO, which meets perhaps only once a month, day-to-day supervision is diffi-

[2] Calvin Clark, *A Survey of Legislative Services in the Fifty States* (Kansas City, Missouri: Citizens Conference on State Legislatures, April, 1967), p. 6.

cult. And with a unit such as the Audit Bureau, no one legislative committee is following up on its reports to make sure that its recommendations are carried out.

Coordinated Use of Personnel. Eagleton found generally good informal cooperation between service agencies of the legislature, but only centralization can make for truly coordinated use of personnel. This will be discussed in detail in sections on the Division of Services and the Policy Research Bureau. Meanwhile, it should be noted that the creation of new bureaus will in no way affect the ability of the Administrator of Services to shift personnel between bureaus to meet emergency needs.

Greater Flexibility. Legislative work loads are often uneven. Often one staff unit is frantically busy, while another is not. Some kind of flexibility in staffing is needed. Only then can the legislature get the most from its total staff.

Centralized Data Collection. It makes no sense to have the Legislative Council and the Reference Bureau compiling research in the same field. Fortunately, there has been relatively little duplication of effort among Wisconsin's legislative services. But with centralization of services, there will be better opportunities for collecting needed information and possible conflict in the future can be avoided.

A Broader Perspective of the Relative Merits of Different Areas of Consideration. Centralization can also help in terms of setting priorities. Which bureau's emergency is most critical? How can the output of one bureau be utilized to help another? Putting one experienced administrator in charge provides a means of resolving these competing claims and problems in a fair and intelligent manner.

These are the general arguments in favor of centralization. But how can centralization work? What controls should the legislature provide to assure its proper functioning?

THE GOVERNING BOARDS

In a discussion of committees we have touched on the proposed Senate and Assembly Operations Boards and the Legislative Council Board (LCB) and the suggestions made for their membership, meetings, and control over standing and joint committees. We have suggested how the LCB would replace the Joint Committee on Legislative Organization, the Legislative Council, and the Ford Committee. We have also described how the Senate and Assembly Operations Boards might neatly interlock to comprise the LCB and thus provide an evenly balanced and completely representative governing body to administer all of the jointly conducted business of the legislature.

We have not, however, discussed the department, divisions, and bureaus into which all staff services are arranged. According to the proposal we are advancing, all employees of the legislature are grouped in a Department of the Legislature, within which are three divisions—the Senate Division the Assembly Division, and the Division of Services. This arrangement has advantages of both substance and terminology. By treating the legislature as one administrative unit it encourages uniform policies for both houses and the joint services that serve them.

By use of the term "Department of the Legislature" it coopts the spirit and convenience of the language used in the Kellett Committee recommendations which led to the reorganization of the executive branch of the Wisconsin state government into fourteen major departments. Within this Kellett concept, as described by the chief of the Legislative Reference Bureau: "The entire operations of the legislature should probably be considered as one 'department' which has as its function the determination of Wisconsin state policy."

Use of the term would also symbolize, perhaps, the consolidation of service agencies, and streamlining of functions, that took place in the Kellett reorganization. It would provide consistency of nomenclature, in that the next level below the department would be a division, followed by a bureau.

Whatever term is used, the concept makes sense. So does consolidating control in the LCB rather than having it dispersed among the Legislative Council, Ford Committee, and JCLO. Under this centralized arrangement, responsibility will be fixed. The LCB will be highly visible. No one will ever have to ask "who's in charge here?"

Eagleton therefore recommends that:

(106) *All joint legislative services staff be organized into a single Department of the Legislature and brought under the control of a single Legislative Council Board.*

The chief function of the LCB would, of course, be the setting of administrative policies for the service agencies under its jurisdiction. Once the policy was set, it could be carried out by the Administrator of Services.

As the governing board for the operations of the legislature, the LCB's responsibilities would extend in many directions. Under AB 1069, it would:

(1) approve budgets for the Department of the Legislature (as is now done by the JCLO);

(2) study means of improving all aspects of the legislature, with particular attention given to fiscal analysis; procedural rules, committee work load, working conditions, and data processing (JCLO, Council, and Ford);

(3) serve as a joint ethics committee (now a duty of JCLO);

(4) conduct demonstration projects (similar to the Ford

Committee) and employ outside consultants (as has been done by the Legislative Council and the JCLO); and

(5) sponsor legislation to implement its findings and recommendations for legislative improvement.

All of these functions are important. The LCB should continue to have the freedom to explore and experiment in new concepts of state government. It was this freedom which led to the authorization of the Mason and Knight* reports and to the intern, caucus, and budget staff programs.

When a problem is exceedingly complex or technical, legislators, legislative staff, and committee chairman should be encouraged to ask for outside help—and the LCB should be the approving authority. Under the LCB's control, it is unlikely that the practice would be abused. "Contracting out of studies and research is still extraordinary behavior for State Legislatures . . ." but "executive departments and agencies, primarily those of the Federal Government, have turned to management consultants, data processing firms, and university personnel with increasing frequency." [3]

The LCB should also have the power to name advisory committees on legislative improvement similar to its power to appoint public members to joint standing committees.

Finally, because of its overarching responsibility for the operations of the legislature, the LCB should be considered as a continuing body. Its decisions and policies should continue in effect until changed by the legislature or subsequent decision of the LCB.

In summary, then, Eagleton recommends that:

---

* W. D. Knight (consultant), *The Wisconsin Study: Second Report of the Committee on Legislative Organization and Procedure* (Madison: Legislative Council, April, 1965).

[3] Alan Rosenthal, *Strengthening the Maryland Legislature: An Eagleton Study and Report* (New Brunswick, N.J.: Rutgers University Press, 1968), p. 108.

(107) *The Legislative Council Board (LCB): (1) deter-mine the type and extent of tasks assigned to the Department of the Legislature, approve its budget, issue reports and make a continuing study of possible improvements in the legislative structure, procedures, and services; (2) be empowered to conduct demonstration projects and hire outside consultants; and (3) be deemed a continuing body to keep its policies and programs in effect until changed.*

All of this discussion so far has centered around the LCB's duties as a governing board. We have not discussed its own accountability to the legislature.

Problems and reports would flow upward from the bureaus to the Administrator of Services who would report directly to the Board at its meetings, plus a formal report each year.

In addition, however, the LCB would report to the legislature on an annual basis. Such accountability is important for both the LCB (the legislature's leadership) and the service agencies (the legislature's experts). Regular reports to the membership will provide increased accountability and keep the LCB and its service agencies more visible. We hope that this will counteract the possible feeling by members that they have no share in the control of staff services.

Eagleton therefore recommends that:

(108) *The Legislative Council Board report annually to the legislature on the problems and progress of the legislature and particularly on the role of legislative service agencies.*

Although the trend is to pool all functions that can be con-solidated, certain functions and employees are inseparably linked to one house or the other. Under the proposed reorgan-ization, these activities and employees are placed under the control of the Senate and Assembly Operations Boards. The power of these boards would be "regulatory, advisory, and policy-making"—the same as governing boards under other statutes. This is a broader mandate than simply directing and reviewing the work of the "administrators" of their respective service divisions. It involves making the decisions necessary to schedule the session in each house each day.

The make-up of each board, as we have mentioned, interlocks neatly with the Legislative Council Board. This has many advantages: the boards in each house are completely aware of what is being done *jointly* through the Legislative Council Board; parochial resistance to the pooling of like functions in the Divisions of Services should be diminished; and personnel policies for each house can be coordinated with the other, as is the intent of having the Legislative Council Board's administrator of services assisting each division in this area.

Under each of these boards is a Senate and Assembly Division. We shall discuss them in a separate section below.

THE SECRETARY AND THE ADMINISTRATOR

Before describing the divisions and bureaus that make up the Department of the Legislature, some attention should be given to their leadership, which is, of course, the crucial element in all organizations.

Two men will be preeminently important in making the new organization effective: the secretary of the legislature and the administrator of services. Some opinion exists for putting all joint staff functions under one man, rather than two. But the more we became immersed in this study, the more we were persuaded that two essentially different *sets* of functions existed: one staff and one line. The staff duties would fall to the secretary of the legislature; the line functions to the administrator.

Secretary of the Legislature

We see the secretary of the legislature serving in the following capacities:

(1) As the (non-voting) secretary of the Legislative Council Board, making certain that its decisions are carried out, that staff work for its meetings is coordinated and completed in time, and that notices, agendas, and minutes are prepared.

(2) As the Legislative Council Board's agent in negotiating contracts and agreements (for Board signature and approval), making certain they are carried through as drawn.

(3) As the chief long-range planner and strategist for the legislature, with enough prestige, foresight, and drive to help make such plans come true.

(4) As secretary to the Board in ethics cases, maintaining the confidential records involved, and arranging for the compiling, printing, and indexing of its rulings as a continuing body of interpretation of the statutes and rules.

(5) As a respected, impartial, and highly knowledgeable informal mediator whose good offices would be available to the legislature in controversies between the staffs of the two houses, between the legislature and the administration, or wherever else they might be needed.

(6) As senior advisor to legislative committees, coordinating their operations whenever necessary. Where conflicts may arise in committee jurisdictions, the secretary's experience and good offices can be important in resolving them constructively, with the Board's approval.

(7) As a public relations officer for the legislature in maintaining its importance before the people of Wisconsin and with other states.

(8) As the person responsible for an orientation program for new legislators.

(9) As the person responsible for any future Washington office that might be opened to represent Wisconsin's interests, including representing the legislature in calls on the Congress and federal agencies.

(10) As the initiator of pilot projects, seeking out foundation support similar to that provided by the Ford Foundation.

(11) As the "eyes and ears of the legislature," with a mandate not only to receive but also to look for complaints about the services and operation of the legislature.

(12) As the co-editor, with the administrator, of the Legislative Council Board's annual report on the "State of the Legislature."

In summary, then, Eagleton recommends:

(109) *As "chief of staff" to the Legislative Council Board, the secretary of the legislature be provided with sufficient assistance to*:

(a) *serve as secretary to the Board in ethics cases*;

(b) *serve as secretary to the Board for its meetings*;

(c) *develop plans for the continuous improvement of the legislature*;

(d) *coordinate, with the Board's approval, the operations of legislative committees*;

(e) *serve as chief architect of a public relations program to bring the legislature to the people*;

(f) *supervise a Washington office for the legislature*; and

(g) *plan and conduct orientation schools for new legislators*.

Administrator of Services

If the secretary of the legislature is the chief of staff, the administrator of services is the commanding general in the field. His is a line position. He would report directly to the Legislative Council Board where control of the Division of Services and its policies is vested. His duties fall into three broad categories: supervision of the Division, administration, and personnel.

To him, as chief operating officer of the Division, the directors of the six bureaus would report directly. He would exercise administrative control over these bureaus and review their work, but respect the essential independence of their viewpoint, i.e., he would exercise no control over their findings.

The bureau chiefs would thus run their own organizations, but would be able to seek guidance from the administrator, particularly when policy direction was needed from the LCB. Under the administrator's leadership, budgets would be prepared, computerization planned and installed, and personnel shifted to meet the ebb and flow of work in various bureaus.

Eagleton, therefore, urges that:

(110) *In carrying out the Legislative Council Board's policies, the administrator of services exercise administrative control over the bureaus and review their work, but without interfering with the essential independence of their findings.*

The administrator's second major area of responsibility would be administration. He should supervise all the pooled housekeeping functions of the legislature, including printing, duplicating, payrolling, mileage and expense accounts, requisitioning, purchasing, maintenance of office machines, maintenance of the document rooms, and the planning, allocation, and furnishing of space—everything, in brief, not tied by law or logic to the separate houses.

Keeping each of these functions separate results in an inefficient system. The payroll and vouchering of expense accounts could be combined to reduce the five to five and one-half persons now needed in separate departments to four persons in a pooled operation, and allow one person to be the disbursing officer for the entire legislature. Consolidating the document room would again provide only minor savings. But added together, and extended over a period of years, the combined savings would be significant. It also behooves the legislature, as guardians of the people's money, to run an efficient operation. Where jobs are eliminated, personnel would obviously be given special preference for re-employment.

The Joint Committee on Legislative Organization has already made a start toward consolidation of administrative and housekeeping functions. Last year it arranged the use of one index clerk for both houses. Earlier this year it proposed an administrative officer, within the Legislative Reference Bureau, to put together a payroll system for the legislature. The move covered only three agencies—Legislative Reference, Audit, and Statutory Revision Bureaus—under control of the JCLO. But others can transfer their payroll function to such an administrative officer by action of their own boards or through full reorganization.

Finally, the administrator would supervise the long-awaited personnel function, which is discussed below. Because that task is important and time consuming, Eagleton recommends that:

(111) *An experienced assistant, with clerical staff, be provided to the administrator of services to handle payrolls, expense vouchers, and reports for the entire legislature, and an assistant to the administrator be provided to specialize in per-*

sonnel in all its aspects, including recruitment, training, job classifications, and the other duties of a personnel manager.

The LCB's annual report on the "State of the Legislature" will also fall heavily on the administrator who will be responsible for reporting on all the problems and progress of administration personnel, and the six bureaus under his supervision —everything, in fact, not covered by the secretary.

The division of responsibility outlined above for the secretary and the administrator differs in some respects from that contemplated in AB 1069. Providing training manuals, for example, should be part of the administrator's responsibility for training personnel. Arrangements for committee facilities, minutes, and reports should also be made part of the administrator's general responsibility for space and personnel, particularly since professional staff for the committees will be coming from the Research Bureau.

But their relationship to each other and to the Board is the chief difference. Instead of the administrator serving under the secretary, Eagleton believes both should report directly to the Board. This preserves the line function of the administrator's position and the staff position of the secretary. It frees the secretary from additional administrative responsibilities, and it reflects the fact that both the secretary and the administrator would be appointed by, and serve at the pleasure of, the Legislative Council Board.

Differences in qualifications for the two positions are primarily a matter of emphasis. The administrator's special forte should be administration; the secretary's should be the wisdom that comes from long study of legislative problems. Otherwise the talents they need tend to overlap. Both officials must have great knowledge of Wisconsin's legislature, executive departments, law, procedures, and substantive issues. Both must exercise tact in performing their tasks and both must possess an unshakable zeal for upholding the legislature's viewpoint. Both must be innovators, and both must cooperate fully with each other. The secretary will have suggestions on administering the bureaus; the administrator on long-range planning. Working together, they can determine whether Wisconsin is to remain in the forefront of legislative modernization.

DIVISION OF SERVICES

The heart of the reorganization of services lies in the merger of existing agencies and subagencies into a Division of Services. This Division, and its two counterparts, the Senate and Assembly Divisions, will do the staff work for the legislature. Of the three, the Division of Services is the "growth sector." All of the joint services of the legislature would fall within this division. It would be composed of the six bureaus shown on Table 6, plus the specialized staff for personnel and administration that is attached to the administrator's office.

Two key matters are at issue in the proposal for a Division of Services: first, the creation of new bureaus, and second, their centralization under one administrator.

The Audit Bureau, Statutory Revision Bureau, and Legislative Reference Bureau already exist under the JCLO. Three additional bureaus are also needed for fiscal, legal, and policy research. Since almost all of the work of these bureaus is being carried on, the major effect of the proposed reorganization will be: (1) to break up the staffs of the Legislative Council and the Legislative Reference Bureaus, reassigning them to the Legal Bureau, the Research Bureau, and the Library and Reference Bureau; (2) to provide statutory authority for these bureaus and the Fiscal Bureau; and (3) to provide the common administrative services and coordination that each of these bureaus needs.

Establishing a total of six bureaus is, of course, a departure from the original structure proposed in AB 1069 last year. But it conforms closely to an arrangement provided in a substitute bill, 1967 AB 1120, for fiscal, legal, and reference library services. It formalizes what already exists de facto. It is, in our opinion, a more accurate reflection of the division of functions the legislature will need in the future. With each service properly labeled, a legislator should know exactly where to go for help.

Each bureau will be headed by a director reporting to the Administrator of services. Each would also be set up by statute so that it could operate continuously, without reorganizing every two years. But the statute would cover only the structure. Procedural and implementing detail would be governed by the Legislative Council Board.

A question arises as to whether the appointment of the new bureau chiefs will require an increase in their salaries. Eagleton has been told that it would not, that the adjustments to be made would be made anyway through the normal process of promotion. It will also be neither necessary nor justifiable to pay all bureau directors the same salary. Differences in responsibility, size of staff, and appropriation justify different salary levels, just as in the executive branch.

The question inevitably comes up as to whether adding more bureaus creates the condition for an accelerated increase of staff in the future—a Parkinson's Law of "creeping incrementalism." The possibility is that it does. But, more important, it will also tend to offset a great increase of work load that has inevitably occurred in every bureau, to say nothing of the better service that the new arrangement would provide. The determination of the administrator of services to run an efficient operation will, of course, be crucial.

The advantages of centralizing staff have already been discussed in general terms. There are specific advantages as well. A great deal of research and some bill drafting are now done in the Legislative Council, as well as in the Legislative Reference Bureau. A more logical arrangement, as noted above, would put all bill drafting in the Legal Bureau and research in the Research Bureau, with the Administrator of Services coordinating both.

If this is not done, and the Council and Reference Bureau are left as they now stand, the possibility exists for duplication of effort. With good talent in short supply separate specialists in the same field are a luxury no state can afford. Certainly one lawyer from the Division of Services should be able to act both as general counsel to a committee and as drafter of the bill needed. Similarly, it seems wasteful for research personnel in the Legislative Council to screen research on special projects done by the Legislative Reference Bureau. Research and screening should all be done by the same trained person.

Arranging services along functional lines will be particularly important when standing committees are set up, as recommended earlier. When professional personnel are needed, their hiring should be coordinated through the Administrator and the Division of Services.

Creation of one Division of Services should also make all services more efficient by smoothing out the peaks and valleys of overload and under-utilization that occurs in organizations that at certain times work against deadlines. Both overload and under-utilization exist in the legislature today. It makes no sense for a small service unit to have a full-time secretary when it might share one with another service unit. Where under-utilization does exist today, it is largely because of unnecessarily rigid separation of agencies and staff.

The fact that the Division is broken down into six bureaus should be no handicap if leadership is available from a skilled Administrator of Services. One potential reorganization presented to the Martin Subcommittee states: "For specific tasks and in each individual case with the prior consent of the director of the respective bureau, the administrator of services may assign personnel from one or more bureaus to participate in special projects."

Eagleton has discussed the matter with some of the present bureau chiefs and finds no reason why personnel cannot be shifted to meet emergencies that might arise. The legislature is not the executive branch. Maximum flexibility should be available to the former.

Other factors also point to the benefits of centralization. They include:

(1) The ability to use lawyer-researcher teams on important issues. Key personnel from the Reference Bureau and the Council now work together in the field of education. Similar collaboration can and should be encouraged under centralized control.

(2) The efficient deployment of staff to points of greatest need at times when it is difficult to hire competent lawyers and analysts.

(3) Increased certainty that the job gets done. When responsibility is divided, some functions are often left undone.

(4) The greater possibility of selling the use of staff to the committee chairman and legislators who could use it. Certainly it would encourage a legislator to seek staff help if he had a clear picture of all the staff services available and knew that there was a centralized source for all of it.

Such centralization of joint services is enhanced when recruiting, training, and other personnel functions are also placed within the division. This is discussed below, under employees of the legislature. Meanwhile, centralization tends to equalize opportunities for advancement in working conditions, in pay and benefits for employees, in fitting the right man to the right job, in increased efficiency with regard to computerization and printing, and in greater economy in routine services and equipment, such as document room and xeroxing facilities.

Therefore, Eagleton recommends that:

(112) *All services, facilities, and equipment for the legislature—other than those specifically attached to the chief clerks and sergeant-at-arms—be brought under a single Division of Services, and that within the Division of Services there be six major bureaus, each headed by a director, for Audit, Fiscal, Legal, Library and Reference, Policy Research, and Statutory Revision;*

(113) *Within this Division of Services the administrator of services be empowered, with the consent of the bureau directors involved, to shift personnel to meet developing needs.*

SENATE AND ASSEMBLY DIVISIONS

Under the proposed reorganization plan, as mentioned above in discussing the operations boards, staffs of the Senate and Assembly would be grouped in two divisions, each composed of a Clerical Bureau and a Sergeant-at-Arms Bureau.

Their functions would continue, as in the past, to include: scheduling each day's business; assuring that all necessary materials are available to members at the proper time; recording legislative action for posterity; and, in the case of the sergeants-at-arms, maintaining decorum.

The chief clerk would become the administrator of the division in his house, with a sergeant-at-arms as his deputy. Each division would be under the control of the Senate or Assembly Operations Board.

The key man in each division is of course the chief clerk who would serve as administrator of the division. The new title is appropriate. As the chief of the Legislative Reference Bureau has pointed out, the term "clerk" is a holdover from the days when only a portion of the population could write and when legislative records were kept with a quill pen. So, too, the sergeant-at-arms is a holdover from the days when force was often needed to maintain decorum.

Chief clerks and sergeants have been traditionally chosen by the majority party on political grounds. Yet the office is universally recognized as one that, almost more than any other, *must* be administered in an entirely non-partisan manner and solely on the basis of competence, loyalty, and experience. It is so administered in most states. Yet, as one authority observed: "The patronage nature of the appointments is all but universal for these posts. Only in Wisconsin is there a clear requirement that the selection shall be on a merit system basis." [4]

Surely, Wisconsin should maintain this tradition. The Wisconsin constitution (Art. 13, Sect. 6) requires both the chief clerks and the sergeants to be elected by each house. Eagleton would hope that the Operations Board of each house would make the nomination of the men to be elected, which should be on the basis of competence rather than party.

Administrative control of each division should be vested in the chief clerk as administrator. The chief clerk should be in charge in law as well as tradition, especially since the functions of the chief clerk and sergeant-at-arms interlock and should, someday, be one. Meanwhile, the chief clerk, while administrator of the division, should have an assistant to be director of a Clerical Bureau, while the sergeant would head the Sergeant-at-Arms Bureau—an arrangement that has the advantage, again, of following the terminology of the Kellett plan for state agencies.

The Martin Subcommittee has urged that both shall serve "for the entire biennial term . . . unless removed by death, illness, or majority vote of the members present." The Sub-

[4] Council of State Governments, *The Offices of Legislative Clerks and Secretaries in the State* (Chicago, 1957), p. 5.

committee has also proposed that the sergeants, in addition to the immunity from arrests they now share with the chief clerks, "may exercise the powers of sheriff concurrent with the sheriff of Dane County" in the capitol building and grounds, a power that is granted in other states and might be of use, potentially, against vandals and other lawbreakers.

In summary, Eagleton recommends that:

(114) *Senate and Assembly divisions be established under the Senate and Assembly Operations Boards, and these divisions be composed of a Clerical Bureau and a Sergeant-at-Arms Bureau;* and

(115) *The chief clerk of each house serve as the administrator of his respective division; an assistant chief clerk and the sergeant head their respective bureaus within that division; and these officials be nominated for their posts by their respective Boards and elected by their houses on the basis of competence to serve for the full biennium.*

EMPLOYEES OF THE LEGISLATURE

Wisconsin's legislature has been fortunate in the high quality of its staff. A study last year of twenty-seven staff members showed that nearly all had bachelor's degrees, one-third had master's degrees, and most of the rest had law degrees or had taken some graduate study.[5] Backgrounds included journalism, government, and college teaching. Direct on-the-job experience, so important in legislative staff work, was excellent. Turnover has been relatively low. Unlike some states where each successive majority installs its own followers, Wisconsin's legislature has kept a relatively high proportion

[5] Warren Rockwood Wade, "The Adequacy of Legislative Staffing in the Wisconsin Legislature" (Master's thesis, University of Wisconsin, 1968). (Xeroxed.)

of its staff, many of whom, of course, are classified civil servants. Eagleton has also been impressed with the dedication and amount of overtime that key staff members put into their work and the respect for actual merit that seems to exist.

Categories of Staff

All two hundred eighty employees of the Wisconsin legislature presently fall into three basic categories of personnel: classified, limited term, and unclassified.

Classified employees are under the state's regular civil service structure. These personnel must pass competitive civil service examinations and receive the security, benefits, tenure, and rights of transfer of other state employees. This grouping includes most of the staff of the operating service bureaus of the legislature—the chiefs and the staff of the Legislative Reference, Audit, and Statutory Revision Bureaus.

There are also employees on Limited Term Employment (LTE). For these positions there is a qualifying exam, conducted by the Bureau of Personnel. They are provided roughly the same pay classifications and benefits as the classified service, except for the "right" to transfer to other agencies, but are limited in tenure to the legislative biennium and/or the pleasure of the appointing body. This grouping includes all but a few of the one hundred ninety-six employees under the chief clerks and sergeants of each house.

In addition, there are unclassified personnel, appointed by the legislature to serve at its pleasure, with or without a qualifying exam. This grouping includes the chief clerks and sergeants, the Secretary of the Legislative Council, the directors of the Legislative Fiscal Bureau, the Council for Home and Family, the caucus analysts, legislative aides (interns), and secretaries and assistants to the leaders.

Some positions, such as caucus analysts and assistants and secretaries to leaders, require party loyalty or a confidential relationship or both. Their supervisors should be able to hire and fire on that basis.

At the other extreme are two groups whose positions deserve some protection from partisanship. The first are those who serve in relatively routine and non-sensitive posts: the clerks, secretaries, and security personnel who must work without partisanship for every member of the legislature, and whose jobs should not be subject to the vicissitudes of party politics over which they have no control. The second group are those experienced researchers, bill draftsmen, and lawyers whose professional talents are indispensible, and who have demonstrated their ability to serve effectively on a nonpartisan basis. Almost all personnel in the Division of Services falls in this group.

Eagleton believes these permanent, year-round employees of the legislature should be part of the Classified Service. This group should also include the bureau directors, three of whom are already under civil service. Having the director of each bureau in the Classified Service, according to AB 1069's analysis, "corresponds to the . . . Kellett reorganization act for the executive branch and will assume . . . that only qualified persons are hired to fill the executive positions."

In order to meet the competition of private employment, salaries in the Classified Service can now move up to a maximum of $29,412—higher than the governor's. Tenure is also provided; yet the legislature has time to make sure it has found the right man since the probationary period can run up to two years.

With such benefits, Eagleton believes the Classified Service will continue to attract superior talent. If it does not, the legislature should not hesitate to change its policy to allow hiring its directors on an unclassified basis.

A merit system is good if the security and benefits it offers tend to attract and keep—rather than repel—good staff. The main problem, in fact, is no longer to keep undesirable staff out, but to bring excellence in. A classified system should not "lock in" an incompetent. This is bad enough in an administrative bureaucracy; it is worse in a legislature—if only because the two hundred eighty employees of the Wisconsin legislature are less than 1 percent of the 37,454 employees of the executive branch.

In the belief that the merit system can meet these requirements in Wisconsin, Eagleton urges that:

(116) *The Classified Service include all personnel in the Division of Services, including the bureau directors, who should be appointed by the Legislative Council Board.*

The remaining personnel in the legislature fall basically into the remaining categories. The largest number numerically would be in the Senate and Assembly Divisions as limited-term employees. These would include most of the clerical staff that carries on the day-to-day procedural work of the session, plus the secretaries to legislators. Some modification, however, is needed in the current appointing practice. In the Senate, a resolution is passed at the start of the session carrying the names of all appointees. Later these persons drop out, are replaced, and changed about, without any similar formal action. Setting up the staffing pattern by resolution, without names, will correct this untidy practice. Similarly, the chief clerks, as administrators, should be given authority to hire and dismiss staff, with the Operations Board available for an appeal to reverse their decisions.

The third category would be unclassified personnel. In addition to chief clerks and sergeants, caucus staff, interns, and confidential aides and secretaries to leaders, Eagleton would recommend including the secretary of the legislature and the administrator of services, and expert consultants who are occasionally needed by committees.

The secretary and the administrator are the two top staff officials of the legislature and should serve at the pleasure of the Legislative Council Board. The highly paid specialist should surely not be required to take a civil service exam to demonstrate his knowledge of the field. Indeed it is his reputation as an expert that causes a committee to seek him out.

In summary, then, Eagleton recommends that:

(117) *Unclassified positions in the legislature include the secretary of the legislature and the administrator of services, the chief clerk and sergeant-at-arms of each house, the caucus analysts, assistants to legislative leaders, and the special professional, technical, or investigative experts that serve when authorized by the Legislative Council Board*; and

(118) *In the Senate and Assembly, staffing patterns be established, by resolution early in the session, setting the number, and type and total cost of positions that are: (1) unclassified and (2) limited-term employees, and within those patterns the chief clerks, as administrators, have the authority to hire and dismiss staff, subject to possible review by their Operations Board.*

Centralized Personnel Management

In the past few years the Audit Bureau and the Legislative Reference Bureau have been transferred from the executive branch to the legislature. It is now time that the personnel function also be set up under legislative control. The trend in Wisconsin and elsewhere has been in this direction, as noted throughout this report. The reason is not hostility or competition or any lack of desire to cooperate. It is simply that our tripartite system of government works best when each branch stands on its own feet.

At present, the Bureau of Personnel, in the executive branch, determines classifications and pay-range assignments for classified personnel with the approval of the Personnel Board. The Bureau also recommends classification and pay scales for LTE and unclassified legislative personnel. It conducts the qualifying examinations for limited-term employees, and it provides applicants to the legislature when vacancies exist for classified personnel under the so-called "rule of three." Under this procedure, the employee must be chosen from the top three qualified applicants.

Recently, recruitment problems have also plagued the Legislative Council, the Audit Bureau, and the Fiscal Bureau, among others. Discussions of pay scales and classifications have taken up valuable time in the Joint Committee on Legislative Organization. References to the need for a personnel manager for the legislature recur repeatedly in minutes of the meetings of the Ford Committee and the JCLO.

If a personnel manager were appointed, as we have urged in our discussion of the administrator of services, several benefits should result. The legislature would be entirely independent of the Bureau of Personnel and the executive branch. It would, of course, continue to collaborate with the Bureau. But it would now develop its own employee classifications, reflecting, in turn, the specialized nature of legislative staff work. There would be a focal point for grievances in the Division of Services (and equally clear lines of authority in the Senate and Assembly divisions). There would be a means for equalizing legislative salaries on an equal-pay-for-equal-work basis, and someone charged with setting up proper classifications. There would be someone to maintain a roster of talent for the legislature, and, most important, responsibility would be fixed for the vital task of recruitment and training.

The administrator's authority should cover the entire legislature. Eagleton therefore strongly recommends that:

(119) *The administrator of services, as personnel coordinator for the Division of Services and the entire legislature, recommend position and pay classifications to the Senate and Assembly divisions; administer necessary qualifying examinations for them; assist them in recruiting their help; and work with the service agencies of other states to establish meaningful classifications, training, and experience requirements for all staff positions.*

Recruitment and Training of Staff

The shortage of bill drafters, auditors, fiscal analysts, and other personnel trained for state government seems to be nationwide in scope. Wisconsin's Audit Bureau has had staff vacancies for years. Bill drafters are almost always in short supply during the session.

The legislature is fortunate in having the University of Wisconsin in Madison as a source of talent. The opportunity this offers should be fully exploited. Surely there is no reason why political science majors in graduating classes, and law school graduates, should not be informed of the opportunities of work for the legislature, in the same manner in which they are encouraged to seek work with major corporations.

The professionalization of legislative staff work can also be encouraged by the administrator, particularly in relations with other states. Just as the International City Managers Association keeps a roster of trained personnel in city management, so too should a regional roster be maintained of personnel trained in state government.

Under an able administrator of services much can be done to make the legislature a more attractive place to work. Good morale doesn't just happen—it is created and maintained by planning and working for it. Salaries, benefits, grievance machinery, and promotions have a major effect on any employee's morale. But morale is also affected by the importance attached to one's job, an atmosphere of high purpose, and incentives that assume a desire for self-improvement as well as more income.

Therefore, Eagleton recommends that:

(120) *Supervisors should have positive control over personnel through the granting of merit increases, promotions, training, and compensatory time off; and negative control, when needed, through reprimand, demotion, and dismissal.*

Under reorganization, training can be centralized for the entire legislature. Techniques used in other state legislatures can be applied. Job training for present employees can be supplied as well as training for new employees.

There is no reason, for instance, why new staff members cannot attend the orientation sessions on operations and procedures when these lectures are given for freshmen legislators. Additional service training should be provided for interns and for staff assigned to standing committees. In New York a school for legislative staff was tried, and in Ohio research applicants assigned to committees were grouped by categories of interest which held more or less continuous briefings, so that each was informed of his colleagues' work.

The value of employees to the legislature can be greatly enhanced by encouraging them to continue their education in fields that apply to their work. Eagleton noted with approval that the Joint Committee on Legislative Organization was willing to pay $100 tuition fee each for three members of the Legislative Reference Bureau to take an extension course in public administration. Corporations in the private sector have found that such subsidies pay dividends.

Training manuals should be an important part of staff training. They exist already for bill typists, drafters, and legislative index clerks. Orientation course material on procedures, such as the *Clerks' Manuals* and the Mason Report can, of course, be adapted to brief employees of the Senate and Assembly. And the Wisconsin *Blue Book* and *The Legislative Reference Bureau Can Help You* can also be used for general orientation. The Council of State Governments *Handbook for Committee Chairmen* can also be helpful for committee staff.

The preparation of training manuals were originally assigned, in AB 1069, to the secretary of the legislature. Surely his experience and ideas would be helpful. But because personnel recruitment and training are duties of the administrator, Eagleton recommends that:

(121) *Appropriate training manuals for staff should be prepared by the administrator of services as part of his training program for personnel.*

CHAPTER VI.

ORGANIZATIONS AND FUNCTIONS OF CENTRAL STAFF

THE LEGAL BUREAU

Bill drafting is the main task of the Legal Bureau, but other functions are also important. These include bill analysis, legal counseling, and assistance in providing parliamentary ruling and in the enrollment of bills.

Because of these additional duties, it is appropriate that lawyers in the Legal Bureau be described as "legislative attorneys" rather than "bill drafters." Eagleton has been pleased to learn that this change has been made and believes that it should make recruiting easier.

Bill Drafting

The National Legislative Conference has described the qualities that make for good bill drafting.[1] Summarized, for any given bill, they involve knowledge of (1) the constitutional, statutory, and case law; (2) the form, style, and organization of the law; (3) a precise awareness of the intent and purpose of the bill; (4) an ability to anticipate how the proposed law will operate as well as its interpretation and consequences; and (5) an ability to translate the bill's purpose into language compatible with all these considerations. Background research and review of related judicial decisions is also often involved. It is clear that the bill-drafting function

[1] Council of State Governments, *Mr. President . . . Mr. Speaker . . .*, Report of the Committee on Organization of Legislative Services of the National Legislative Council (Chicago: The Council, 1965), p. 42.

has many levels of sophistication. Mathematicians speak of "elegant" solutions. The same can be true in drafting a bill.

The policies of the bill-drafting service have been clearly described in the Mason Report and need no further description here. It will suffice to say that every effort is made to serve the needs of the requestor. The services are non-partisan, confidential, and, upon request, include research.

All bills go through the bill-drafting service. A high proportion are taken from the requestor's written or oral request and drafted from start to finish. Others have been drafted outside by legislators, state agencies, private individuals, or lobbyists, and are simply reviewed and jacketed by the bill drafting service.

In part because bill drafting is a specialized skill, a nationwide shortage of experienced personnel exists. Vacancies have existed in the Legislative Reference Bureau over most of recent years. The result has been heavy overloads on the bill-drafting service during the session. Meanwhile, the number of bills drafted has increased steadily over the past ten years as the following figures show:

Legislative Session	Drafts	Bills	Joint Resolutions	Resolutions	Laws Enacted
1955	4,164	1,503	256	74	696
1957	4,635	1,515	253	84	709
1959	5,571	1,769	272	84	696
1961	6,268	1,592	295	67	689
1963	6,214	1,628	251	120	580
1965	6,975	1,818	293	86	666
1967	8,190	1,700	215	61	355

Although it is apparent that the total number of bills and amendments drafted has doubled in the sessions from 1955 to 1967, the number of bills introduced has increased only slightly and the number enacted into law has actually declined. The difference between total drafts and the number of bills, joint resolutions, and resolutions introduced is attributable to the number of amendments, substitute amendments, and proposals that were drafted but never introduced. This number increased from 2,331 in 1955 to 6,214 in 1967 and represented an additional and essentially unproductive work load for the bill-drafting service.

Although the right of a member to have a bill drafted is traditional, it is probable that the total number of drafts could be reduced without disadvantage if members were reminded of this upward trend and asked to hold down their less important requests.

Under present rules (JR 18) the fifty-first calendar day after the opening of the legislature has been specified as a cutoff date for introducing any new bill. After that date, bills can be introduced only in two ways: (1) by the Assembly Committee on Rules, the Senate Committee on Legislative Procedure, or by certain joint committees (interim, special, or select); or (2) if the bill has already been requested, with full instructions, from the bill-drafting service.

Removing this cutoff date and allowing introductions at any time would undoubtedly reduce the rush of requests made by members to reserve their right to introduce a bill on a given subject after the deadline, under alternative (2) above.

Will removing this device delay the introduction of many bills and thus increase the log jam of bills at the end of the session? Perhaps slightly. Legislators could no longer tell their constituents that it was "too late" to introduce a bill for them. But they could tell them it was too late, from a practical viewpoint, to get a bill considered in committee or on the floor. There would still be an advantage to early filing. Surely as a means of reducing extreme and concentrated pressures on bill drafters, the legislature should experiment with dropping the fifty-first-day cutoff date for the introduction of bills. It should then make an assessment at the end of the session as to the effect of this change on the number and log jam of bills.

If this procedure does not work, another method might be tried on an experimental basis. This would reinstitute a modified form of Joint Rule 18 and specify that after the cutoff date, approval would be required from the Operations Board of the member's house before a measure could be introduced under the member's name. The request should be made to the Board in writing. This is a variation on the present procedure in Wisconsin under alternative (1) above, and the method used in New York and in other states which provides that after a certain date, no bills can be introduced except from a privileged committee. If bill drafting were overloaded, the Operations Board would reject the proposal. At that point, if the member were still interested, he would be forced to seek a committee to introduce the bill under its own name.

Another factor contributing to unproductive work load in bill drafting is the high proportion of bills requested and drafted but never utilized. In 1967, almost 2,000 bills, joint resolutions, and resolutions were prepared by bill drafters and introduced. A full 1,800 more were also drafted but died at the hand of the requestor. The following breakdown is illustrative:

700 were jacketed and delivered, but never introduced;
300 were jacketed but the requestor never picked them up;
800 had intermediate drafts completed, but the requestor never advised on further action to take.

According to the above figures, 1,100 were never even reviewed by their requestors, but simply allowed to rest in the files of the LRB. Surely, this constitutes a waste of staff time.

Again, Eagleton would recommend voluntary methods at the start to cut such extravagance. Every member should be made to know that for almost every bill introduced another was also drafted but died at that point. Some reminders ("Is this bill necessary?") could point the way. Eagleton therefore recommends that:

(122) *Attempts be made to reduce overloads on the bill-drafting staff during the session by experimenting in the following ways:*

    (a) *dropping the fifty-first-day cutoff date on the introduction of bills; or*

    (b) *requiring committee approval for the introduction of bills after the cutoff date; and*

    (c) *encouraging members to give bill drafters enough time, and reminding members of the wasted effort involved in unnecessary drafts.*

Bill Analysis

Surely one of the most useful of all services to the legislature is the brief and simple explanation which is prepared by the bill draftsman and printed with the bill. These analyses save untold hours of work for those persons who must deal with the bill. This is particularly true in Wisconsin, where bills that amend statutes are unique. In other states, the entire surrounding text of a section is shown when making a change. But Wisconsin law is divided and subdivided into small subdivisions, and only the immediate subdivision directly affected is amended and shown. The result of this arrangement is that the bill is often unintelligible without either the surrounding text or an adequate analysis.

Bill analysis was started in the 1967 session and is still a relatively new operation. Under present procedures, the analysis is prepared by the bill draftsman and returned to the requestor, with his bill, for approval. Despite this seeming guarantee of accuracy, bill analyses are not yet a complete success. Several former legislators have criticized it. As one put it:

> It tells what the author meant the bill to do, because it is compiled from the author's instructions to the bill drafters; but to tell what the legal language of the bill *really does*, it would have to be prepared by a review board which read only the text and then wrote a summary without knowing what the author had intended.

The bill-drafting service is aware of these shortcomings and is now revising its bill-drafting manual and procedures to make analysis more accurate.

It is also important, as in fiscal notes, that new analyses be prepared in engrossed bills and joint resolutions, where changes have been extensive, before these bills go to the other house. Similarly, as Speaker Froehlich has indicated, it is important that bills drafted outside the legislature be analyzed "by competent staff members whose loyalty is to the legislature and not to the department sponsoring the legislation."

Therefore, Eagleton recommends that:

(123) *Bill analyses be continued and strengthened, and extended to cover: (a) a review of those analyses done outside the legislature, and (b) engrossed bills and joint resolutions that contain substantial amendment.*

Legal Counseling

In addition to bill drafting and bill analysis, the lawyers in the legal bureau are needed for general legal counseling to the legislature. Such counseling falls into several main areas:

legal opinion on the constitutionality of bills and amendments; providing legal counsel to standing committees reviewing administrative rules and regulations; representing the legislature in proceedings before a court; and providing legal counsel to other service agencies, such as the Fiscal and Audit Bureaus, within the Division of Services.

Legal opinions have normally been provided formally by the Attorney General's office and informally by the legal staffs of the Legislative Council and the Legislative Reference Bureau. A transfer of this function to the Legal Bureau would cut one more tie of dependency to the executive branch, and should be made for this reason alone. This has been the trend in state government. Such a transfer should speed up and give greater control by the legislature to securing legal opinions. Nor would it abridge the legislature's right to additional opinions from the attorney general, by resolution. Opinions on the constitutionality or legal implications of a bill should be in writing and should be published in the journal.

Eagleton therefore recommends that:

(124) *The responsibility for rendering legal opinions to the legislature be formally transferred from the attorney general to the Legal Bureau, without the legislature surrendering its right to secure additional opinions from the attorney general.*

If reorganization goes through, an important new function of the Legal Bureau should be the provision of staff counsel to standing committees in general and particularly in the drafting of new legislation and reviewing administrative rules. Here it would be desirable for the lawyers specializing in education, for instance, to handle both bill drafting and counseling and to work closely with the committee, including attendance at meetings. Such integration of staff with the committee structure holds great promise for making the legislature a true body of experts.

The Legal Bureau's responsibility for representing the legislature and legislative committees in court proceedings would be intermittent. Where easily handled, there should be no problem. But on major cases, involving extended proceedings, the legislature through the Bureau, and under the authority of the Legislative Council Board, should have the right to retain outside counsel or request the aid of the attorney general.

Finally, the Legal Bureau should provide informal advice to the legislators on their constituents' problems with state agencies. Some of these complaints require legal advice, and the Legal Bureau, we believe, is the appropriate source in the legislature for this help. Three qualifications should be added, however: A constituent's complaint should always involve an agency of the state or the operation of present statutes or administrative rules. It should involve a *legal* aspect, and an attempt should have been made *first* by caucus staff to handle the problem. The Legal Bureau, in brief, can supply collateral help to legislators. But it is a relatively highly paid and busy staff and should never have *primary* responsibility for dealing with complaints of constituents.

Under the proposed reorganization, Eagleton recommends that:

(125) *The Legal Bureau provide legal counsel to standing committees in their consideration of bills, and in reviewing the rules and regulations of administrative agencies;*

(126) *Have primary responsibility in representing the legislature in court proceedings;* and

(127) *Provide informal legal advice to legislators on constituents' complaints involving government agencies.*

Serving as Parliamentarians

The United States Congress and a number of states have officially designated parliamentarians for each house. In Wisconsin, lawyers on the bill-drafting staff are now fulfilling that role, but the task, in our opinion, should be assigned explicitly to a continuing, statutory Legal Bureau.

Rulings of the speaker, which the parliamentarians would provide at his request, are to the rules what court decisions are to the statutes. In the United States House of Representatives, for instance, the monumental volumes of Hinds' and Cannon's *Precedents* alone have aggregated more than eleven thousand such rulings covering almost every parliamentary situation that might arise. Although state legislatures need no such elaborate documentation, the accumulation and indexing of these precedents can be a continuing and valuable service. Assembly Rule 94 (2) provides:

> Reference to established precedents of both houses, to long-established customs, to Opinions of the Attorney General interpreting rules and precedents, or to other leading parliamentary authorities may be used in the interpretation of both these and the rules in Jefferson's manuals.

The members can, of course, appeal these rulings and suspend the rules. But the precedents have served as invaluable guidelines to orderly and effective procedure.

The Legal Bureau could also assist the chief clerk in compiling and publishing the precedents of both houses. The Senate precedents, for example, have not been published since 1953.

Eagleton recommends, therefore, that:

(128) *The Legal Bureau should be formally required to provide parliamentarians for each house, and assist the chief clerks in recompiling rules and precedents.*

Enrollment of Bills

Enrollment is the putting together of the final version of a bill, with amendments which have been made, for the governor's signature. The chief clerks have had the legal responsibility of getting the bills to the governor, with the Legislative Reference Bureau providing the mechanical assistance.

In 1967, AB 1120, a companion measure to AB 1069, proposed a Legal Bureau with many of the functions listed above. It also directed the Legal Bureau to enroll bills, joint resolutions, and resolutions requiring enrollment thereby restoring a section of a statute enacted in 1966, which had been inadvertently repealed in a general revision of the printing laws earlier in 1967. Since AB 1120 did not pass, Eagleton urges that the legislature correct this unintended error and continue the practice of assisting the chief clerks by supervising the enrollment and printing of bills from camera-ready copy.

REFERENCE AND LIBRARY BUREAU

With the creation of the Legislative Reference Library in 1901, Wisconsin became the first state to provide information services specifically designed for the legislature. As the first such facility of its kind in the United States, the Legislative Reference Library has brought honor to the Wisconsin legislature for over half a century. Today the overwhelming majority—80 percent—of those questioned by Eagleton describe its successor, the Legislative Reference Bureau (LRB), as "very effective." Another 16 percent say it is "somewhat effective," while only 4 percent believe it is "not very effective." Although these comments pertain to the Bureau's entire operation, including bill drafting, it was clear from other interviews that the library and reference function ranked high in their estimation. Comments include such words as "good," "courteous," "very helpful." The service has been particularly helpful to legislative leaders and to younger members seeking to become expert in specific fields. With the advantage of over sixty-five years of continuous experience, it has been possible to refine the Bureau's work to a high level of efficiency.

Library. Everything is done to make the library easy for legislators and the public to use. Like other special libraries, the collection in the LRB's four compact floors of stacks is highly specialized. All books, government reports, and clippings are selected to provide information on the legislature's current and anticipated future problems, or to illuminate significant actions in its past. New material is selected from checklists of government publications, ten daily newspapers, and three hundred monthly publications. Some twelve thousand items are clipped, mounted, and catalogued each year. In addition to state documents, audit reports, voting records, and a complete legislative service for the current session, the library maintains drafting records on all bills since 1927, as well as a subject index of all legislation introduced in the Wisconsin legislature since 1895.

Keeping this collection usable and up to date also requires the indexing of items, a function as important as the process of selection. Those working in this field should have two years of library school in addition to an A.B. degree.

Unlike many other states, the Bureau makes a specialty of cross-indexing material, with up to a dozen entries on a given article. This not only provides better service to the legislators, but conserves precious space. The latter problem is severe. With the physical confines of the LRB unchanged in forty years and with valuable new material accumulating at the rate of six feet of shelf space per week, it is almost impossible to move documents out to the Historical Society fast enough to contain the incoming flood.

The answer, of course, is microfilm—both to conserve space and to save for posterity those unique records now threatened by decay. The value of this preservation effort is not solely for the historians. During consideration of a change in the Constitution's $100,000 debt limit, it was pointed out that the tax commission report of 1899 was the only document with a table of assessments for the whole state since the beginning. An annual sum of $12,500 is now being asked for microfilming unduplicated documents prior to 1930. The Joint Committee on Finance approved this proposal in 1967. Eagleton supports this project and recommends that:

(129) *As a means of preserving rare documents, the legislature continue to provide funds for the microfilming of selected materials.*

Reference. Reference is one of the major functions of the LRB. It is provided to all who ask. Thousands of requests pour into the LRB each year by letter, personal contact, and telephone. They come from every source: legislators, government agencies, private organizations, Wisconsin citizens, school children, and persons from other states. They range from simple queries handled routinely by a printed form, to time-consuming research. In general, requests fall into the following categories: (1) history and background of Wisconsin law; (2) information on Wisconsin state government and finances; (3) comparison of Wisconsin programs with similar programs in other states; and (4) library research to provide information on solutions already attempted in other states, but still in the discussion stage in Wisconsin.

Requests from legislators average about one hundred a

month when the legislature is in session. Many involve answering letters from legislators' constituents. Although the majority of all requests can be handled in a routine manner, those which require more effort pay off through multiplied distribution, or the amplified effect of having the research used as background for a bill, or as part of a speech or a newspaper story.

In servicing requests, priorities are followed to accommodate the legislative leadership, committee chairmen, members, and government agencies before other needs are met. Requests from school children for general information are usually filled on a classroom basis, but when school children seek information on some hard-to-find item, the library does provide them with an answer.

Over the past ten years, an average of some eighty-five hundred requests have been made on the LRB each fiscal year. The trend is up. Such totals make Wisconsin's LRB one of the two or three most-used facilities in the nation. For the fiscal year 1965, the only year when comparisons are available, Wisconsin's own all time high of 10,923 requests is approached only by Maryland and Pennsylvania with ten thousand requests each, and Texas and Massachusetts with six thousand. The same survey showed the LRB with an expenditure of $85,416, compared to the national average of $124,-638.[2]

These figures, of course, cannot be taken without some qualification. What constitutes a request? How many other functions, if any, do research and reference personnel perform? How much overhead is covered by expenditures? And so forth. Even if these figures are rough approximations, it is apparent that Wisconsin is getting full value from the LRB.

[2] Calvin W. Clark, *A Survey of Legislative Services in the Fifty States* (Chicago: Citizens Conference on State Legislatures, April 9, 1967), pp. 14–15.

As its chief pointed out to the Martin Subcommittee, "our researchers are the overtime champions of the legislature."

The line between research and reference is narrow. In its research function the LRB is perhaps best known for the factual reports it issues intermittently through the year. These are prepared on the LRB's own initiative, by request of a legislative committee, or are triggered by information requests from agencies or individual members. Since staff time is at a premium, they are developed only when need and interest is evident. They are factual, non-partisan, and avoid advocacy. Distribution is by request. Output in a biennium averages perhaps ten Wisconsin Briefs (short summaries of specific subjects of high immediate interest), eight extensive Research Reports (major studies, running fifty pages or more, that require considerable research), and fifteen Informational Bulletins (comprehensive but of intermediate length). At present, four researchers and a deputy chief of the LRB work on these materials and carry on the non-clerical aspects of the reference service as well.

Of particular importance is the Summary of Legislation prepared last year by the LRB in two parts. This should be continued under the sponsorship of the Reference Library Bureau and be coordinated with the Summary prepared by the Fiscal Bureau on the impact of the budget bill as passed by the legislature each biennium.

Two additional functions of the Reference Library Bureau are the indexing of bills and the biennial publication of the *Blue Book*. The latter job, and publication in off years of its new companion volume, the *Wisconsin Book,* has been handled in the past by the chief of the LRB and his deputy. Most of the work was done between sessions, when work was slack. But slack periods are becoming fewer and farther between.

The *Blue Book* is excellent, but as its editor has pointed out it could be better. An editor is needed to work full time to update and refine its eight hundred fifty pages. The book not only serves as the basic reference volume on the state's government, but is also a vital information link between the state and its people. Producing it within the Reference Bureau is appropriate in every respect. The *Blue Book*'s contents are the substance that the Bureau works with in its day-to-day operations.

The Reference Library Bureau should also handle the indexing of bills, not only for its own information but also as a service to the chief clerks in their preparation of the bill status reports. This ties in with the library's traditional function of maintaining an index by subject for years.

In summary, Eagleton recommends that:

(130) *The Reference Library Bureau be staffed to meet the increased demand on its reference service; continue, as in the past, the preparation of briefs and informational bulletins as a practical means of informing the legislature on current problems; assume the functions of indexing the bills for both houses; and provide a full-time editor for the* Blue Book.

RESEARCH BUREAU

Good research is indispensable if legislators are to legislate intelligently. Historically, Wisconsin's research services have been strong. We believe they still are. But even greater demands will be made on research personnel if the legislature is to meet the needs of the future. Research in the legislature has been divided between the LRB and the Legislative Council. Much of the research function of the LRB has been described in our discussion of the Reference Library Bureau.

The Legislative Council research staff of six persons, and the interns under its supervision, have been another major resource for research. Under the proposed reorganization, the

Council, as a coordinating agency, would be replaced by the Legislative Council Board. The Council staff would become part of the Division of Services with its personnel assigned to the Legal or Research Bureaus. This would create a pool of highly trained research personnel. It is from this pool, in the Legislative Research Bureau, that staff would be assigned to standing and joint committees under the proposed system of standing and interim committees.

The availability of professional staff is critical if the new committee plan is to work. On this, nearly everyone agrees. Simply holding hearings does not allow committees to make meaningful changes or delineate alternatives. Committees become little more than a rubber stamp for policies originating elsewhere. Part of this deficiency can be met by staff specialization, but part must come from additional personnel needed to man the new committee structure.

The committee staff proposal under 1967 AB 1069 makes sense. Under this arrangement, professional staff from the Division of Services will be assigned to standing committees with the prior approval of the Legislative Council Board and with the approval of the respective committee. Administratively, employees will remain under the Division of Services. This arrangement provides great flexibility for finding the right staff for each chairman, encourages the development of a truly professional cadre of legislative experts, and offers both more security and job opportunity for employees. Security for the employee comes from working for the Division rather than one chairman. Opportunity comes from the possibility of working for various committees, with the accompanying challenge of each new assignment.

The different levels of experience and talent for committee staff should be recognized within the Research Bureau. These levels range, in a state such as New York, from "compilatory" research at the beginning level (much of which will have already been assembled by the Reference Library Bureau), to "functional" research within a given field, to "program" research for developing a complete legislative program, and finally to "negotiating" research, whereby staffers serve as impartial mediators when the occasion demands. These different roles indicate the opportunities for advancement that lie within the legislative research function. This is as it should be. If the legislature is to be significantly strengthened, its committees must be professionally staffed.

Under the proposed reorganization, the Legislative Research Bureau would conduct in-depth research needed for drafting bills for committees and members. It would appraise bills for committees, prepare information or research bulletins for duplication, and summarize and digest public hearings before committees in the same manner that the Legislative Council now prepares minutes of interim committee meetings. This latter function should be done in cooperation with the secretaries to committee chairmen who take minutes at committee meetings.

In summary, Eagleton recommends that:

(131) *The Legislative Research Bureau be adequately equipped to supply staff to standing and joint committees from its pool of experienced personnel*;

(132) *Assignment of professional staff to committees be with the approval of the Legislative Council Board and the standing or joint committees involved*;

(133) *Preparation of in-depth research on pending or proposed measures be continued for committees and members*; and

(134) *Summaries and digests of committee hearings be prepared as part of the permanent record of the legislature.*

REVISOR OF STATUTES BUREAU

Statute revision is like pruning and weeding a garden. Without it, a brambly undergrowth creeps into most law—to almost everyone's disadvantage. Wisconsin, in 1909, was the first state to establish a Revisor of Statutes. It has been continuously revising its statutes ever since. A share of credit must go to the code revision committees of the Legislative Council in areas such as highways, election law, insurance law, and others.

Against a 1965 national average expenditure of about $57,500 for the revisor's function, Wisconsin's expenditure was $46,500. With merit increases the Bureau's budget request for 1969–70 is $65,400. This will not involve a $28,-000 project, now under way, for a new volume of the Wisconsin *Annotations* with court decisions from all courts that interpret the statutes. The benefits of clear and consistent law definitely make the investment in the revision function worthwhile.

Two types of bills are prepared by the revisor. One type is the correction bill. Correction bills are entirely non-substantive. They are needed, for instance, when two bills amend the same section and both pass. The correction bill simply establishes that both bills are correct and that one does not correct the other. In such a situation, if there is any doubt, the revisor informs the two sponsors and secures their approval.

Comment was made to Eagleton by several legislators that such bills should not be amended on the floor. Eagleton agrees. If the revisor is trusted and if the appropriate committee has approved the bill, it should be put on the calendar and recommended for passage as a correction bill. If legislators understand this to be a correction bill that changes no law in a substantive manner, it can be amended in committee, in consultation with the revisor, provided it makes no substantive change. But it should be protected from change on the floor.

The other type prepared by the revisor is the revision bill. Revision bills clarify, simplify, eliminate contradictions and obsolete language, and thus occasionally involve some minor changes in the actual substance of the law. Because of this they can legitimately be amended on the floor, though this should occur only with an awareness by the members of why the bill was put on the calendar.

There is general agreement that the earliest possible consideration during the session of bills from the revisor is also helpful. Normally, there is no public pressure for or against such revision. Nor is there reason for the bill to be held to await the formation of public opinion. Committee consideration, under the new structure, hopefully will have taken place during the preceding interim. Early passage helps reduce the end-of-session log jam and clears the way for an omnibus correction bill, in the closing days, to refine legislation enacted during the session.

The revisor's office, always a highly independent entity, was placed under legislative supervision in 1963. Despite the need, similar to the auditor's, for continuing the independence and non-partisan objectivity of the revisor, it makes sense to have it administratively part of the Division of Services. This aids the further integration of all staff services and expedites the shifting of personnel in and out of the revisor's office to meet its fluctuating demand for proofreaders and other help.

In summary, Eagleton recommends that:

(135) *The rules of the Senate and Assembly prohibit amendment of correction bills from the floor; correction bills continue to be clearly distinguished from revision bills; and both correction and revision bills be considered as early in the session as possible.*

FISCAL BUREAU

The first states to have a budget system were Ohio in 1910 and Wisconsin and California in 1911. At the time it was a "good government" reform. Back in those days, state budgets were less than 1 percent of what they are today. Yet, even then, some method was needed to bring appropriations and revenues into line with public needs and resources. The executive budget was then, and still is, the answer.

The problem has been that state legislatures have failed to provide intelligent budget review. Instead, they have been "reduced to nitpicking, pork barrel logrolling, frenzied, frustrated across-the-board budget slashing, or a polite 'amen' to the governors' budgets." [3] Primarily, this failure was due to lack of time, staff, and continuity. No legislator could be expected to analyze hundreds of pages of a governor's budget. Nor did he or his associates have the resources to evaluate the programs involved. Nor was there even a continuity of service in the legislature that would allow expertise to develop— membership on finance committees turned over with each election. The result was abdication. The legislature either "rubber-stamped" the budget, or cut it almost blindly. Yet there are encouraging signs of change. Today some forty-one states maintain staff for fiscal review. In California, a full-time staff of forty-one operates on an annual budget of over $554,000.

[3] Albert J. Abrams, in *State Legislatures Progress Reporter* (New York: National Municipal League, February, 1966), p. 6.

Fiscal Review in Wisconsin

Wisconsin's experience has been similar to that of other states, and its legislators have been aware that they were not getting enough fiscal analysis to compete with their bureaucratic leviathan.

Wisconsin's involvement with fiscal review was launched in 1963. Staff has grown from a single director in 1963 to a current authorization of a director, seven analysts, and two clerical employees, roughly the average for a state of Wisconsin's size.

The authority of the Legislative Fiscal Bureau (originally known as the Budget Staff) was derived from the Legislative Programs Study (Ford Foundation) Committee, but it has functioned as staff to the Joint Committee on Finance. Administrative control was in the hands of the Ford Committee; payrolling and office supplies were handled by the Legislative Council. General policy direction was also in the hands of the Ford Committee, but day-to-day operations were guided by the co-chairmen of Joint Finance. In February, 1968, it was redesignated the Legislative Fiscal Bureau.

The Bureau describes itself as a clearinghouse for fiscal information, which it provides to Joint Committee on Finance and all of the committees and agencies in the legislature, individual members and their constituents, and, to a limited extent, the general public. It has been directed to perform the following functions:[4]

(1) Analysis of agency operating budget requests;

(2) answering of individual legislative fiscal information requests;

(3) Evaluation of legislative proposals for fiscal effect;

[4] Legislative Reference Bureau, "The Wisconsin Legislative Fiscal Bureau" (Madison: Bureau Memorandum, 1968), p. 2.

(4) In-depth study of selected program areas or statewide policy areas;

(5) Continuing review of agency budget and programs;

(6) Analysis of agency capital budget requests;

(7) Estimating of revenues.

In fulfilling these functions it has analyzed two major budgets, processed an increasing number of requests, and conducted in-depth studies on subjects such as state-supported laboratory test charges, the state's institutional building program, compensation of citizen-member boards, the correctional camp system, hospitals, motor vehicle travel by state employees, and various programs at the University of Wisconsin.

The director of the Bureau, questioned in appearances before the Martin Subcommittee, estimated savings resulting from the Bureau's work at ten to fifteen times the Bureau's cost. This ratio is based on savings of some $3.1 million stemming from Bureau recommendations, against budgeted Bureau costs of $187,926—all during the current biennium. Other reductions totaled more than $5 million where decisions were based, at least in part, on the Bureau's recommendations.

An independent analysis of Bureau records by Eagleton shows that of seventy specific written analyses by Bureau staff on 1967 AB 99, the budget bill, about thirty had considerable and direct impact, and another fifteen some direct impact on decisions made by the Joint Finance Committee.[5] There is little doubt that staff analysis resulted in savings of several million dollars. Also important is the deterrent effect of fiscal analysis. Agencies tend to budget more stringently when they know their budgets will be scrutinized by the Bureau and by a

[5] Data from a study of the impact of legislative staff now being conducted by Professor Alan Rosenthal, Rutgers University, 1969.

caucus staff. This is true in California, and there is evidence that it is also true in Wisconsin. Eagleton's survey of legislators gave the Bureau a particularly high rating. Two out of three of those interviewed believed the Bureau to be very effective.

The Bureau's shakedown cruise is over. Ford Foundation matching support, which it used to receive, has now expired. It has demonstrated its ability, and it has also shown itself to be indispensable if the legislature is to fulfill responsibly its historic role of appropriating funds and levying taxes. It is now time for the legislature to fund and strengthen its operations for the future.

Statutory Authority for the Fiscal Bureau

The Bureau's first need is clear statutory authority. At present, it is derived from Chapter 13.49 establishing the Legislative Programs Study (Ford Foundation) Committee. This authority, while perhaps adequate during the Bureau's early years as a pilot project is now clearly insufficient. The Ford Committee will probably cease operations as the last of Ford funds are used up. The Bureau can and should be integrated into the over-all reorganization of legislative services now under consideration. And, most important of all, the Bureau requires, we believe, adequate statutory authority in order to maintain its day-to-day operating effectiveness vis-à-vis the administrative agencies.

This need has been demonstrated by various obstacles thrown in the Bureau's path in the past: the failure of a state authority to submit information until it knew who had requested it from the Fiscal Bureau; the delay encountered in getting answers from other agencies; and the failure of still other agencies to comply with the spirit as well as the letter of the Bureau's request.

At the root of these difficulties lies the fact that agencies of the administrative branch were unclear of the Bureau's authority and function. They were thus guarded or unwilling to respond to the Bureau's requests in any way that might set a precedent for weakening the administration's own historic right to administer its own programs. Such fears are, of course, groundless. Oversight, not harassment, is the Bureau's job, and the sooner the ground rules are clear to all, the easier it will be for everyone concerned to get on with their jobs.

Under last year's version of Assembly Bill 1069, the Bureau would have been established as a function for fiscal analysis of the Legislative Services Division. The Bureau would serve as staff for the Joint Finance Committee as it does now. The Bureau's director, under the proposed reorganization, would serve as non-voting secretary of the Joint Committee. All this is as it should be. But we also believe that the Bureau, as a semi-independent creature of the legislature, has a role to play separate and apart from Joint Finance. We can visualize a point in the future when Joint Finance will have a staff of its own, responsive to the committee's majority perhaps, which will be separate and apart from the Fiscal Bureau.

Both the Legislative Audit Bureau and the Statutory Revision Bureau are given such special status. The Fiscal Bureau, in our opinion, plays the same quasi-autonomous role and is no less important. By making it a bureau within the Division of Services, it moves one step closer to the same kind of independence enjoyed by the other two bureaus.

We are hoping, of course, that a total of six bureaus, including the Fiscal Bureau, will be established in the Division of Services. But even if this proposal fails, the Fiscal Bureau should be given this status.

Assuming the Function of BOGO

In our chapters on committees, we have described the Joint Finance Committee's assumption of the powers and duties of the Board of Government Operations (BOGO). In general, these are: (1) to supplement appropriations to state agencies under special conditions; (2) to transfer funds between programs and appropriations; and (3) to make recommendations to improve the administration of state agencies. A $4 million budget is set for these purposes.

Under BOGO, at present, the non-voting secretary is ex officio and is the secretary of administration or his designee. Under the proposed reorganization, the director of the Fiscal Bureau would serve as non-voting secretary ex officio, bringing this function under legislative control.

Under Wisconsin law, a generalized pre-audit function to ensure that agencies are spending funds only in accordance with law (and the governor's budget) has been accomplished through quarterly allotment requests filed with the Bureau of Management. Review of these requests provides an early warning system as to whether agencies are meeting their goals within their budgets. If the agency is in trouble, it may need to request a supplemental appropriation or a transfer of funds. Or if the need has declined, a program surplus may be developing. In any event, it is a valuable measure of agency activity.

Under the proposed reorganization, the secretary of the Joint Committee on Finance would automatically receive all allotment requests. This would enable him to follow impending deficiencies, surpluses, transfers, and other irregularities. If, in reviewing these allotments, he believes any estimate to be in conflict with legislative intent, he is to notify the co-chairmen of Joint Finance.

The Fiscal Bureau's efforts to follow transfers led to a

small controversy with the Department of Administration in early 1966. As described in the minutes of the Ford Committee for February 22, 1966, the director of the Fiscal Bureau "felt that the commissioner of the Department of Administration takes the position that the statutes are very vague with respect to what type of information should be made available to the legislature's staff, and it is a matter of legislative responsibility. The commissioner has felt that there is no specific statutory provision outlining their responsibility in this area."

The need for such statutory authority thus seems clear-cut. No difficult adjustments are involved in this proposed change. The co-chairmen of the Joint Committee on Finance serve ex officio on BOGO. At BOGO's request many applications to BOGO are now being looked at by the Fiscal Bureau.

Present practice in Wisconsin leaves the authorization to determine legislative intent regarding quarterly allotment with the Department of Administration. But under the proposed bill, the Joint Committee on Finance can make a "study, investigation, or review" of any allotment requests to which it objects.

Budget Analysis

No legislative function is more important than passing a budget. No staff function is more important than the Fiscal Bureau's budget analysis for Joint Committee on Finance and the legislature. With the 1965 and 1967 budgets behind them, and experience accumulating in other states, a pattern is emerging on the ideal operation of a Fiscal Bureau. Such a bureau should furnish: (1) continuous year-round work by expert analysts following specific programs and agencies; (2) studies in depth, spot research, and review of interim appropriations and transfers with those programs and agencies; (3) attendance at the governor's executive budget hearings to gather information (Fiscal Bureau personnel should attend as *observers* rather than to comment or to influence the budget at this point); and (4) direction and guidance for Joint Finance at public hearings on the budget.

At present, hearings are too often arranged to meet the convenience of the administration. Less important portions of the budget are often discussed first, when the committee is fresh and has time to listen. Sometimes this is desirable as a "warm-up." But it should not automatically consign more important subjects to a later period during a heavier crush of work. If adequate consideration is to be given the most important items, the co-chairmen, with the Bureau's help, should arrange the schedule.

As Joint Committee on Finance comes down to voting on specific portions of the budget, the Fiscal Bureau attempts to sharpen and clarify the options available for committee decision. It presents background memos of fact, actual recommendations, and alternatives from which the committee can choose. Alternatives are particularly important, not only for different levels of programs that different budgets would finance, but for *alternative programs*.

It is not that legislators lack for alternatives. Proposals are made constantly to kill, curtail, or increase a program. The special value of the alternatives offered by a good fiscal bureau is that they are limited in number, they are specific, and they are based upon information and study. No one else has the capability to do the job so well. Certainly, as D. J. Doubleday states, the agency in charge of the program and committed to it is "not likely to respond creatively to generalized requests for alternatives." [6]

There are other functions that the Fiscal Bureau should

[6] D. J. Doubleday, *Legislative Review of the Budget in California* (Institute of Governmental Studies, University of California, Berkeley: 1967), p. 77.

perform in analyzing the budget. One involves projecting costs beyond the current biennium. Many authorizations and appropriations have both a clear-cut immediate cost and a long-range cost that is difficult to avoid once the first step is taken. Capital budget requests are an example. "The legislative authorization for construction of buildings automatically 'locks in' certain corresponding operating budget requirements." [7] The Bureau should work closely with the Building Commission, for example, on the kind of jail that should be built when trends in penology are running counter to the old "maximum security" approach.

The Bureau should also keep an eye on federal grants. In some states, notably New York, this has become a particularly controversial issue. Grants that start at $100,000 in the first year of the program often escalate rapidly into many times that amount. Another function of the Bureau's budget analysis should involve an objective assessment of the probable effects of reductions in the budget. Still another would call attention to, and comment on, those items in the budget previously denied by the legislature—although flagging of these items should be part of the governor's budget-making responsibility too.

California's budget analysis fills one thousand pages, and covers every item in the budget. This is too much. The Bureau should not even attempt going into such details. Instead it should spend its energies where it has most chance of effecting practical improvement. This makes it important for the Audit Bureau, standing committees, and individual legislators to bring suggestions to the Fiscal Bureau on where it can best direct its energies.

[7] Legislative Reference Bureau, "The Wisconsin Legislative Fiscal Bureau," p. 3.

Final Budget Report

The Fiscal Bureau, we believe, should also prepare a summary at the end of the session on the impact of the final budget and revenue program enacted. This is in line with forward-looking legislative modernization efforts in other states. It is also in line with the Joint Committee on Finance's duty to report to the legislature, in a joint resolution filed within ten days after passage of the budget bill, its recommendations on fiscal policy for the next biennium. Although such reports have not been filed in recent years, it would seem important to have such a recapitulation, particularly with a backlog of other appropriation measures awaiting consideration. Such a recapitulation should be coordinated with the Reference Library Bureau's summary of all legislation.

Revenue Estimating

The Bureau should also implement the Ford Committee's directive that it work up a regular quarterly or semi-annual estimate of state revenue. The value of having this service, independent of other agencies, is pointed up in the Bureau's record to date on annual estimates. For at least one period (1966), its projections were some $28 million closer to subsequent actuality than the Administration's own estimates. All authorities agree that the legislature of a state is at the mercy of the governor without such independent estimates.

Relations with Other Agencies

The Bureau's role as legislative staff for all fiscal affairs places it in the center of a web of interrelationships. Elsewhere in this study, Eagleton has recommended that standing committees utilize the services of the Fiscal Bureau when considering the budget and when working on new legislation, and that all agencies and members of the legislature suggest to the Bureau those programs that most need examination.

An important relationship already exists between the Fiscal Bureau and the Committee to Visit State Institutions, which has asked the Bureau to provide staff for its work. This relationship is a two-way street. The committee, on its visits, can provide eyes and ears for the Bureau.

Another of the Bureau's important relationships must certainly be with the state auditor. Essentially, each bureau can be of great help to the other. The Fiscal Bureau, as the staff of Joint Finance, can follow up Audit recommendations to check on what action has been taken. It would have no power to force any change. But it could report to Joint Finance on corrective action taken or not taken. Such reports are, we believe, essential to responsible legislative oversight. The two Bureaus should also report special situations to each other. And both should cooperate in helping to establish performance standards, which are discussed in the next section.

The Fiscal Bureau should also have the authority to request special audits. This would be done only with the approval of the Joint Committee on Finance and the Legislative Council Board. It is in line with practice in Utah and in other states.

Looking Ahead

A 1967 bill (S80) called for a Scanning Council for "long-range public policy research" on problems that might be confronting the state twenty and thirty years hence. It specifically required that staff "not be burdened with such tasks of a short-range nature as one customarily assigned to the Legislative Council or the Legislative Reference Bureau."

The bill did not pass. But it poses the question of whether the legislature should look far ahead, or whether it should leave such long-range planning to the executive branch alone. Long-range planning could involve the implications of the thirty-hour week, electric automobiles, automatically controlled highways, and similar problems of the distant future. Or it could involve more immediate questions. What is the effect of capital spending plans on the state's debt structure? How dangerous is it to defer construction, in light of construction costs rising each year? Is some construction "too good"—i.e., built to last longer than the facility will be needed?

Where do lease-back arrangements become advantageous? What are the state's budget trends? What are the economic forecasts for the state? How is Wisconsin faring by comparison with other states? The economy as a whole? Is the state getting its share of federal government contracts? Grants-in-aid? How are different regions of the state sharing in the state's economy and the state's spending? These are the hard questions. It is questionable whether any operating agency dealing with current problems can handle them. And it seems undesirable to place this burden on the Fiscal Bureau, concerned as it is with practical situations that can save money, or maximize results for the state.

Yet they deserve mention. Someone should look far enough ahead on revenues and spending to anticipate crisis—if possible.[8] Someone should alert the legislature when the state's options for the future are being foreclosed.

Many of these problems will be handled automatically by the substantive work of standing committees. Some can best be handled by the appointment of an ad hoc citizens' committee. But the Fiscal Bureau—closer, perhaps, than any other

---

[8] A further reason could be to prevent the "politicizing" of these estimates in the future. In New York the governor and the comptroller frequently come up with conflicting estimates. The same conflict existed between Governor Ronald Reagan and former Speaker of the House Jesse Unruh in California. Having a bipartisan or independent viewpoint on the state's growth, for instance, could be a contribution. This is the approach taken by the Joint Economic Committee of the United States Congress.

service agency to these problems—should also be encouraged to seek these solutions.

To do it, we would urge that the Bureau be permitted to hire part-time specialists on such problems, or to retain outside consulting firms. Approval, as with special audits, should come from Joint Finance (which has this privilege) and the Legislative Council Board.

Fiscal Notes

Fiscal notes originated in Wisconsin in 1955. Since then all but five states have adopted the practice of "price-tagging" legislative proposals with estimates of their effects on revenues and/or appropriations. The National Legislative Conference has recommended their use. As the Legislative Reference Bureau has noted, fiscal notes have become "the outstanding innovation in legislative procedures in recent years." In Wisconsin, at least, it is difficult to recall how a legislature did its job properly before fiscal notes were available. In theory, at least, they seem indispensable.

Yet as the Tax Foundation has pointed out, in actual practice fiscal notes have been disappointing in some states. New York and Maryland adopted fiscal note procedures in 1964, repealed them in 1965, and subsequently restored them. Missouri and South Dakota, after several years' experience, modified their procedures. Of ten survey respondents in states using fiscal notes, four thought they were of "little or no value." [9]

Eagleton's survey showed that three out of four members of Wisconsin's legislature felt that fiscal notes were a "very effective" innovation; another quarter felt that they were "somewhat effective."

[9] Tax Foundation, Inc., *State Expenditure Controls: An Evaluation*, Research Publication, No. 3, 1965 (New York: The Foundation, 1965), p. 45.

In many states the whole question of fiscal notes has also become "politicized." If those preparing the note are opposed to a bill, they will hike its "price tag"—and the legislator has no appeal other than to attack the figure on the floor. Similarly, when an agency administrator desires a bill and is fearful that it may fail at passage, he may underestimate its cost and hope that a later deficiency appropriation can be arranged.

Such practices, while perhaps commonplace in other states, seem infrequent in Wisconsin. Yet allegations of such abuses have been made as well as complaints on procedures. Our judgment is that fiscal notes are being handled routinely and well in Wisconsin and that what abuses may exist are far less than in other states. Still, improvements can and definitely should be made.

Some of these improvements are important and go to the heart of the entire fiscal note program. Others simply put into statute or joint resolution certain procedural steps that are now, or should be, taken. Either way, these recommendations are important, for preparing a fiscal note can involve a great deal of work. Many fiscal notes are prepared; nine hundred nineteen were prepared for the 1965 session, and seven hundred forty-two for the 1967 session.[10] These figures are conservative. For the Legislative Reference Bureau, the major source of requests for fiscal notes, does not request a fiscal note except where the requirement for one is clear-cut. As Paul Mason comments: "Naturally, most legislation has some fiscal implication, and if the requirement were liberally applied . . . (it) would undoubtedly create a . . . burden on the legislative process." [11]

[10] In 1965, three hundred of the bills for which fiscal notes were prepared were not introduced; in 1967, one hundred seventeen.
[11] Paul Mason, "The Wisconsin Study: Report of the Committee on Legislative Organization and Procedure" (Madison: Legislative Council, January, 1964), p. 17–12.

Under present procedure, the Legislative Reference Bureau, or the presiding officer, or chief clerk of the house involved, or a member (by point of order) may request a fiscal note on a bill. The bill in turn is forwarded to the Department of Administration, which plays the key role as administrator and expeditor of the entire program. The bill is then forwarded from the Department to the primary agency or agencies involved. The agency is given five days to prepare a fiscal note, or fifteen working days, *maximum*, if the department grants extra time.

A memorandum from the Department of Administration instructs administrative units on how to prepare such notes. It is a model of clarity and comprehensive detail. Departmental worksheets are, by tradition, attached to the note that is ultimately prepared. Every precaution seems to have been taken in this procedure to safeguard objectivity, secrecy, and the rights of the author of the bill.

Yet the majority of legislators and staff to whom we talked felt that the Department of Administration had too much control over the content and timing of fiscal notes. We concur.

It is proper that the affected state agencies work up estimates, that they be asked "to exercise a high degree of objectivity," and that they be afforded a "clear-cut channel to inform the legislature of their fiscal needs as applied to the proposal." [12] But the basic responsibility for administering and expediting fiscal notes should be legislative. Fiscal notes are part of the legislative function, and the legislature, through the Legislative Fiscal Bureau, should request them and decide how much time can be allowed for their preparation.

This arrangement would not change the present arrange-

[12] Legislative Reference Bureau, "Fiscal Note Manual," Informational Bulletin 64–12 (Madison, December, 1964).

ment by which a fiscal note originates. The original request would still come from the Legislative Reference Bureau (the Legal Bureau under the proposed reorganization), the presiding officer, chief clerk, or member, upon a point of order. But once initiated, it would go to the Fiscal Bureau for transmission to the appropriate agency. Once in the agency, the Department of Administration may, of course, exercise some form of internal control. But the note comes back to the Fiscal Bureau which transmits it to those concerned.

The Fiscal Bureau does not attempt to analyze the fiscal note at this point. But a member should be able to have the Fiscal Bureau prepare a separate analysis and fiscal note if he so desires. Arranging to handle this program will take a little time, but the Fiscal Bureau is already covering the administrative agencies. The Bureau is specifically concerned with revenues and appropriations. It is the one legislative staff unit which can review the fiscal estimates of the administrative agencies with expertise, a skeptical and searching eye, and some knowledge of the agency's past performance relating to accuracy in estimating future costs. It should also help speed up the production of fiscal notes. Staff work for the legislature has a sense of urgency during a session that is often lacking within a state's bureaucracy.

The Ford Committee, which has had statutory authority for the Fiscal Bureau, has already specified that the Bureau provide an "evaluation of legislative proposals for fiscal effect." The Bureau, accordingly, has reviewed fiscal notes, and, in those instances where requested, it has presented alternatives or suggested changes to modify the fiscal impact or eliminate ambiguous or inconsistent provisions. This arrangement has worked well and should be continued.

Some further refinements are necessary, however. Chief among them would be a requirement for a new fiscal note on a committee substitute amendment, or on a bill, amended and passed in one house and ready for engrossment, where the amendments have substantially increased the obligations of the state.

At present Joint Rule 24 (2) states that "notes are required on original measures only and not on Substitute Amendments or Amendments," but that Joint Finance "may, on the basis of additional information, attach . . . a statement of the fiscal effect . . . as amended. . . ." It is significant that this option has rarely, if ever, been used by Joint Finance.

Although it would be almost impossible to have a fiscal note prepared on each amendment, it should be possible to have a fiscal note on an engrossed bill going from one house to the other. Amendments, after all, can change a bill completely or nullify it. This point is already recognized in the statutes covering procedure for legislative consideration of bills on retirement systems and tax exemptions, the two subjects that require special fiscal impact procedures different from those for all other bills. A provision requiring fiscal notes on amendments was put into use in Missouri in 1965.

Still a further change would ask that fiscal notes disclose, where possible, the short-term variations and long-range implications of a money bill. As the National Legislative Conference has pointed out, "a fiscal note which does not reveal whether such costs will increase at an abnormal rate is of questionable value. To be of value, the note must reveal whether the cost figure is for only a portion of a year or whether, for any other reason, the annual cost will increase disproportionately." [13]

The memorandum of the Bureau of Management regarding the form of fiscal notes advises the author to "explain long-range effects, if any" and later adds that he "may, with pro-

[13] Council of State Governments, *Mr. President . . . Mr. Speaker . . .* , p. 33.

priety, indicate the cumulative long-range effect, if such effect
is known."

Still another refinement would formalize an important procedure now followed by state agencies as a matter of tradition. This would require that state agencies attach worksheets
to fiscal notes showing the calculations used to formulate fiscal figures. This custom, not always followed in other states,
seems both good practice as well as an expression of good
faith and is therefore entirely in keeping with the fiscal note
tradition in the Wisconsin legislature.

In summary then, Eagleton recommends that:

(136) *The Fiscal Bureau be set up as an independent
agency within the Division of Services;*

(137) *All estimates of quarterly allotments submitted by
state agencies to the budget director of the administration also
be submitted to the secretary of the Joint Committee on Finance (director of Fiscal Bureau);*

(138) *The secretary of the Joint Committee on Finance review all estimates and advise the co-chairmen of the Joint
Committee on Finance, if he has reason to question whether
legislative intent has been properly interpreted, or if he has
reason to believe the allotment is more than is needed to
carry out the intent of the legislature;*

(139) *The Fiscal Bureau assist the Joint Committee on
Finance in establishing the sequence and timing of subjects
taken up at hearings on the budget;*

(140) *After enactment of the budget, the Joint Committee
on Finance provide a summary projecting and describing its
impact on the state;*

(141) *The Fiscal Bureau be able to request special audits by the Audit Bureau with the approval of the Joint Committee on Finance and the Legislative Council Board*;

(142) *The Fiscal Bureau, with the approval of the Joint Committee on Finance and the Legislative Council Board, be authorized to hire outside consultants as needs arise*;

(143) *The role of administering, expediting, and "policing" the preparation of fiscal notes be transferred from the Department of Administration to the Fiscal Bureau; or,*

(144) *At the option of the presiding officer, a member be able to have a fiscal note analyzed by the Fiscal Bureau and printed and distributed in the same manner as an amendment to a bill*;

(145) *Where amendments have apparently increased or decreased state revenue, appropriations, or fiscal liability, the engrossed bill be required to carry a fiscal note similar to an original bill*;

(146) *Fiscal notes include estimates of fiscal impact on the next biennium wherever appropriate and possible*; and

(147) *State agencies attach worksheets to fiscal notes showing the calculations used to formulate final figures.*

LEGISLATIVE AUDIT BUREAU

Just as the Fiscal Bureau examines the present and future, the Audit Bureau looks at the past. Both Bureaus are vital in assisting the legislature in its oversight of Administration. They are, in fact, the major staff resource for this purpose.

In the period from September 1, 1966, to March 1, 1968,

the Audit Bureau has conducted sixteen audits of major departments or funds, forty audits of medium or small departments, and one special study on federal aids. These have been fiscal audits and have been concerned primarily with the accuracy of an agency's finances rather than its efficiency or effectiveness. As far as they go, they have been both necessary as a safeguard and constructive as a means of catching errors and recovering money for the state. Examples of these recoveries are found in the Bureau's audit reports. They include situations where:

> The state made an advance to the city of Madison for a construction project. It was never carried out. The funds were not returned until the auditors' report called attention to them.
>
> Overpayments of $295,228 were made to municipalities for highway aids.
>
> An unspent balance from an earlier appropriation was kept by a department as a "kitty" of available funds.

Each of these items is a one-time recovery. Disclosure, as the acting chief of the Bureau has pointed out, undoubtedly will prevent similar errors in future years. Audit reports are transmitted to the governor and to the department involved. A copy is also filed with the Legislative Reference Bureau, where it is available to the press. Corrective action is usually prompt.

Although monies recouped between September, 1966, and March, 1968, totaled some $318,750, or a major portion of the cost of the auditor operation, it would be wrong to calculate the value of a post audit on the basis of the amounts recovered. Far more important is its influence as a corrective and a deterrent.

Bureau personnel feel that their activities undoubtedly help to keep state government clean. Auditors are of course called in when there is any hint of irregularity. They set up controls for the handling of cash receipts, and their presence is felt in many ways by both the potential embezzler and the careless employee.

The Department of State Audit was created in 1947, in the executive branch, as part of the general reorganization of budgeting and accounting for the state government. Into the department were brought various accounting functions performed by the secretary of state and the municipal auditing functions from the Department of Taxation.

To head the department, a state auditor was appointed by the governor, with the consent of the Senate, for a six-year term. His activity, as it evolved over the years, fell into three main areas: (1) audits of municipalities, on a reimbursable basis; (2) annual audits of the state treasurer and other units handling money and accounts; and (3) audits of remaining state agencies, on a frequency of at least once every three years.

Under a law effective September 1, 1966, the auditor's staff was split. The municipal audit staff was left in the executive branch. The state auditor and the remaining functions were transferred to the legislature as the newly created Legislative Audit Bureau.

Frequency of Audit

Annual audits are conducted on the stewardship of the state's money-controlling agencies: the Treasury, Investment Board, Central Accounting, and Retirement Fund. The remaining agencies are audited only every three years. This means that two years are skipped entirely—though, if discrepancies are discovered, the auditor follows the records back into these years. As set up in 1947, all departments were to be audited every two years. But an increasing work load, and chronic shortages of staff, stretched the span to three years, and it has become increasingly difficult to keep up. Compared to other states, this three-year cycle is neither the best nor the worst. Some states audit all agencies only every four years, others audit every two years, and still others audit some agencies annually.

Almost all observers prefer an annual audit. This reduces the chance of an irregularity becoming a major problem. It discourages laxity and helps to keep the state government on its toes. It is also particularly important where there is little in the way of an internal audit program—within the Administration—that is being used as a means of executive control.

The main need in the future, however, is to adjust the frequency of the audit to the budget cycle and the requirements of performance auditing. Skipping two years and picking up only every third year will hardly mesh with estimating accomplishments under a biennial appropriation. At this time, however, one must be realistic. There appears to be a nationwide shortage of qualified auditors. If staff is not available to conduct even the present program, there is little point in conducting more frequent audits. Eagleton favors a two-year cycle. As the acting chief of the Audit Bureau has pointed out, a one-year cycle is not efficient, except when a team makes the audit together. Otherwise, on a one-year basis, an auditor would "meet himself coming out."

Staffing

As with the Legislative Council, with bill drafting, and with various other legislative services, the Audit Bureau has been hobbled by staff shortages from the start (1947). This has unquestionably been the Bureau's biggest single problem. The same is true in other states across the nation. The problem is also complicated by a nationwide shortage of accountants in private firms, where salaries are usually higher.

There are only a few states where personnel needs are being met adequately. California's Auditor General has the power to set the salaries of his own employees, who are not under civil service. Over half are certified public accountants;[14] some of the others have taken C.P.A. exams; and all supervisors are experienced, with many from national C.P.A. firms. Michigan's auditors are under civil service, but its salary rates are more competitive. Illinois, which went through a scandal with its state auditor in the early 1950's, contracts out nearly all of its auditing, at considerable expense, and other states have moved in this direction.

In Wisconsin, recruitment has been difficult. Lapsed salaries caused by vacancies have averaged more than $25,000 per year in recent years. In 1967–68, salaries and fringe benefits, which were allotted but not expended, totaled over $50,000. By April, 1968, there were five vacancies out of twenty-four budgeted positions. Three staff members, in fact, received better offers from other departments of the state government.

For the 1967–68 fiscal year, the auditor had planned on conducting fifty-one audits requiring 4,550 man days. The actual figures brought these totals down to forty-four audits and 3,260 man days, a reduction of nearly 30 percent.

Meanwhile the work load continues to increase. At the University of Wisconsin in Milwaukee, with no internal auditors, a huge increase in enrollment (4,281 to 15,219 in ten years) calls for two additional auditors. At the state universities, two more are needed, since the Bureau is one year behind now, even on a three-year cycle.

Budget figures call for increases as follows:

[14] So are nine out of sixteen accountants in Wisconsin's Audit Bureau as of March, 1968.

	Man Days	Budget
1967–68	3,260	$240,237
1968–69	3,900	313,300
1969–70	4,800	412,800
1970–71	5,100	442,800

About 15 percent of the increases are required to maintain present levels. The balance of the increase would be spent about equally on more financial and program auditors.

By contrast with many other states, Wisconsin is spending relatively little on its post-audit activities. A recent compilation cites averages for the twenty-five states that are able to give a separate figure for legislative post-audit. These figures show a $345,714 average annual expenditure and an average of twenty-seven technical and six clerical employees.[15] We are necessarily wary of comparing such figures because of differences in the scope of each state auditor's job. But we are certain that Wisconsin has not been overspending. Indeed, according to the acting state auditor, some sixty auditors would be needed if each department were audited annually.

Increasing computerization of state government may ease some of the auditor's job in the future. Otherwise, all the pressures are toward increased responsibility for the Audit Bureau. The federal government has asked the states to audit, under federal guidelines, the National Defense and Student Loan Fund—to the irritation of state auditors across the country. Wisconsin has done three out of nine such audits already. The requirements of performance auditing, an almost completely extra function, will undoubtedly increase year by year.

Because staffing has become so pre-eminently important to the Audit Bureau, a personnel expert for the legislature

[15] Calvin Clark, *A Survey of Legislative Services in the Fifty States,* p. 42.

would be particularly valuable. The Bureau currently needs help in recruitment. It should not be dependent on the Bureau of Personnel, which has its own recruiting problems. The Audit Bureau will also have increasing need for a person with expertise in performance auditing, where employee evaluation is an important measure of an agency's control system. Such a person need not work full time for the Audit Bureau. But he should be an employee of the legislature. Such a person could also contribute—though not directly—to a training program for the Audit Bureau as it moves into performance auditing. Other states are investing in this area. The state of Washington is reportedly spending $30,000 for audit staff training, and Michigan $51,000. Wisconsin's proposed budget for 1969–71 calls for only $2,000 per year, a figure which should be increased if a good training program could be set up.

Direction for the Audit Bureau

Of the twenty-nine states that have a post-audit service primarily responsible to the legislature, eighteen have legislative committees supervising the program. In Colorado, for instance, the influential Legislative Audit Committee provides such supervision. During 1967, it spent sixteen days in committee activities; met with sixty representatives of state agencies; and reviewed one hundred audit reports. Its own annual report summarized these reports for the legislature, described action taken on each finding in these reports, and made numerous recommendations on the conduct of state government.[16] A similar detailed report by California's Joint Legislative Audit Committee gives figures on the number of recommendations therein, and the percentage of recommen-

[16] Legislative Audit Committee, State of Colorado, "Third Annual Report."

dations accepted.[17] In Illinois a Legislative Audit Commission, composed of five members from each house, is required by statute to receive auditors' reports and make recommendations to the legislature concerning them.

In Wisconsin, the supervising agency is the Joint Committee on Legislative Organization (JCLO), which the present statute (13.90) provides "shall act as the policymaking board of the . . . legislative audit bureau" and "determine the types of tasks to be assigned . . . within statutory limitations of the quantity and quality thereof."

From a reading of the minutes of the JCLO it would appear that little such direction has been requested or provided.[18] A major reason for this lack of direction was of course the fact that both the Audit Bureau and the JCLO were awaiting legislative reorganization and the appointment of a new state auditor. But there was a further reason too. The JCLO is the right committee to appoint a new auditor and to approve any request for staff. But it is *not* the committee to get deeply involved in the substantive aspects of audits. This direction would be best provided by the Joint Committee on Finance which has much to gain from, and give to, the work of the Audit Bureau. The Audit Bureau needs Joint Finance to publicize its reports and recommendations as is done in California and Colorado. Joint Finance needs the Audit Bureau as its eyes and ears on the performance of state agencies—the largest reporting system available to it.

This is not to diminish the traditional and necessary independence of the auditor's office. It has nothing to do, of course, with fitting the Audit Bureau into the Division of

[17] Joint Legislative Audit Committee, State of California, "Biennial Report," 1965–66.
[18] The JCLO did, however, spend a great deal of time in 1967 discussing performance auditing and filling the position of State Auditor which had been vacant for two years until September, 1968.

Services, where it should be for the sake of administrative efficiency. But it does mean a far closer collaboration between the legislature and the auditor on substantive matters than has been the practice in recent years.[19]

In California the Joint Audit Committee approves the schedule of audits planned. We are not certain this is necessary in Wisconsin. But surely Joint Finance could publish, annually, a list of all agencies subject to audit, the date of the last audit and period covered, the proposed date of the next audit, the number of recommendations made in the last audit and the action, or inaction, resulting therefrom.

Joint Finance could also suggest areas of study to the Audit Bureau as it does to the Fiscal Bureau. It could in addition be the vehicle for transmitting a review of the auditor's reports to the legislature. With its imprimatur on the message of transmittal, its interpretation of the findings, and its recommendations for the followup, much more attention would be focused on these reports. The Committee, in effect, would be studying, screening, and predigesting these reports for the full legislature. The information gleaned from them would of course be of great value to Joint Finance in all of its activities: in considering the budget and appropriations bills for the agencies involved, in its BOGO function of considering supplemental appropriations, and as a supplement to the work of the Fiscal Bureau.

With standing committees operating on a continuing basis, Joint Finance should schedule time, out of session, for this work. When irregularities are uncovered by the Audit Bu-

[19] There is precedence for collaboration. When the state auditor was still in the executive branch, the statutes required a close collaboration between the auditor and Joint Finance. The auditor sat in on meetings, was asked for and made recommendations, and took notes for followups. The role of the auditor has declined, but can be restored—and must be if the Audit Bureau is to provide performance auditing.

reau, Joint Finance should be interested in correcting them, and in finding out how such irregularities originally developed.

The Audit Bureau, in effect, needs a legislative sponsor that will call attention to its findings, use its staff on current problems, and call attention to its shortages of personnel. If proof were needed, it is contained in the findings from Eagleton's survey. The Audit Bureau is the least visible agency of the legislature. Asked if they thought the auditor's office "should be strengthened and the functions it performs expanded," many legislators agreed, but a large majority were neutral or undecided or did not respond to the question.

Under Wisconsin law, the auditor shall prepare a biennial report due on December 1 of each even-numbered year, "including recommendations for efficiency and economy in the expenditures of appropriations made by the legislature." We believe such reports should be made annually. This is the practice in Michigan. This is the timing for the reports of the Legislative Council Board covering all legislative services. But mainly, it is needed because change will be occurring rapidly in Audit Bureau activities, and because it is important that the Bureau be accountable to Joint Finance and the state.

The presence of someone from the Audit Bureau at all hearings and meetings of the Joint Committee on Finance is important. Michigan has two men assigned as legislative liaison. Under such an arrangement the auditor would then incorporate minutes and other comments about an agency or program into the auditor's manual for the next audit of that agency. This would avoid the situation where auditors have sometimes questioned an agency, only to be told: "We covered this with the Joint Committee on Finance at the budget hearings." It would give auditors clues on what to look for, particularly in performance auditing and it would help pin down legislative intent. Ideally, the man auditing the state university would attend the hearing where it was being discussed.

If the Fiscal Bureau has the privilege of requesting a special audit with the approval of the Joint Committee on Finance and the Legislative Council Board, surely the Committee itself should have this power. The present law provides that the Audit Bureau shall "make such special examinations . . . as the governor or the legislature directs." It was under this authority that the governor recommended the special examination of the federal programs of the Industrial Commission.

Similarly, if other standing committees (and bureaus, with approval) can hire outside consultants, surely the Audit Bureau should be able to retain outside accounting firms. For financial auditing, this might be a means, however expensive, of meeting the manpower shortage. If an outside firm were retained, it might audit the legislature's own accounts. Illinois, after a scandal in the auditor's office in 1956, has used many outside firms for regular audits. Michigan uses them to conduct a financial audit at the University, and then goes in and does a performance audit with its own men.

Performance Auditing: Definition and Background

The aim of better legislative services is to provide legislators with an increased awareness of the conditions and consequences of their decisions. Performance auditing, particularly when combined with program budgeting and fiscal analysis, is a major step in this direction.

Lennis Knighton, one of the leading authorities on the subject, defines performance post-auditing as a means of examining whether administrators have faithfully, efficiently, and effectively carried out the programs of the state. *Faithfulness* refers to whether program execution conforms with legislative will. *Effectiveness* refers to whether program objectives have been achieved. *Efficiency* refers to whether it was done with the least cost combination of resources and with a minimum of waste.[20]

Three types or levels of auditing are suggested: the fiscal-legal, program, and performance. In a rough sense, they parallel the three key words above. Fiscal-legal considers the faithfulness of execution; program auditing looks at the faithfulness and effectiveness; and performance auditing takes into account all three. Each builds on the others, and all are important.

Fiscal-legal auditing is the traditional government audit. Auditing of "the books" is familiar to everyone in business. The auditor, in most situations, checks out the *financial* transactions of a company, after the fact, and works up his balance sheets and profit and loss statements. In government, the *legal* aspect is added. Expenditures are examined to make sure they are made within the law, within the allocation available, and that they are certified by the proper person to make the expenditure.

The *fiscal-legal* audit is the form that has been traditional in Wisconsin and in every other state. If both the fiscal and the legal aspects were administered in accordance with the legislators' expressed will, one could say the program had been administered faithfully.

Program auditing continues the necessary fiscal-legal or "regularity" audit and adds another step. The fiscal-legal audit asks the question: How much did we spend? Was it spent legally? The program audit asks still another question: What did we get for our money? Did we meet our goals? In other words, was our program effective? The emphasis here is on output as well as input, on achievements as well as expenditures. It goes deeper than checking the "authorized signa-

[20] Lennis Knighton, "The Legislative Post-Audit of State Government" (East Lansing: Michigan State University, 1968).

tures" and into the basic decisions operating management has made.

Performance auditing asks the preceding questions and adds still another: Could we have done it better? Was it done efficiently—using the least cost combination of resources and with the least waste?

As can be noted, none of these groupings is exclusive. Both program and performance auditing assume a fiscal-legal audit; and a performance audit implies a program audit as well. All three types of audits also search for evidence of effectiveness and efficiency as well as faithfulness. For none of these audits imposes any restrictions on an auditor's making recommendations for improvement in administration. Performance auditing is currently a topic of great interest in state government. But progress is difficult to assess and seems limited to only a few states.

California is following "a performance auditing format" but has not as yet released any of the performance audits it has completed. Hawaii, according to Knighton, has a promising system. And New York has for several years been conducting what Comptroller Arthur Levitt calls "integrated audits."

Michigan's new constitution of 1963 specifically provided that its "auditor general shall conduct . . . *performance* post-audits," and in the years since it has embarked on an ambitious program. It is expanding its staff to one hundred seventeen auditors—about five times the size of Wisconsin's staff—and it budgets to allow twelve working days a year for training each of its auditors. In Michigan, it is interesting to note, the auditor-general became an early and ardent advocate of a program budgeting.

No discussion of performance auditing would be meaningful without a mention of Wisconsin's pioneering work in setting up its budget on a program basis. This was effective in

1965, following several years of study and experimentation in selected departments. Under the traditional line budget approach that it replaced, the governor presented a budget in terms of *what is to be bought*: personal services, materials, etc. Under the program approach, the budget is broken down into programs to be carried out—or services to be provided and for whom. Subsections explain by what means this is to be accomplished. In the shorthand of budgeting we might call it "what, for whom, and how?" Many advantages have resulted: more flexibility for administrators (expenditures are not locked into the iron grid of the line budget); more understanding of the budget in general (an accent on goals and methods, not positions and equipment); and, most important, a greater opportunity for the legislature and the governor to see the whole picture in focus, to weigh the options, and actually to formulate policy.

Eagleton's survey found overwhelming support for the program method of budgeting. All but one legislator surveyed approved it and 62 percent thought it "very effective." A companion step to the program budget was taken in 1965 when a statute was enacted creating the Audit Bureau and providing that the Bureau "shall review the *performance* and program accomplishments of the agency . . . to determine whether the agency carried out the policy of the legislature and the governor during the period. . . ."

As mentioned above, the Audit Bureau has been handicapped by continuing staff shortages since the law took effect. Little has been done to implement this directive to review "performance." Indeed, it has been difficult enough for the Bureau to keep up with its traditional financial-legal audit. There has also been the long search for a state auditor to direct this function. Now, however, with this appointment made, and with the expectation of additional staff, the Bureau should be able to move ahead. How should it proceed? What will be its needs? What are its chances of success?

The Problem of Measurement

Two perceptive memoranda prepared for the JCLO have defined many of the terms and focused the issue of performance auditing in Wisconsin.

> A *program budget* . . . isolates, the costs of x kinds of services to y numbers of individuals. The *performance budget* . . . (goes) . . . one step further . . . (and) . . . presents the costs of x kinds of services to y numbers of individuals at z cost per individual.[21]

The performance budget, by establishing a unit cost, presumes some established performance standards, or creates them as a goal to meet. This is meaningful in situations where the work is uniform and repetitive and can be "quantified" —that is, the job is either done or not done. Examples are the cost per collection in a municipal garbage service, or the processing of license applications, or the planting of a seedling.

The measurement is *quantity*, and one can go from there to a comparison with similar operations and to decisions on whether to reduce service or buy new trucks, or computerize the operation, and so forth. No auditor would have any difficulty checking quantified data. But the problem becomes difficult when *quality* is involved. One can develop costs for maintaining someone in a mental institution, and this figure has value in budgeting, but it tells nothing of the success in

[21] Memorandum to JCLO by Dale Cattanach, "The Performance Post Audit," October 27, 1967. This memorandum and one prepared by Bruce Gebhardt and George C. Kaiser, "The Program and Fiscal Audit of State Agencies," March, 1968, are the basis for these definitions and many of the comments in this section. (Typewritten.)

treating the patient. As the Cattanach memorandum points out:

> In many cases the measurement of the real heart of a program (e.g., the treatment of mental illness, the rehabilitation of the criminal offender, the "higher" education of Wisconsin residents), i.e., its accomplishment of stated objectives, lies almost solely in the area of quality. How good is the program? Is it curing mental illness or rehabilitating criminals? Would doubling the appropriation mean a doubling of the accomplishment level . . . ? All these . . . questions remain unanswered. . . .

Some projects—particularly in the anti-poverty field—are experimental and difficult to measure. Two programs, for example, seek to make disadvantaged youth employable. A relatively low cost per youth in the Neighborhood Youth Corps must be compared with a four-times-higher cost per youth in the Job Corps, where food and lodging must be provided. Costs such as these must be the basis for future decisions. But the administrator of the Job Corps cannot be blamed if his program costs more. Nor should the program be killed until all the returns are in.

David Novick of the Rand Corporation, one of the authorities in the field, has summed it up: "Quantitative aids are of great importance, and we want to quantify as much as we can. But . . . computers and quantitative methods are not decision makers. They are, instead, aids to the decision making process . . . aids in illuminating the issues." [22]

His comment is echoed by others. Non-quantifiable considerations are profuse in health, education, welfare, and most of the other programs dealing with people. The point of this discussion is probably obvious: if the men in government departments who *plan* and live with these programs have trou-

[22] David Novick, *Program Budgeting* (Washington, D.C.: Howard University Press, 1967), p. xxiii.

ble developing quantifiable measurements of efficiency, it is difficult to assume that auditors can.

Different Approaches to Performance Auditing

Although all thoughtful observers seem committed, quite properly, to the performance audit approach, there seems to be some divergence of views on how to achieve it—and how much of the task should fall on the Audit Bureau. One viewpoint tends to put all the responsibility for performance auditing on the auditor. The other places a major share of the burden on the administrative agencies and their budget makers. According to the Cattanach memorandum:

> establishment of any meaningful kind of performance audit is practically impossible without a performance budget. This is so because any kind of evaluation of performance that is not just a subjective value judgment needs a set of standards with which to measure the performance being evaluated . . . performance standards . . . must be established by the program administrators who have the most expertise.

The Joint Legislative Audit Committee in California shares this latter viewpoint. Also, the Deputy Auditor General of Michigan has noted that "any unit . . . must measure its performance in terms of what it expects of itself. These standards must be established by the operating department, but they should be subject to review by outside parties." [23]

Eagleton believes both viewpoints are correct. Initiating performance standards must lie with the operating agencies. But the auditor must go beyond his financial-legal audit whether or not these standards are established.

Eagleton also believes that standards should be part of the budgeting process. Indeed, the task of setting performance

[23] Franklin C. Pinkelman, "Michigan's Use of the Program Audit", *State Government*, Summer, 1967.

standards—of working out the measurements of efficiency and all of the other problems of quantifying—should be handled just as appropriations are now handled: the operating agency should have the initial responsibility; the Bureau of the Budget experts should provide their expert counsel; the Fiscal Bureau should subject it to searching examination and present all alternatives; Joint Finance and the relevant standing committees should review it as a key part of that agency's budget; and the Audit Bureau should audit it.

Where the data can now be quantified, the auditor should start immediately. Where it is not quantified, but it is possible to do so, an attempt should be made.

There are, of course, many government activities where direct comparisons can be made of output and cost against the unitized costs of previous years. These would cover such projects as the number of cattle inspected, the miles of highway maintained, or the number of children served in a program.[24] The state's program budget discusses similar figures. Audit reports should also include them, but test them too.

What Kind of Audit for Wisconsin?

The literature of accounting is full of different terms for audits that go beyond the financial-legal audit. "Management" auditing, "operational" auditing, "efficiency" auditing, and "integrated" auditing each have their separate sponsors. Yet each involves analysis of the same factors involved in Michigan's "program" audits. The heart of the matter lies not in the terminology but in what the audits cover.

Perhaps the most impressive audits we have seen are those of the Michigan Department of Mental Health and the New York Department of Mental Hygiene—each running over

---

[24] In Michigan comparisons are made between university branches on classroom utilization, laboratory utilization, academic personnel utilization, and so forth.

forty thousand words of succinct analysis, covering everything from fire protection to use of federal surplus foods, with literally hundreds of practical recommendations for better management.[25]

Throughout these and other reports run common questions—

Inventory Control. Is there a control to keep inventories from becoming too large? Is operating equipment numbered, tagged, and recorded on control cards? Are discrepancies between inventories and book balances being successfully investigated? Are valuable drugs under effective control?

Procurement. Are bidders' lists up to date? Are procedures being used to get the lowest prices?

Personnel. Are daily time sheets kept? Is staff being reduced commensurate with declining work load?

And so forth. These problems are the same from agency to agency—and often from state to state: student bookstore cash controls have been found wanting in Wisconsin—and in New York. Inmates are getting improper receipts for their personal property in Michigan—and in Connecticut.

Wisconsin's present financial-legal audit is, of course, vitally important. In Eagleton's opinion it should—in fact, *must*—be continued. But the common-sense auditing of management controls, cited above, should also be launched, regardless of what name it is given.

Undertaking this additional auditing will be in some ways a natural extension of what the Audit Bureau does today. An examination of forty-four recent audits conducted by the Bureau shows that twenty-one contained narrative comment and recommendations in addition to the audit figures. Most such

[25] We are indebted to Albert Lee, State Auditor of Michigan, for copies of their audits; and to the Honorable Arthur Levitt, Comptroller of New York State, and Martin Ives and Francis Rivett of the New York Department of Audit and Control, for various reports and advice.

comment had to do with financial controls (speeding up deposits, etc.). But a few involved such matters as using data processing equipment to control departmental programs, revising the control of printing paper inventories, and disposing of twenty-five thousand inactive accounts in the state Teachers' Retirement System. It is in matters such as these that the Bureau must become involved. To do this, the Audit Bureau will need additional staff even beyond those increases requested, a comprehensive training program, and a mentally adventurous and inquisitive attitude.

Despite the impressive audits done in New York and Michigan, the field is still in its infancy. There is, as yet, no model. New techniques are still being developed. Thus Wisconsin has an opportunity, again, of providing pioneering leadership. Happily the investments needed, like the basic investments in the Audit and Fiscal Bureaus, should bring multiplied returns.

Inter-Agency Standards

Many housekeeping and maintenance functions are common to many different programs: feeding inmates, cleaning office space, maintaining a truck fleet, heating buildings, and so forth. Sharing these figures should be of value to the Audit and Fiscal Bureaus as well as the Department of Administration. Where the auditors found an operation far out of line, further investigation could be made.

Similar exchanges of data should be made with other states wherever possible. Surely the auditor and his representatives should attend all possible conferences where such information was available.

Electronic Data Processing

Before computerized systems are set up in the administrative agencies, the Audit Bureau should be given an opportun-

ity to comment and provide advice. This is particularly true
where internal auditing procedures are weak.

In Michigan, two auditors were assigned to become expert
in EDP and asked to work up a questionnaire used to evaluate data processing systems. They were also asked to train all
the audit staff "to audit through the computer rather than
around it."

Internal Audits

No one we talked with in the legislature felt that the administrator's internal audit system was strong enough. There
was evidence, in fact, that the Audit Bureau was slowed down
considerably in some of its audits by the lack of an internal
audit system. The result was frequently to overburden the
higher-paid auditors with checks of routine financial transactions.

Part of this problem, we are told, is the difficulty in hiring
this type of staff. We would suggest, however, that the legislature and the Department of Administration examine this
problem. As Knighton and others have pointed out, a strong
internal audit staff is indispensable for successful performance auditing. Each audit report, in the future, should specifically note the extent and thoroughness of an agency's internal
auditing procedure.

Relations with Fiscal Bureau

Some states, like New York, have an auditing operation
which completely overshadows its legislative fiscal analysis.
Others, like California, have a fiscal analysis that has been
superior to its auditing operation. In Wisconsin there is the
opportunity for great strength in both.

We have already urged that the two bureaus collaborate
closely with one another independently and through their
work for the Joint Finance Committee. We feel certain this

will occur. Education experts in both bureaus will consult on performance standards, on following up audit report recommendations on a given agency, and on followup investigations in general. Each can advise the other on what to look for. There should be no overlap on their basic missions, as there is more than enough work for each to do. The Fiscal Bureau is concerned, as we've said, with the present and future, with budgets and alternative programs, and generally with substantive matters. The Audit Bureau is concerned with the past, with financial and management controls—and thus primarily with procedural matters. But both are concerned with efficiency, economy, and effectiveness in state government. It is virtually impossible to distinguish between what auditors do in Michigan and New York and what the Fiscal Bureau does in Wisconsin.

Eagleton therefore suggests that informal operating guidelines be drawn up between the bureaus, with the help of the administrator of services and the Joint Committee on Finance (ultimate authority being, of course, in the Legislative Council Board). Our suggestion would be that the Audit Bureau, in its audits, constantly seek to uncover problems which, if it can't solve them readily, are referred to the Fiscal Bureau. An example would be a revenue-producing unit of government that is losing money, although similar operations are successful. Why? If the answer is not uncovered in the course of the audit, the problem should be referred to the Fiscal Bureau.

The Audit Bureau reports that no recidivism studies are being made of the released population at correctional youth camps. Why? The Fiscal Bureau follows up—and reviews the proposed recidivism study as well. The process, of course, would also work in reverse. The Fiscal Bureau, in its studies of a certain program, might suggest to the Auditor that certain management procedures need review.

Although the Joint Committee on Finance should review the work of the Audit Bureau, the review should not come from the Fiscal Bureau. It should come, instead, from special staff provided by the Administrator of Services or from a special Audit Advisory Committee.

An Audit Advisory Committee

Some states have established audit advisory committees. The advantages to Wisconsin at this time, would be, we believe, far reaching—particularly as the whole legislative auditing operation moves into new and untried areas. Duties of such an advisory group, established by the proposed Legislative Council Board, would include:

(1) advising on problems that arise in auditing state agencies, particularly as the Bureau begins to look at management controls;

(2) providing a link with the professional accounting community and affording a means of exchanging ideas and information between these experts and the Audit Bureau;

(3) providing a professional review of the Audit Bureau itself and the adequacy of its reports;

(4) assisting on problems of recruitment of personnel.[26]

Membership would be drawn from the profession. There are fifteen hundred CPA's licensed in Wisconsin. A minimum of five members would be desirable. The JCLO has already drawn on the services of at least one member of the Accountancy Board (which sets standards for the licensing of accountants) and a former commissioner of the Department of Administration who has given generously of his time. The more management experts who can be drawn into voluntary assistance to state government the better.

[26] Most of these functions are adapted from a description of Illinois' Advisory Committee in Lennis Knighton, "The Legislative Post-Audit of State Government," p. 60.

A capable staff person to provide services for such a committee should be available as needed—probably part time at the start. Such a person could be assigned by the administrator of services with the approval of the Legislative Council Board.

Summarizing our discussion of the Audit Bureau, Eagleton recommends that:

(148) *The Audit Bureau:*

    (a) *conduct audits on a two-year, rather than a three-year, cycle;*

    (b) *be provided funds for performance auditing staff even beyond its budget request for the next biennium;*

    (c) *report annually on its operations;*

    (d) *be empowered to use outside accounting firms with the approval of the Joint Committee on Finance and the Legislative Council Board.*

(149) *The Joint Committee on Finance assume "sponsorship" of the Audit Bureau's work and:*

    (a) *provide periodic comment on audit reports and make recommendations thereon to the legislature;*

    (b) *report on the status of the auditor's recommendations;*

    (c) *collaborate with and keep the Audit Bureau fully informed of all its actions.*

(150) *The responsibility for developing performance standards be part of the planning and budgeting function of*

the operating agencies, with the assistance of the Bureau of Budget and Management.

(151) *As a first step toward performance auditing, the Audit Bureau should*:

(a) *audit an increasing number of management controls*;

(b) *begin assembling figures on basic maintenance costs*;

(c) *appoint specialists for data processing*;

(d) *encourage internal audits.*

(152) *An Audit Advisory Committee be established to advise the auditor on problems and standards for audits of state agencies and to comment constructively on the work of the Audit Bureau.*

CHAPTER VII.

SPECIAL NEEDS
AND ASSISTANCE

ADMINISTRATIVE AND SECRETARIAL AID
FOR LEGISLATORS

To do his job properly a legislator must be almost constantly accessible to his constituents. He must pass his own legislative program, campaign, attend meetings, and earn a living. Few persons are busier. Yet personal help to the individual legislator is still the exception rather than the rule across the land. As of the end of 1966, less than one-fifth of all state legislative bodies provided their members with a private secretary, and even a stenographic pool was available in only twenty-eight senates and thirty lower houses. Except for the majority members of the New York State Senate, only California provided a research assistant for each legislator.

Wisconsin also felt the pinch. As a former legislator told us:

> We're asking one hundred thirty-three men and women to work in impossible conditions. That's why I didn't run for re-election. Each should have a secretary. I shared one with eleven assemblymen; I had to take my work back to Milwaukee and dictate to my own secretary. Each should have a research assistant too, but if we can't afford that, there should be one research assistant for each three legislators. We're being penny wise and pound foolish in economizing on staff.

Conditions have changed somewhat since this man served in the Assembly. There is now a secretary for every two senators, and one for every four assemblymen, in addition to secretaries for the speaker, president pro tempore, and majority and minority leaders and assistant leaders. The speaker has an administrative assistant. Caucus staffs offer additional assistance. Eagleton found sentiment in favor of more help—but not to the extent of a secretary and/or administrative assistant for each legislator. There is simply not yet that heavy a burden on the average member.

Administrative Aides

Proposals have thus been made that one aide serve several members—or that there be one from each of the thirty-three Senate districts to serve the senator and the three assemblymen, too. Again Eagleton does not believe such a plan to be practical under current work loads. Thirty-three additional members of the staff seems too many—to say nothing of the complication when the members in a Senate district are of opposite parties, or one or more assemblymen want the senator's seat.

There is still the problem that some members need help in handling their mail and phone calls as well as their constituents' problems. The constituents deserve such help. So do members if they are to spend as much of their time as possible on important legislation. To perform this administrative aide function without waste, Eagleton urges that each of the caucus staffs be expanded to include at least one person to serve as an "ombudsman" or caseworker, following the designation used in the United States Congress, on constituent problems in each house.

These personnel should be experienced in state government. Perhaps they should be lawyers with a background in practice before administrative tribunals. This staff could provide truly expert help—better, in fact, than that provided by the average administrative aide.

These caucus caseworkers could take over some of the more complicated correspondence problems faced by the members. Centralizing such work in each caucus would also be efficient since the same research and writing could be adapted to meet the needs of more than one member. There would be advantages in having all contacts with state agencies on behalf of constituents channeled through a few persons.

All caucus staff is responsible to its party leadership. But these new personnel would have, as their first duty, the provision of administrative help to these leaders, to help reduce their constituent burdens, and free them for party leadership activities.

The leaders, in general, are the busiest men of any legislature. Yet, in Wisconsin, only the speaker has an assistant. As one senate leader has been quoted:

> I am overwhelmed with detail that simply does not get done. As I become overloaded I tend to produce less—not more—because of the normal tendency to spin my wheels by shuffling more papers and seeing more and more people come through my door.[1]

A leader's secretary, acting as a typist-receptionist, cannot handle all this detail. Certainly the casework should be lifted from his shoulders. Hiring one or more case specialists for each caucus staff would, we believe, provide the solution. This staff should be expanded, as needed, to handle all the casework brought to it by the members.

Secretarial Help

As noted above, the present arrangement of secretarial help for members allows a secretary for every four assembly-

[1] Warren Wade, "The Adequacy of Legislative Staffing in the Wisconsin Legislature (Master's thesis, University of Wisconsin, 1968.) (Xeroxed.)

men and one for every two senators. The system seems to be working adequately. In fact, virtually every legislator interviewed in our survey agreed that the increase in secretarial help was one of the most important improvements made by the legislature in recent years. But the demand for secretarial help is increasing, and the needs of individual legislators vary. Some require a disproportionate amount of typing, some almost none. Comments have been made to Eagleton that the old pool arrangement actually worked better.

Eagleton has no perfect solution but suggests that the three division administrators in the Department of the Legislature be encouraged to experiment with various answers. The easiest would involve a continuation of the present arrangement plus a pool of extra girls to handle overflow. Still another might entail a limited pool of three girls to perhaps nine assemblymen. One of the three girls would be in charge and would equalize the work load, which should be measured periodically for each pool. The amount of help per member could be increased as sessional work loads increased and cut back between sessions—when some secretaries would prefer to return to being housewives, and when some help could be shifted to work for joint committees. Such an arrangement might combine some of the flexibility of a pool with the personalized service of a private secretary: each girl would answer the telephone for two or three assemblymen, but be available to work on typing overloads of the whole group. Seating arrangements and telephone service are probably the bottleneck.

It is therefore questionable whether any neat theory will work out in practice and the need is greater than ever for staff flexibility and experienced personnel management to bring services into line with needs.

As we have pointed out previously, secretaries to leaders would be, like caucus staff, unclassified. Secretaries whose time was shared by several members, and whose loyalties were therefore divided, would be classified as limited-term employment and supervised by the chief clerks, as administrators of the Senate and Assembly Divisions. The clerks, in turn, would work with the administrator of services and his assistant for personnel in recruitment, training, and utilization. Through such combined and careful effort, some of the turnover that has plagued the secretarial force for the two houses might be cut. Putting secretaries on a full-time basis, and shifting them to meet fluctuating work load, would be a move in that direction.

CAUCUS STAFFS

Caucus staffing started as part of the Ford Foundation program in 1963 that also provided pilot programs of interns and budget staff. It was transferred to the legislative payroll on February 1, 1967, and employees are unclassified. Our survey of members showed great satisfaction with the effectiveness of the caucus staffs, and they represent one of the most successful developments of recent years. Over 60 percent of the members thought the caucus staffs very effective and almost 40 percent thought them somewhat effective. In fact, only one out of seventy-four legislators interviewed was unimpressed by caucus staffing. Republicans and Democrats, senators and assemblymen all agreed.

There seem to be a number of reasons for the legislature's satisfaction. The caliber of caucus staff has been high. Instead of paying off loyal supporters, party leaders have hired the best personnel they could find. These personnel have been visible to their party members. The quality of their work has been generally high. Their analyses of bills have been clear and concise, and their writing of speeches, press releases, and constituent correspondence has helped many members directly. Among Democrats, the analysis of the Republican governor's budget by the Assembly caucus staff is a source of pride and provides an opportunity for meaningful opposition. Alternatives are presented, and the key issues are explored more thoroughly as a result.

Still, there were a few criticisms on the concept of partisan staffing. One came from a former legislator who felt that any partisan staff would be abused and used for campaign purposes. To us this does not seem cause for concern. Indeed, confining partisan activity to caucus staffs tends to keep such requests from being made on other service agencies of the legislature.

There was also the comment that caucus staffs come between the legislator and the service agencies of the legislature, who do not like having their material "sifted through partisan hands on the way to the legislator." This, of course, may be true. But there is not much that can be done about it except to encourage the legislator to use the Reference Library Bureau or the Fiscal Bureau directly. It seems obvious to us that giving objective, non-partisan information to a constituent is quite often the best politics anyway—as caucus analysts will agree.

How can caucus staffing be improved? Eagleton has already mentioned that staffs should be expanded to provide one or more case specialists for its members in each house. It has also been suggested that greater efficiency might be achieved if caucus staffs were pooled for each party—to provide one staff for the Republicans in the Senate and Assembly and one for the Democrats in the Senate and Assembly.

This might make bill analysis easier and more efficient and should eliminate duplication between one party's staff work in the two houses. It might also provide better working quarters than now exist for Assembly caucuses.

To effect such a plan would require a single staff director, appointed by the party's representatives on the Legislative

Council Board. Other staff would be appointed by the director with the consent of his party leaders. These might include a budget specialist, a person to write press releases and radio scripts and organize their production and distribution, a specialist for casework, and two or three analysts who could assist in all areas and work on key issues as they arise. Such work on key issues might involve following a bill from the very beginning—through committee deliberations, caucus consideration, and floor debate in both houses. Eagleton therefore recommends that:

(153) *For each party caucus staffs from the Senate and Assembly be merged, at least on an experimental basis, to provide greater efficiency.*

(154) *A director of caucus staff be appointed by his party's members on the Legislative Council Board.*

(155) *The director, in turn, appoint the rest of the caucus staff with the consent of his party members on the Legislative Council Board.*

LEGISLATIVE INTERNS

State legislative internships started in California in 1957. They were modeled on the successful congressional internship program, launched in 1953. Today some fourteen states have initiated the program with mixed results. Some states that expressed interest have never gotten their programs off the ground. On the other hand California has already achieved considerable success. After eight years of the program, records showed that two out of five of the first eighty-eight interns had held positions with the legislature after their internships had been completed, and one out of five was still employed. Most became highly placed committee consultants, one became Assembly chief clerk, and many others went into local or federal government service.[2]

The legislative intern program in Wisconsin was started in 1965, on the basis of matching support by the state and by the Ford Foundation. The program's aims were three-fold: (1) to provide valuable experience for students in law, political science, and related fields; (2) to provide supplementary staff for the legislature; and (3), perhaps most important, to provide a pool of talent for recruiting permanent staff.

The program was set up by the Ford Committee but put under the direction of the Legislative Council. Interns were drawn from the University of Wisconsin. Most were continuing their courses in the law school, or in graduate school. The majority were assigned to standing committee chairmen.

Four interns served part time in 1965, five in 1966, and eight in 1967, at pay scales of $2, $2.25, and $3 per hour. Seven law school graduates were scheduled to start full time September 3, 1968. Total costs will now be assumed by the legislature.

Results have ranged from fair to good—depending on the job, the committee chairmen, and the intern. Some legislators felt the help they received was superior. Some interns felt their efforts were effective. But the pattern was uneven. Generally, there was more dissatisfaction with the intern program than with other innovations which had been made by the legislature. About 20 percent of the legislators interviewed felt interns were very effective, but almost 30 percent thought quite the opposite, that they were not at all effective. Dissatisfaction came from those in charge, from those who had used interns, and interns themselves.

The most pressing need, from everyone's viewpoint,

---

[2] For these and other facts on the California Program, see "California's Legislative Intern Program" by Speaker Jesse Unruh, *State Government,* Summer, 1965, pp. 155–157.

seemed to be centralized day-to-day supervision of the program. Although placed under the Legislative Council, no extra staff was provided to supervise the program. The result was an extra responsibility for the secretary of the Council, who was the first to point out the inadequacy of the arrangement.

Lack of day-to-day guidance was particularly acute at the start of the internship. One stated that he did nothing the first month but attend committee meetings where he hardly knew what was going on. No orientation was provided, as one intern put it, on "how to look things up." Others felt they had to look for things to do, that what they were doing was not being read, and that, therefore, they were not making a meaningful contribution.

Relations with committee chairmen were crucial to success. One intern had "an ideal working relationship with his chairman" who "had had some prior experience using staff." Another also felt his chairman used him "objectively." Yet another felt his chairman was "not fully appraised of the intern program," and another even questioned whether some members of the legislature really wanted research done on their problems.

Lack of office space near the Legislative Council was also a problem. The interns of the past year have been located in one large room on the fourth floor of the capitol. This arrangement was good for morale and allowed for certain efficiencies in providing secretarial help and filing. But it was too far from the Council's offices to allow for quick answers to problems that constantly arose.

Even more difficult was the part-time nature of the work up to this time. As researchers know, a certain "start-up time" is required each day. Efficiency is reduced when "start-up time" must be included in the two or three hours that an intern works each day. Changing the program from part time to full time is a major improvement.

If intern morale was not as high as it should have been, part of the reason would seem to be in the gap between expectations and reality. No program, if it is to operate successfully, should be oversold. Or if it is, every effort should be made to bring reality closer to expectations.

Still another factor was probably the difference in attitude between some of the university students and some of the legislators toward each other. Acceptance by each group for the other should grow, however, as time goes on.

There was a range of opinion on what kind of academic training made the best intern. Some felt law students were particularly qualified. Others felt they were legalistic and narrow, and that a political background was best. The viewpoint, Eagleton observed, seemed to depend somewhat on the respondent's own training. From the record, however, it would appear that interns of many backgrounds can be qualified. In California, for instance, 46 percent were trained in political science, 33 percent in law, and the remainder in journalism, history, sociology, economics, criminology and other areas.

Opinion also split on the best preparatory or probationary work for interns. Some felt law students would be wasting their time as messengers. Others felt this was the ideal method of breaking in a new man.

Finally, some of the interns were critical of the term "intern." From their actual work experience with the legislature, they felt they were not apprentices. They would prefer to be called "legislative aides" or to be given a similar title which would get them more attention when dealing with state agencies.

A good intern program has great importance, we believe, for the future of good government in Wisconsin. As the president pro tempore of the Senate has pointed out, it should get the same support from the legislature that private corporations provide in their college recruitment and training programs.

Eagleton would put the whole program into the Research Bureau, since most interns would be grouped in the Division of Services talent pool, and referred from there to standing committees, or possibly to caucus staffs. The director of the Research Bureau could run the program or put a deputy in charge. Interns who serve as research aides or caucus analysts would receive guidance and counseling from the same person.

Under the supervision of this director, an orientation program for interns would take place in the months before the session started, familiarizing them with the work of the legislature and resources available. If, for instance, interns started in July, they might spend July and August being rotated through the Reference Library Bureau and the Fiscal Bureau, and the Revisor's and Legal Bureaus if they are lawyers. September through December could then be spent on interim joint committee work. And a "permanent" assignment to a committee or caucus staff could be made in January.

Later, with the approval of the Legislative Council Board and the help of the administrator of services, résumés on these new interns would be circulated to those committee chairmen and others who had requested intern assistance, in an attempt to match the intern to the proper supervisor. Preferably, interns would be assigned only to positions where they could work under a professional staff person who could provide better day-to-day direction than a busy committee chairman.

Fitting the right intern to the right chairman and professional staff person would be the director's most important job. Where they are properly matched, the program works well. To promote a proper relationship, all concerned should have a clear understanding of their responsibilities to each other. The chairman, or his professional staff person, should be willing to help teach the intern. The intern should be introduced, at the first meeting, to the committee, and his job explained to the members. Work requests from the members should channel through the chairman or the intern's immediate staff superior on the committee.

A number of challenges face the director of the intern program if it is to work to its full potential. One is training the job supervisor on how best to use his intern's talents (it is of course indispensable that on-the-job supervisors be willing to teach the intern and constructively criticize his work). Another is to provide the intern with a rounded experience. The orientation and rotation experience will help greatly in this respect. But the director can also act as a guidance counselor and attempt to expose the intern to bill drafting, assisting the clerks at the front desk, building "debate" books on a bill, writing press releases in a caucus, and similar tasks. Being able to follow a major bill all the way through is particularly important.

Still another task of the director would be to run periodic seminars for interns. Legislators, staff experts, and academic people can be invited to speak. But the main value of such getogethers (if we are to learn from California's experience) will probably come from exchanging ideas on current problems in legislative work.

Course credits for interns, a much-discussed subject, are desirable. But they should not become a *sine qua non* of the program. Law school students cannot receive credit and law school graduates don't particularly care about additional scholastic credit. This, again, is a matter where the legislature and the university will have to feel their way.

Whatever happens, periodic reports should be made on the

intern program. Interns and supervisory personnel should also be asked to submit an assessment of the program at the end of each intern's term of work. And the director should recapitulate progress and problems annually for inclusion in the annual report of the administrator of services.

For the major structuring of the intern program, Eagleton recommends that:

(156) *The director of the Research Bureau, or his deputy, be made general director of the intern program, be given the time and support to make the program work, and be available to interns and their immediate supervisors each day;*

(157) *An orientation and rotation program be worked out to train interns at the beginning of their employment;*

(158) *Training of interns be continued on the job with the help of their immediate (staff) supervisors, seminars, rotation of their work as desired, and counseling by the director of interns; and*

(159) *Interns be given a title (research aide, e.g.) other than intern when they assume a regular assignment.*

AN ORIENTATION PROGRAM FOR LEGISLATORS

An average of 28 percent of each incoming Wisconsin Assembly since 1953 has been new—freshmen who have never served in either house of the legislature before. (The percentage for the Senate is, of course, smaller, since many senators had served before in the Assembly.) Compared to other states, these figures are low. The normal turnover is about 50 percent, with reapportionment pushing totals to 70 and even

80 percent in some states.[3] However low these percentages for Wisconsin may be in relation to other states, they are nonetheless substantial. Since freshmen need several months to "learn the ropes" and since the legislature is in session an average of only about one hundred thirty meeting days per biennium, it is obvious that presession orientation is important. The same is true of training staff and legislative interns. The sooner they "know the ropes" the sooner they are able to function effectively.

Orientation conferences are not new. Massachusetts held the first one in 1933. More than half the states said they had some form of orientation program by 1954. But the real effectiveness of many of these programs has still to be developed.

Wisconsin's first formal Orientation Conference was held in January, 1967, for two and one-half days in the middle of the week before the legislature convened. Along with Illinois and Iowa it was one of three pilot programs sponsored by the American Political Science Association, with help from the Ford Foundation. Twenty-eight new legislators were invited, of which twenty-five had had no previous legislative experience.

The twenty-five were surveyed later and their replies summarized by the Legislative Council.[4] It was a tribute to those who spoke at the sessions and to those who planned and guided the conference that every aspect was approved as helpful, including time, length, subject matter, tours, later meetings, and the materials prepared for it. Where change was suggested, it clearly favored *more* of the same type of program and information.

[3] Council of State Governments, *American State Legislatures: Their Structure and Procedures* (Chicago: The Council, 1967), p. 16.
[4] "Summary of the Responses to the Questionnaire on the 1967 Pre-Session Conference" (Madison: Wisconsin Legislative Council, August, 1967).

Timing

The majority favored a session of about the same length (two and one-half days). But there were many who wanted the session lengthened. Our own view would be to have the content dictate the length of the session, but to keep any one conference to not more than three and one-half days. More than that might exhaust the participants. Other sessions could be scheduled at a later date.

Concerning dates for the next conference the new legislators in 1967 voted for holding it at the same time—just before, or concurrent with, the opening of the legislature in January. We would like to see the conference held earlier, in late November or early December, before the tempo of legislative activity begins to pick up. This would give new legislators an opportunity to meet each other, discuss leadership and committee choices, and get organized before the opening days in January.

Meeting early also allows for an additional conference in early January. This reduces the chance of boredom developing in the first session. It allows legislators to come back with sharpened questions. If committee assignments have been made, it allows some of the orientation period in January to be used for briefing members on the issues of their committees. Under the new committee structure this could be very fruitful.

Later meetings could be held after the session actually gets under way. An evening meeting was held two weeks after the session had begun in 1967 to explain certain state aid formulas. This too received favorable comments and suggestions that similar meetings be set up to cover other complicated and important subjects and background data on tax and budget questions.

Location

The facilities of a state park are used for orientation conferences in Kentucky. A state university campus has been used elsewhere. The capitol itself is, of course, used in most states. There are advantages to each. In our opinion, housing and feeding all legislators together in an informal and relaxed atmosphere is one of the important factors. This encourages getting acquainted, making and renewing friendships, and even helps establish an esprit de corps. It is also important to have the meetings in Madison. Several legislators in 1967 suggested that a tour should be arranged of the capitol itself. Legislators should be taught how to use the library and other facilities. Interns and other new staff personnel should attend the orientation meetings.

The Content of the Meetings

Duane Lockard comments that "no training session can teach what experience teaches by slow pedagogy," [5] and this is surely true in the legislature. But some initial learning can help later processes. In terms of content, we believe that orientation sessions should cover four basic areas: (1) how to operate one's office, including a suggested filing system, a control system for correspondence, building a mailing list, and using dictating facilities; (2) how to operate the machinery of the legislature, including facilities to use for handling constituents' requests, how to gather background research, and how to have a bill drafted and introduced; (3) how to keep one's constituents informed via publicity and newsletters; and (4) important substantive issues facing the state. This conforms to the views of the freshmen participants of the 1967 conference.

[5] Duane Lockhard, *State Legislatures in American Politics* (Englewood Cliffs, N.J.: Prentice-Hall, 1966), p. 106.

All talks were deemed helpful. But a majority favored having more discussion of procedures and "how to": how to introduce and pass a bill; how to maintain constituent relations, and so forth. Everything should be done to expedite the handling of each legislator's "errand boy" chores. As one observer has noted, some legislators "have no conception of how to use staff services." [6] As another man told Eagleton, "while the physical setup has been improved, with offices and more secretaries, the legislators are not using the improvements."

As the Legislative Reference Bureau had pointed out, this is a nationwide problem: "Through a desire to handle all their affairs personally, inexperience in directing staff, or simple distrust, individual legislators may be unwilling or unable to make effective use of these services." [7] Yet they must if they are adequately to perform their important lawmaking functions.

The best way, of course, for anyone to learn is by doing, and the more the program allows for the legislator to answer mail, request a bill draft, or contact an administrative agency, the better.

Since some techniques, such as securing publicity and mailing newsletters, involve potential partisan advantage, we would recommend that caucus staffs handle this portion of the program with each party's members being briefed in his own caucus. Caucus meetings could also cover the party's position on substantive issues, a supplement to lectures that would be held within the conference on issues such as education.

One of the talks at the conference should be on the subject

[6] Wade, p. 39.

[7] Legislative Reference Bureau, "Legislative Staffing and Services," Informational Bulletin 48–4 (Madison, May, 1968), p. 1.

of legislative ethics, preferably by a member of the proposed Joint Legislative Ethics Committee. Some do's and don'ts could be provided that would be helpful, particularly on dealing with state agencies.

Field Trips

A visit to a state office building housing a major state agency has some marginal value, but nothing like a visit to a state mental hospital, penitentiary, school for the retarded, welfare office, or slum area. These are the areas where there is literally no substitute for firsthand observation, and where increasing amounts of state funds are being committed. As one legislator told us: "An office is an office, but visiting the disturbed children's floor of a hospital is something different."

In New York state, legislators, newspaper editors, business executives, and others are invited by county councils of social agencies to accompany welfare workers on their rounds in local areas. One participant is assigned to each welfare worker. At the end of the day, all participants reassemble to compare experiences and discuss their impressions. The program is an outstanding success. Most of the participants have never visited slum areas or talked to welfare recipients before. For them the day is an eye-opening experience of great help in understanding such social problems.

In Mississippi such field trips are mandatory. A new law providing a pay raise for legislators directs each of them to "attend at least two meetings of the board of supervisors of the county . . . at least two meetings of the city or town board of aldermen or city council . . . visit the universities and state senior colleges and also each of the eleemosynary and penal institutions of the state . . . [and] study the educational programs of the common schools, colleges and public schools and visit in the public schools of his/her county or district." [8]

Our recommendation would be to try these trips on an experimental basis at first. Like other parts of the orientation program, such trips should be kept open to experienced legislators as well as freshmen. Buses and other forms of group transportation should be provided where possible.

A Buddy System

Continuing guidance to new legislators, particularly on matters of procedure, can also be provided by an adaptation of the "buddy system," used in the army and in summer camps, which teams up a new legislator with an experienced man. To make it work best, the buddies should be members of the same party.

Under optimum conditions, these men would be seated next to each other and have offices near each other. Seating is particularly important. The freshman is often uncertain of the parliamentary situation and does not wish to appear stupid, or wish to slow down debate, by asking for help publicly. Similarly, he may be unaware of a political nuance that only experienced men have caught. Providing him with a source for whispered consultation can often be of great value.

Orientation Manuals

Wisconsin has already developed so many documents helpful to the legislator that part of any conference might be to simply present the Wisconsin *Blue Book,* the Report of the Committee on Legislative Organization and Procedure (*Mason Report*), the *Legislative Reference Bureau Can Help*

---

[8] *The State Legislatures Progress Reporter* (New York: National Municipal League), June–July, 1967.

You, and Speaker Froehlich's article on "How a Bill Is Passed." [9]

But it would still be worthwhile to pull these and other materials together into a comprehensive, indexed manual. Distributed at the start of an orientation conference, such a manual could be used during these sessions and permanently thereafter. Some or all of the material it contained could also be available for staff training.

Seminars

With the big state agencies and the state university in Madison there is also an exciting opportunity for continuing the educational process. This could be done through occasional evening seminars open to legislators and persons from the university and government. Keying it to state government problems would keep such a program distinct from other evening programs at the university.

Expenses

Food, lodging, and transportation should be provided to all legislators participating in the orientation conference. All legislators should be invited. Many of the conference sessions can provide new information to experienced members as well as freshman.

Everything should be done to stimulate attendance. When one considers the investments made by private industry in training salesmen of an industrial product or a customer's man in a brokerage house, an investment in a legislative orientation conference seems small indeed.

In summary, Eagleton recommends that:

(160) *An orientation conference for new (and old) members be held as soon as practicable after election day, with an*

[9] Available from Legislative Reference Bureau.

*additional session in early January if desired, together with
subsequent evening meetings*; and

(161) *The conference cover how to operate a legislator's
office, how to use the legislative services available, how to
keep one's constituents informed, and provide background information on substantive issues; one segment of the conference be used to discuss legislative ethics; field trips emphasize
visits to hospitals, penitentiaries, slum areas, and other locations that have not normally been seen by new legislators; a
"buddy system" be tried to assist new men, particularly on
problems of procedure on the floor; orientation manuals be
prepared for use during the conference and later; evening
seminars on major social problems be considered in cooperation with the University of Wisconsin; and food, lodging, and
transportation be provided all legislators for the meetings.*

PUBLIC INFORMATION

The complexities of contemporary problems and the speed
with which they change make it imperative that state government today be responsive, flexible, and able to act promptly.
To do so means putting responsibility on those elected officials who can act, and relying on the voters to retire those
officials who fail this trust.

But putting our trust in our elected representatives requires
that legislators be visible and the people informed. Visible
legislators and an informed public are two sides of the same
coin. Wisconsin deserves both, and in fact it has more of both
than most states: a vigorous and attentive daily press; a
unique and excellent tradition of keeping all committee meetings open to press and public; and an electorate that ranks
above average in terms of education.

Yet, it is probably still not enough. The public's interest is
focused on Washington and City Hall. These are the power

centers that attract attention. Consider the Gallup Poll taken just after the November, 1966, elections. Only one-quarter of the people said they knew who would represent them in their state senates and assemblies, half knew who their congressman would be, and almost three-quarters knew the name of their mayor. And even these figures were high compared to a Roper Poll taken at the same time. In New York City, for example, 79 percent said they had voted for state assemblyman, but when asked if they remembered the name of the man for whom they voted, only 8 percent replied affirmatively.

The truth of the matter is that only a minority of the people ever have direct contact with their legislature. Most impressions of it are fragmentary and are often based on attention-getting incidents. Few know how it works. Wisconsin's legislature, like every other state's, needs to inform the people. As the Utah Legislative Study Committee stated:

> A legitimate expenditure of modest public funds for a report to the people is in order. It is easy to conjure up possible miscarriages of such an effort, to discuss this suggestion summarily, or to rely on our public-spirited communications media to carry the whole burden of informing the public. But total inaction . . . carries with it . . . a penalty—a continuation of the decline of the Legislature as a branch of government.[10]

Fortunately, informing the public on the legislature also provides publicity for legislators, and, as one of Wisconsin's leaders remarked, "the more exposure you can give legislators, the better."

Eagleton believes several steps can be taken to make the legislature more visible and the public more aware.

First, the press. Although legislators agree that press coverage is generally very good, anything to make it better

[10] *Final Report,* December 28, 1966, p. 38.

should be encouraged. The present press room is small and could be better. Even more desirable would be a radio-TV studio with proper lighting and acoustics for interviews and press conferences—where individual legislators can tape shows for local distribution at minimal cost. The closer a small interview room is to the floor, the better.

Radio-TV coverage should also be expanded for major committee hearings—a particularly desirable step as joint standing committees develop expert knowledge in their chosen fields. Such coverage would be especially helpful in the months when the legislature is not in session. By that means, its activities could be kept before the public.

Live coverage of floor debate on TV should also be encouraged when vital issues are being discussed. Nineteen state legislatures allow televised debate. It should be controlled, for the sake of fairness, by rules of the house. Members should be advised when the proceedings are telecast.

The problem with TV is air time for telecasts. Very little debate will probably be used, except perhaps on educational TV stations. But this is not true of radio. Greater coverage can perhaps be arranged there.

The legislative newsletter is still another device for keeping the public informed. Newsletters can be printed inexpensively by photo-offset, with a standard masthead and pictures of the capitol and the member. Some legislatures maintain a mailing room and provide members with an allowance for a given amount of such mail (over and above daily correspondence) in each session. Copy must be factual and non-partisan. It must be different from the material worked up by caucus staff for partisan purposes. The material is quite often prepared by press aides to the leadership as a report of action taken during the session. Members can select the items they wish to use. Mailings should be made at the end of a session. No mailings should be allowed within the six months period before an election involving the member as a candidate.

Under a new program in Oklahoma, civic organizations may request speakers who are experts in a specific area of government, for example, the chairman of a subcommittee on conservation, to address a conservation group. Speakers are accompanied and introduced by the local legislator of the district and no fee or expenses are charged to the organization. A similar device can be used to great advantage in the months between elections and the middle of a session. Local hearings can be held within a district, where all local organizations and individuals may testify on matters they believe should be taken up by the legislature. The event can be scheduled for a Saturday, or one or more weekday evenings. Heavy publicity should precede and follow the event. Organizations should be sent written invitations, and witnesses scheduled in the order that acceptances are received. Sufficient copies of their statements may be requested for the press and the legislators who are present.

Still another means of bringing the legislature to the people is through a film. New York and several other states have had films produced of their respective legislatures in action. New York's took ten days to film, cost $45,000, and has been shown on TV, seen in theaters, and viewed in New York schools. Since teachers in many states know less about state government than about any other branch of government, such films have been particularly helpful. The film should be available for use on TV, by organizations, and by members and other candidates for meetings. It could also be a valuable teaching aid in the schools, particularly as a supplement to the visits that children regularly pay to the capitol. For those who come when the legislature is out of session, the screening of such a film would bring the empty chambers alive. The goal, as with other techniques mentioned here, is maximum exposure.

Tape recordings are also a useful medium. We are told that the radio department of the University of Kentucky offered a series of programs on the proposed state constitution to those who supplied blank tapes. A similar series could be done on Wisconsin's legislature.

If, as mentioned above, the secretary of the legislature should undertake an information program, part of his efforts should involve Wisconsin's schools. The Reference Bureau already provides informational materials. Speakers and a film and tapes would be of additional help. Still other projects, such as debates and essay contests on the legislature, are also possible.

A program for groups visiting the capitol during the off-session should also be worked out—a film showing, perhaps, at 11 A.M. and 3 P.M.; taped recordings in the rear of the chambers describing how the legislature operates when in session; a suggested reading list on Wisconsin's state government.

The League of Women Voters is an invaluable resource to most state legislatures. Many of the projects above could perhaps be launched with their help. In Maine, the League sponsored a TV quiz show with questions on state government that could be answered by the participating public. Two TV stations and five professors of government helped produce it. Commercial sponsors were secured. Thirty-eight state legislators and a state government class at the University of Maine made up four panels. An official test form was published in the newspapers. Observers described it as fun, interesting, and informative.

For all these efforts where media are involved, it would do well for the secretary, or some other representative of the legislature to meet periodically with the capitol press corps, including, of course, the radio and TV representatives, to discuss their needs in covering the legislature. Their cooperation is, of course, indispensable.

A Transcript of Debate

Just as the *Blue Book* and the research papers of the Legislative Reference Bureau have a multiplied effect through use of their material in speeches and articles, so too would a verbatim transcript of debate provide a valuable new source of basic data on the legislature. Up to this point it has not been included in the long catalogue of the legislature's needs. But Eagleton is convinced that a detailed record of legislative activity must come, that it is feasible now, and that its benefits to the state would spread in all directions. Consider the following points:

(1) *Memory is fallible.* Experiments have shown that we forget half of what we learned within twenty-four hours, and half of the remainder within the next thirty days—on simple information. With thousands of words spoken in the legislature, the proportion retained is undoubtedly far less. Because debate is so ephemeral, its whole value is reduced proportionately. Yet hundreds of hours of study and preparation lie behind the words spoken on the floor. Putting it another way, Eagleton believes if it is worth saying it is worth saving.

(2) *Accuracy.* It is easy to be misquoted. Having a transcript—and allowing members to correct the form, but not the substance, of their remarks—insures that a member's comments are accurately reported. False charges, alleging what a member said, simply cannot be made.

(3) *Visibility.* Constituents should have the privilege of looking up what their representatives said on issues, as well as how they voted. Perhaps only one in one thousand will do

so. But for that one the matter can be of the utmost importance. A democracy works properly only when the people have access to information on the issues and how their representatives responded to these issues. Whatever beclouds a clear line of vision between the citizen and his legislature hurts both.

(4) *Historical record.* The Wisconsin Historical Society's only record of debate must now come from two sources: newspaper articles, which are frequently fragmentary and sometimes garbled; and the papers of legislators that have been turned over to the Society, but which frequently lack information about their views on issues, even those on which they have been highly influential in debate.

(5) *Legislative intent.* With a properly indexed transcript, judges, auditors, agency heads, and attorneys could all get a better idea of what the legislature intended in passing a bill. Judges today search the bill record for the sponsor's intent. As the director of the State Historical Society has written: "At least one former Supreme Court Justice has indicated . . . that the transcript would be invaluable to the Court in determining legislative intent." Or as an important staff member told us: "Sometimes a single phrase is important . . . such as the sponsor's comment that his bill is patterned after a certain law in another state." Attorneys also need such background. As the director of research for the Missouri legislature has put it: "I get calls about once a month from attorneys asking for transcripts of committee hearings that would show legislative intent, but I have none." [11]

There are objections to transcripts. Most frequently one hears that it could "turn into a Congressional Record," a pile of newsprint filled primarily with irrelevant materials. This argument can be met. No privileges to insert additional mate-

[11] Carl M. Schmidt, *American State and Local Government in Action* (Belmont, Calif.: Dickinson Publishing Co., 1966), p. 125.

rials or extensions of remarks should be allowed in the transcript.

There is the objection that legislators already have too much to read. This is, of course, true. But for those who must occasionally be absent, a transcript is also a valuable way to catch up on what has happened.

The main questions are, quite properly, how it would work and what it would cost. Six states have daily transcripts of one form or another, and ten have partial transcripts or allow for them on request. It has been recommended for Illinois. In Maine, an experienced court reporter is assigned to the House of Representatives, for example, for the session. He takes all debate in shorthand and supervises three girls who record all debate on discs. The recorder is attached to the public address system console. As each member is recognized and speaks into his own microphone, his words are recorded. The shorthand is used only as a "backup" in case of failure in the recording process. Girls work in relays, recording a disc, removing it and typing, double space, onto standard sheets of paper. Typed material then goes to the printer, is set on a linotype, gathered into an eight-column, full-page newspaper form, and then some four hundred "horse blankets" are delivered to the legislature the next morning. This is the proof. Members offer corrections needed. These are made and the type reassembled for printing in book form (see the excerpt and sample index in Exhibits A an B).

The transcript for Maine's two houses, in the five-month 1965 session, was printed in two volumes totaling 3,223 pages and requiring eight inches of shelf space, about the same as Wisconsin's *Journal* for the session. Costs ran to $90,000: approximately $28,000 for transcription, $7,700 for advance proof sheets, and $55,500 for typesetting, indexing, printing, and binding three hundred and twenty-five copies of the complete *Legislative Record*. Maine's Legisla-

EXHIBIT A: SAMPLE OF THE *LEGISLATIVE RECORD* OF THE MAINE LEGISLATURE

tant thing to me and extremely important to the people that I represent. I do not view this as a take it or leave it proposition. I will support any reasonable tax to support uniform local tax effort and I for one was rather disturbed that priorities were arranged the way they were with respect to the agreement which has been talked about so much in our papers.

I do not view the telephone tax as being a good tax and I don't think it is because of the many good sound reasons that have been stated in opposition to it, but I do say to you that I don't take this as a take it or leave it proposition. That I intend to support any reasonable tax which will lead to the possibility of the coming into being of the uniform local effort and I simply want the record to be clear that when I vote for the indefinite postponement of this bill I am not voting against the uniform local tax effort.

The SPEAKER: The Chair recognizes the gentleman from Portland, Mr. Cottrell.

Mr. COTTRELL: Mr. Speaker and Members of the House: I think we should basically consider some of these principles of taxation that are used by all states. New York State, you know, now has a sales tax and an income tax. New York City has an income tax and a five per cent sales tax. Our opportunities to increase our income through taxation are simply to broaden our sales tax, increase it to four and a half percent or five percent or to have an income tax. Now, we can put a tax on coal and oil. We already have a sales tax on electricity and gas. Or we can put a sales tax on the telephones. I think that in doing it we are accepting one of the principles of broadening our sales tax. It's painful, but at least it's not going to increase our property tax if we do get this money on the uniform effort for our schools and a lot of you people who I hope some day have an opportunity to serve on the Taxation Committee which we call really an exemption committee, of all the bills put in, most of them are for exemptions. There are very few wanting to tax.

Now, it seems to me it's just as simple as that. Broaden your sales tax, increase it or have an income tax and this seems at this point the best thing to do, a sales tax on the telephone.

The SPEAKER: The Chair recognizes the gentleman from Lewiston, Mr. Jalbert.

Mr. JALBERT: Mr. Speaker, I would pose a question to the good dreaming gentleman from Cumberland, Mr. Richardson, what is his alternative?

The SPEAKER: The gentleman from Lewiston Mr. Jalbert, has posed a question to the gentleman from Cumberland, Mr. Richardson, who may answer if he so desires.

Mr. RICHARDSON: Mr. Speaker, one of the many proposals that I have heard and I am not a member of the leadership of the Majority Party is that we increase the tax on cigarettes. I smoke. I happen to believe it's a filthy habit and I would be very much in favor of increasing the tax on cigarettes.

The SPEAKER: The Chair recognizes the gentleman from Lewiston, Mr. Jalbert, who requests permission to once again address the House. Is there objection? The Chair hears none. The gentleman may proceed.

Mr. JALBERT: Mr. Speaker, if the gentleman from Cumberland, Mr. Richardson, had chosen to study this matter as thoroughly as he studies insurance measures, he would have found out that if we hike the cigarettes from two to four cents, which is what he would have to do to get his uniform tax effort law, it would become as regressive a tax as the tobacco tax is concerned. And I might say before I close that I am speaking for myself and I think I have got quite a lot of company. The same thing goes that I told the gentleman from Cape Elizabeth, Mr. Berry, to you. This is not an alternative. This is not a threat, this is a promise.

The SPEAKER: The Chair recognizes the gentleman from Enfield, Mr. Dudley.

Mr. DUDLEY: Mr. Speaker and Members of the House: I feel kind of pleased to be able to go along

Pickerel, see Perch, pickerel . . .

Pike, Rep. Sumner T.
Bills ... 236 (3), 237, 295, 298, 1149
Committees 53, 109
Remarks 347, 352,
411, 416, 474, 607, 777, 1300, 1463,
1470, 1512, 1523, 1546, 1722, 1723,
1802, 1806, 1817, 1845, 1879, 1880,
1907, 1960, 1961, 1966, 2080, 2081,
2144, 2158, 2195, 2326, 2374, 2459,
2472, 2475, 2533, 2534, 2536, 2596,
2599, 2661, 2684, 2753, 2760, 2902,
2986, 3030

Pilot programs for school entrance
age 104, 123, 320, 344,
358, 390, 475, 488, 2719

Pineland Hospital and Training
Center
Admission procedures ... 179,
221, 538, 568, 587, 625, 690, 707
Governor Muskie Building ....
.... 3086, 3122
Gymnasium ....
.... 131, 159, 2442, 2481
Indigent dischargees ... 179,
221, 538, 568, 694, 704, 2071, 2546,
2571, 2667, 2742, 2842, 2874
Recreational aid ... 196, 247, 1673,
1677, 2180, 2206
See also Incorrigibles

Piscataquis County
Register of Probate ....
.... 107, 143, 1923, 1931
See also Fishing — Ice fishing —
Aroostook and Piscataquis;
Muskrats

Pitts, Rep. Samuel L.
Bills 177, 180, 182 (2), 365,
Committees 25, 53, 1407
Remarks 615, 1170, 1211

Pittsfield School District, incorporating Athens 1317, 1420,
1871, 1919, 1995, 2074, 2242, 2256,
2457, 2487

Planning and zoning laws ....
.... 236, 265, 796, 813

Plante, Jerome G.
Election and oath of office ... 14
Birth of, and bond for, his daugh-
ter 2863, 3110
Praise for Welcome Back Day ...
.... 937, 953
"Remarkable performance" ...
.... 3099
See also House of Representatives
—Clerk

Pleasant Mt. Ski Development vs.
Mendell 2849

Pleasant Point, see Indian Reservation

Pleasant River, see Scallops

Plumbers 195, 248, 912,
919, 946, 1001, 1117, 1131, 1181,
1410, 1455, 1552, 1576

Plymouth Capital Finance Company
...... 237, 283, 754, 801, 814, 860,
929, 946

Pocket vetoes, see Acts held by
Governor

Poirier, Ernest J. 17

Poisons, see Hazardous substances

Poland, see Lower Range Pond

Police Compact, see New England
Police Compact

Police officers, in fresh pursuit ....
195, 247, 686, 759, 781, 2175, 2224,
2256, 2343, 2352, 2524, 2634, 2773,
2826, 2833, 3001, 3030

Policemen and firefighters, professional immunity ....
.... 296, 356, 2136, 2165

Political parties, see National con-
ventions

Poll taxes 299, 425, 1791, 1821

Pollution, see Air pollution; Andros-
coggin River; Dunstan River;
Halfmoon Pond; Penobscot River;
Sebasticook; Water pollution

Poor persons, see Indigent; Over-
seers of Poor; Paupers

Porcupine bounty ....
.... 105, 142, 167, 193, 438, 450

Portable stoves, see Stoves

Porter, Frank 1439

Portland
City Council
Compensation of members ....
133, 161, 600, 645, 671, 707, 757,
786
Election of members 31,
57, 145, 167, 193, 217, 261, 272
Officials, conflicts of interest ....
.... 134, 161, 535, 546
Police and Fire Departments ....
1187, 1226, 1834, 1908, 1916, 1921,
2063, 2081
Public Library 131,
159, 503, 542, 546, 589, 660, 676,
School Committee 73, 83,
197, 217, 227, 251, 302, 310
Superintending School Committee
134, 161, 1251, 1297, 1318, 1371,
1467, 1488
Water District
Compensation of trustees .....
213, 266, 640, 688, 703, 741, 844,
861
See also Cumberland Water District and Portland Water District
See also Lally, Edward F.

Portland Pipe Line Corporation ...
73, 83, 215, 239, 249, 271, 324, 333

Ports and harbors, see Channel lines

Post-audit statement, see Counties
—Reports

Postage stamp allowance ....
.... 32, 58, 1133, 1184

Postage to advertise hearings .....
.... 32, 58

Posting land, see Hunting

Potato Blossom Festival ....
135, 163, 320, 345, 359, 390, 475, 489

tive Research Committee is now working with IBM, however, to produce the *Record* "much more inexpensively." [12]

In Connecticut, eight copies of a typewritten transcription are made as a reference for legislative intent, at a cost of approximately $17,000 for the session. Members have an opportunity to validate their remarks. The public can check on debate at the state library.

The Wisconsin Historical Society estimated the cost of a one-month experiment in the Wisconsin Assembly at $750 for three typewritten copies, an admittedly low cost which involved only two girls typing from tape. A completely accurate record, delivered the next day, would undoubtedly run considerably higher. Yet, costs can be, we believe, far lower than Maine's. The time surely will come when reporters can stenotype directly onto magnetic tape, which can be run through a computer programmed with a cathode ray tube to provide any type of photo-composition desired. This would save two steps now performed in Maine, a typewritten version and a typeset printed version.

Until this is perfected, Eagleton recommends having a typist listen to tapes of the debate and type directly onto a special keyboard that turns out coded magnetic tape. From this tape, all kinds of photo-composition can then be arranged— for a daily proof sheet for the members' validations; for an ultimate bound volume similar to Maine's; or, if desired, for a separate journal deleting the debate and reporting only on actions taken.

All of this, of course, can be tied in with the computerized bill drafting, electronic voting, and weekly and cumulative bulletins for a total accounting of everything that happens in the legislature.[13]

[12] Eagleton is indebted for this information to Mrs. Bertha W. Johnson, Clerk of the House, and William H. Garside, Legislative Finance Officer of the Maine State Legislature.

[13] For these comments, Eagleton has drawn on the advice of Auto-

Savings can result from such a transcript. Maine and Pennsylvania have eliminated a separate journal. Observers from both the executive and legislative branches might feel they could follow the legislature's deliberations by reading the transcript the next day, rather than sitting in the gallery all afternoon.

Committee Minutes

Not only was general support for a transcript of floor proceedings in the two houses indicated in Eagleton's discussions with legislators and staff, but nearly everyone pointed out the even greater need for a record of deliberation in standing committees. Eagleton strongly agrees. About three-fifths of state legislatures, to one degree or another, maintain records of committee hearings and proceedings. Indeed, it would be ironic if any substantial reorganization took place in Wisconsin without taking this simple and obvious step.

A model of what is needed, we believe, lies in the excellent minutes provided by the Legislative Council for interim committees. These contain everything important that occurred, and underscore action taken, without including unnecessary detail. Secretaries to committee chairmen should be trained in this type of concise reporting. Doing it well depends on understanding the subject. It is to be hoped that this kind of specialization will occur under the new committee structure. Such reporting is particularly important in Joint Finance, especially as it takes over the BOGO function. Indeed, without such minutes, both the Fiscal Bureau and the Audit Bureau will be severely handicapped. The proceedings of important committees could also be taped as a double check for accuracy. This may require the addition of microphones to some committee rooms. To assure that adequate minutes are taken,

---

matech Graphics Corporation, New York, specialists in computerized photo-composition.

an amendment should be offered to Joint Rule 6 on the Record of Committee Proceedings.

Eagleton, therefore, recommends that:

(162) *Both houses have a verbatim transcript of proceedings; daily proof sheets be available for validation the next day if possible; and the entire record be indexed and bound at the end of each session;* and

(163) *Minutes be prepared for all standing and joint standing committee meetings.*

CHAPTER VIII.

ETHICS AND CONFLICTS OF INTEREST

Someday serving in the state legislature may become a full-time job with annual sessions, higher pay, and a smaller legislative body. When that happens, legislating ethics will be much easier. One will simply ask legislators to cease practicing before state agencies or accepting any other outside income for work that is in any way connected with the government. Legislators will even be asked to divest themselves of investments in "regulated securities." The break can be fairly clean. But until that day comes, legislators will find themselves with almost unavoidable conflicts of interest. Such conflicts exist at all levels of government. But they are perhaps most difficult to handle at the state level. Work is hard, sessions are long, pay is low. There are the complicating factors of expenses, pressures, and private interests too.

State legislators are usually the least well known of elected government officials. Often, where visibility is least, irregularities are most prone to develop. Furthermore, there is the cost of being a legislator. The public knows of the cost of political campaigns. But it rarely takes into account the cost of being away from one's permanent job, the cost of keeping up appearances involved in public office, the costs of contributing to every local cause because it is expected of an official, and even, at times, the extra cost of servicing constituents.

The pressures and responsibilities on a state legislator are also very great. In Wisconsin he must approve a budget of some $1.4 billion. He must decide how and where the money can be raised, as well as vote on hundreds of other bills, many of which bring powerful economic forces into play.

It is the rare state legislator, indeed, who has not felt the pressure on him in the competition between the savings banks and the commercial banks, the truckers and the railroads, the municipalities and their employee associations. Shall optometrists as well as opthalmologists be able to prescribe and fit contact lenses? Shall drugstores be licensed to sell packaged liquor, or only liquor stores? Shall the "full crew" law be retained on railroads? Shall single contracts be let for state construction projects or separate contracts for each subcontractor? Millions of dollars turn on such decisions. The public rarely hears of them. Frequently, a well-organized pressure group, back in the home district, stands ready to vote against those who stand in its way.

Finally, there is the complicating factor of the legislator's permanent job—the job that he had before becoming a legislator, the job he will return to, full time, if defeated, and the one with which he supports his family. The lines of work from which legislators can be drawn are relatively few, for they must be flexible enough to allow for time off. Most big corporations are not so flexible—or they are so competitive that executives cannot afford to leave. The result is that self-employed lawyers, farmers, and insurance men, because of their occupations, normally lead all other occupations for legislators. Lawyers and farmers have made up the majority of the state Senate for the past ten years. Together they comprise about two-fifths of the members of the Assembly. Many of the other occupations of state legislators are also among those that can be directly benefited by state legislation. Or, if they are lawyers, they find themselves directly concerned with representing clients before state agencies.

The result is a *private* economic interest that can be at odds with public interest. The private interest can cause a difficult and real division of loyalty for the legislator. Or it can threaten such a division. Or at least it can create the *appearance* of such a division.

Where all of these factors are present, corruption can flourish. Massachusetts, Florida, Louisiana, Texas, and Illinois have all been touched by scandal in state government in recent years. Just as organized crime moves in where law enforcement is lax and officials can be bought, so, too, do special interests move in when the moral tone in the state capitol becomes flabby.

In California in the early 1950's, it was a popularly held opinion that a lobbyist ran the legislature until exposed by *Life* magazine. In Illinois, State Senator Paul Simon wrote in *Harpers*, in November, 1964, that one experienced colleague estimated that "one third of the members (of the legislature) accept payoffs."

Neither of these states is noticeably different from Wisconsin as to the level of education of its population, or per capita income, or the character of its people. But over a period of years the moral purpose and tone of the state government had been allowed to weaken, and the results were costly. The cause, in Eagleton's opinion, was not because the people of the state possibly elected men of inferior moral stature. The fault lay, in our opinion, in the rules, leadership, climate, and ethos of the legislature itself.

Today, California's legislature has become a model of independence and excellence and has passed one of the most comprehensive ethics bills of any state. Illinois is on its way to the same. A sweeping modernization of its legislature and a new code of ethics have been developed.

Why haven't more states and units of local governments adopted ethics laws? The answer, probably, lies in the fact that it takes a good scandal to arouse public opinion.

Most legislators have far greater independence of mind

than the average citizen. Many are very concerned about the ethics issue. But they are also far busier than the average person. Under these circumstances it is often easier to "go along" than to depart from prevailing custom. This is particularly true when changing the customs can mean a major battle, a battle which would probably bring powerful vested interests into play. It could mean the sacrifice of other parts of a member's program. In brief, a full-scale effort is not something to be taken on lightly.

There is also an overriding further consideration. This is the problem of recruiting the best men for the legislature. Many of these men are lawyers, some practicing now before state agencies. The tougher the conflict-of-interest laws, the more difficult it may be for a man to run. The job market from which legislators are drawn is already restricted, as we have pointed out. The number of legislators dropping out because of the frustrations of legislative work is already too high. The net result, after agreeing on the need for complete integrity in office, is that ethics laws should interfere as little as possible with the member's ability to make a living from his permanent line of work.

Eagleton and the Benson Subcommittee[1] have taken this position. We have also recognized the need to use the legitimate expertise and special knowledge that farmer-legislators bring to agricultural problems, insurance members bring to insurance problems, and other specialists contribute in their fields. The ideal ethics code is the one that enables the expertise to be used, but keeps the inherent special interest conflict under control.

[1] "Report of the Subcommittee on Ethics and Conflict of Interest of the Joint Committee on Legislative Organization on A Code of Ethics, and Guidelines for Legislative Conduct," Chairman: Senator Benson (Madison, September 19, 1968).

ACTION IN OTHER STATES

Bribery, election fraud, and corrupt practices are relatively easily defined and covered in the statutes. Conflict-of-interest and other legislative acts are not so easy to define or control by legislation. Many states have considered such measures. Only a few have enacted such legislation. Among them are Texas (1957), Washington (1959), Kentucky (1960), Minnesota (1961), Massachusetts (1962), New York and Louisiana (1964), California and Florida (1967), and New Jersey (1969). Few violations have been reported in these states since enactment. Having the laws on the books seems the best deterrent. The provisions of these laws vary from state to state, though many are copied from other states. No one state has adopted all the best features that are available.

Unethical conduct by legislators involves the substitution of a private interest for public trust. It usually involves, or arises from: (1) soliciting or accepting gifts (bribes); (2) interest in state contracts; (3) representation before state agencies; (4) improper use of inside information; (5) inside lobbying; or (6) private financing of expense funds. These situations may arise singly or in combination. Means of combating them, outside of criminal statutes, involve disclosure of interests, codes of ethics, principles of ethics, ethics boards, and penalties.

LEGISLATIVE ETHICS IN WISCONSIN

Compared to many other states, Wisconsin's legislature has been free of scandal. Old hands at the capitol agree that the legislature is unusually "clean." Members pride themselves on this reputation. Where ethics questions have arisen in the past, newspaper coverage has been exceptionally heavy. Had the legislature enacted a code of ethics at some point in the past, these incidents might not have occurred. In each case the member, or staff official, would have known fairly specifically whether his activities were or were not allowed under the code. In case of doubt, he could have secured a ruling from an ethics board.

Interest in a legislative code of ethics has been high in the past few years. According to an article in the *Madison Capital Times*, October 11, 1967, ethics proposals were introduced in 1953, 1957, and 1959.

Former Governor Gaylord Nelson and the Wisconsin Federation of Women's Clubs in 1960 proposed other codes, and the 1961, 1963, and 1965 sessions also received proposals. All failed, as did recommendations which came out of a 1965 study, and a series of bills which went to hearing in October of 1967.

The Benson Subcommittee's work has followed that of earlier legislative groups. A bill and joint resolution were drafted for the Subcommittee by the Legislative Reference Bureau and discussed at Subcommittee meetings. All provisions of the bill and joint resolution were adopted unanimously by the committee. All witnesses before the committee have supported the bill's provisions as far as they went.

THE BENSON SUBCOMMITTEE'S BILL AND JOINT RESOLUTION

The Benson Subcommittee deliberately kept its code of ethics short and somewhat general, laying down guidelines but relying on the proposed Joint Legislative Ethics Committee to fill in details later.

The preamble notes that the public is entitled to have "confidence" in the Wisconsin legislature and that its members must be "impartial and independent" and not use their office for "private gain." It also notes that "Wisconsin lawmakers are citizen-legislators" entitled "to maintain economic interests which do not conflict with the public interest."

The Subcommittee's draft also lays down four "thou shalt nots" as a code of ethics. In brief, "a legislator or a legislative employee" shall not: (1) accept any gift, favor, or service which might "improperly influence him"; (2) use his official position to obtain special privileges; (3) disclose, or use, confidential information for personal gain; and (4) engage in any business where the principal duty is lobbying.

The draft also calls for the establishment of a Joint Legislative Ethics Committee of eight members, two members to be chosen from each of the four party caucuses. The Committee would select its own chairman from the majority party members or co-chairmen from different parties when party control of the legislature was divided. It also could employ staff from outside the classified service.

The Committee is empowered to: (1) conduct formal or informal investigations, with hearings, upon an affirmative vote of three members from each house; (2) report such investigations, with recommendations to the house involved; (3) recommend changes in statutes and rules pertaining to ethics; (4) issue advisory opinions to legislators or employees upon written request; and (5) publish such opinions with names deleted.

The rights of the accused are carefully protected. Complaints must be sent to the accused by registered mail prior to filing with the committee and prior to committee action. The rules of criminal evidence apply. If the accused is exonerated, the appropriate house will pay all reasonable expenses that have accrued for his defense.

The Benson Subcommittee also approved a draft of a Senate joint resolution outlining "interpretive principles" to guide the JLEC. The first of these specified that a legislator's action on issues and constituent requests is lawful until proven otherwise. The second exempted from the code compensation for published works, for free meals, travel expenses, or speaking engagements, provided a public statement of details was filed within thirty days with the clerk of the legislator's house.

All witnesses at the hearings supported the proposed legislation in general. The attorney general asked changes in certain provisions. Nearly all witnesses asked for additional provisions or the inclusion of more specific detail. Testimony offered by these witnesses is included in the comments below on specific areas of the bill.

ACCEPTANCE OF GIFTS AND FAVORS

Section 3 (A) of the proposed code reads: "A legislator or legislative employee shall not accept any gift, favor, or service which may reasonably tend to improperly influence him in the discharge of his duties in or for the legislature." This is similar to the codes in Florida and Texas and close to that of New Jersey. It also relates to both Wisconsin's bribery and lobbying laws. A discussion of bribery laws came up at the Subcommittee's hearing in Madison on August 14, 1968.

Prompted by the Subcommittee's own question at the hearing, Attorney General Bronson LaFollette asked rhetorically "whether the bribery law as interpreted by the Wisconsin Supreme Court permits legislators to accept expenses from special interest groups." The answer, under some circumstances, he said, was "yes." He went on to explain: "The critical question is whether he accepts property or any personal advantage, which he is not authorized to receive, pursuant to an understanding that he will act in a certain manner in relation to any matter which . . . might come before him."

The attorney general then pointed out that many legislators might have a private employer interested in legislation, but that this would not involve the bribery statute. The legislator would be *authorized* to receive salary and expenses because they were not "*pursuant to an understanding*" that he would act in a certain way. He added that the bribery laws are in a state of confusion, because of a Wisconsin Supreme Court decision which ruled that "corrupt intent" or a "guilty mind" must be proved as well. To correct this interpretation, the attorney general plans to submit a bill to the 1969 legislature.

While Wisconsin's lobbying laws aim at the lobbyist, they also protect the legislature from improper situations. In Nevada, the gambling casinos go all out to entertain members of the legislature. In New York, legislators are given free passes to racetracks to distribute to their friends, and not long ago the savings banks of this same state invited legislators and their wives on a cruise to Bermuda. Fortunately, in Wisconsin the laws are stringent. All lobbyists must be licensed by the secretary of state, must be listed in the Senate *Journal,* and must report expenses monthly. Most important, none is allowed to furnish "any food, meal, lodging, beverage, transportation, money, campaign contributions or any other thing of pecuniary value" to any legislator or official or employee of the state.

Both lobbyists and members of the legislature complain about these provisions. Critics charge that they are unrealistic, because they drive lobbying activities underground, prevent friends from even buying drinks for one another, and encourage "penny-ante chiseling" whereby a lobbyist slips his guest cash to pay the check in order to evade the food and drink provision.

New York's ethics law exempts gifts under $25. An Illinois commission has recommended prohibiting gifts exceeding $100. Suffolk County, in New York State, exempts any "gift or gratuity" of an "inconsequential nature," which has been interpreted as less than $4. Former United States Senator Paul Douglas of Illinois has gone further, putting the cutoff point at $1.50.

All such exemptions would allow lunches and occasional drinks, and might be popular as an amendment to the lobbying law. But Eagleton would urge against a change. It is far better to retain the present ban, irritating as its provisions may seem in practice. This very nuisance factor, it seems to us, serves as a constant reminder of the need for rigorously correct relations between those who hold a public trust and those with a private interest.

If the lobbying laws help to protect the legislator, so too would a small amendment to the proposed code protect the lobbyist from unscrupulous lawmakers. This change would broaden the language to read "a legislator . . . should not *solicit or* accept gifts, favors or services . . ." (emphasis added).

Although the bribery and lobbying laws would tend to stop most attempts by outsiders to influence legislators, it is still well to have this provision pinned down in an ethics code aimed at the recipients of these gifts—legislators and legislative employees. If we are to follow the attorney general's opinion, the bribery law is not now airtight. Even if it were, the stigma and the punishment of the bribery conviction—or even a prosecution—is so great that prosecutors in courts are unlikely to invoke so powerful a weapon against many types of official impropriety.

In Illinois there is an additional prohibition in the bribery law against accepting a fee or reward which is not authorized by law. The reward is closely related to the bribe. Again, both the donee and donor should be reached under the code of ethics and the bribery statutes.

The language of the proposed Wisconsin code should be broad enough to cover a wide range of improper activity.

Surely the prohibition against accepting a "gift, favor, or service" should also prohibit acceptance of economic opportunities (law cases, investments, contracts), for the legislator knows or should know that an attempt is being made to influence his official conduct. A similar ban should apply to accepting excessive compensation or an excessive price from a person with a legislative axe to grind.

In summary then, Eagleton recommends that:

(164) *The proposed code of prohibition on acceptance of any "gift, favor, or service" be adopted;*

(165) *The bribery law be strengthened through enactment of a bill eliminating "corrupt intent" or "guilty mind" as a necessary condition for finding violation;*

(166) *The present lobbying law's ban on even small gifts be maintained without change;*

(167) *The proposed code be amended to prohibit "soliciting" as well as "accepting" gifts, favors, or services after the fact, or to influence subsequent acts;* and

(168) *The prohibition on "favors" include restrictions on the granting of economic opportunities as well as excessive compensation to legislators and employees.*

SPECIAL PRIVILEGES

The second provision (Section 3 (B)) of the proposed code states: "A legislator or legislative employee shall not use or attempt to use his official position to obtain special privileges for himself or others."

Securing special privileges normally occurs in two areas: legislators representing clients before state agencies and legislators helping clients obtain state contracts. Each is an area where a conflict of private and public interest can occur.

Representation before State Agencies

The legislator has traditionally helped his constituents when they have had problems with state agencies. Surely nothing should interfere with this function. It is when the client pays the legislator that the situation changes. The danger here is that an agency will give undue deference to a legislator's client because the legislator is in a position to affect the agency's budget, personnel, and policies. This may not be the fault of the legislator himself. It can also occur, without any encouragement by the legislator, when personnel in the executive branch automatically agree to requests from legislators in an attempt to please them rather than to serve the public interest.

The Benson Subcommittee considered the matter of appearances before state agencies but left final decision to the JLEC. Fairly explicit opinion, however, did exist within the Committee. This favored a ban on a legislator's appearing for a fee before agencies subject to any committees on which he served.

Under this arrangement, a legislator would be free to represent clients in the courts and before any agency, but without compensation. He could also appear for compensation before all agencies except those dependent for approval on a legislative committee on which he served as a member.

Thus, a member of the Assembly Banking and Insurance Committee could not apear as a paid representative before the Insurance Commission, where he has influence in selecting commissioners and judging their work. The question then arose as to whether such a rule would keep a lawyer-legislator with particular expertise from serving on the committees covering the field in which his expertise lay. If he served on such a committee, he would not be able to practice before the executive agency involved. The question was not solved, but it served to point up one of the problems of an effective ethics law. How stringent should one be on practice before state agencies since, over the years, many talented lawyer-legislators undoubtedly will seek part of their livelihood from such fees? Because of this problem many states have tended to go slow in this area.

A number of states now limit representation before state agencies. Under New York law, legislators are banned from representing clients before the Court of Claims and before any agency for a contingent fee. California bars acceptance of fees for appearances before nearly all state licensing and regulatory agencies. Minnesota, New Jersey, and Illinois fall somewhere in between, with each of them prohibiting appearances when client interests are adverse to the state.

The Subcommittee was not persuaded that this ban was necessary. Not all states make this prohibition. Gaining special advantage as a legislator is unethical under any conditions. Perhaps it is less likely in a court of record. But Eagleton feels the question should be examined in the future, particularly where legislators must negotiate settlements out of court.

Still other questions exist. One involves the lawyer-legislator on the Finance Committee, who goes over the budget of every agency. Would he be unable to appear for a fee before any state agency? Would this affect the willingness of some members to serve on Finance?

What of the member who was himself the principal? Should a farmer-legislator on the Agriculture Committee be banned from appearing before the Agricultural Marketing Board? Surely the conflict here would be as great as when a legislator represents a client. Yet a complete ban would not seem desirable except when the benefits such as franchises or licenses are in short supply and might be influenced by the legislator's position.

What of the lawyer-legislator who belongs to a firm whose other members appear before a state agency? Drew Pearson spoke of one New York congressman's law firm which shares the same door and same receptionist and facilities with another firm. One firm includes the congressman's name and one firm (which handles federal cases) does not.

New York and California laws provide that the legislator-partner not share "directly or indirectly in the fee." This is a desirable prohibition. So is having partners other than the legislator handle the case. But the best arrangement, of course, is simply to have the legislator's law firm avoid taking on business that might create conflict of interest. This, it is suggested, would be an example that the law firm itself supports high ethical principles—and would be in line with rulings of the Committee on Professional Ethics of the American Bar Association (ABA). Based on ABA canons, a law firm cannot represent a client before a legislative committee when a member of the firm is serving in the legislature—even if the member does not share in the fee.[2]

What of the legislator who, without being paid, exerts undue influence on an agency on behalf of a constituent, or as a favor to a politician friend back home? Does not the private interest here run counter to the public interest? This problem is met in some areas by making all communication between legislators and agencies a matter of public record. This can be handled by requiring all communications in writing (which is easier), or a record of all phone calls.

Texas does not ban representation but requires full disclosure of all compensated appearances before regulatory agencies when a request is being made. New York asks some of its

[2] Opinion 292 *45 American Bar Association 1272* (1959).

regulatory agencies to maintain a public record of all compensated appearances before them.

Eagleton favors making all legislator contacts with state agencies a matter of public record when those contacts involve action on a particular case. The legislator who needs to expedite the granting of a liquor license for a constituent should make his representations a matter of public record. This will also serve to keep agency personnel from *imagining* that they are being subject to undue influence. Also agency personnel should be aware that they should not give undue weight to representations from legislators.

Contracts with the State

Members of the Benson Subcommittee felt that legislators should avoid contracting with the state. Eight states have provisions in their constitutions that no legislator shall have an interest in any contract authorized by the legislature,[3] and general prohibitions have been used for many years at various levels of government. Among statutory provisions, some states prohibit only contracts with the legislature itself, or contracts on which the legislator must vote. Others require public notices and competitive bidding.

New York prohibits legislators from holding licenses from the racing commission and bans any connection with firms doing business with the state's racetracks. California prohibits legislators from receiving commissions on insurance placed on behalf of the state. California also exempts contracts from a general conflict-of-interest prohibition if the legislator's interest is "remote" when it is disclosed to the legislature and voted in its official records, and thereafter, if the

[3] Citizen's Conference on State Legislatures, *State Constitutional Provisions Affecting Legislatures* (Kansas City, Mo.: The Conference, May, 1967), p. 21.

legislature approves the contract without the vote of the member involved. His interest is "remote" if he owns less than 3 percent of the corporation's stock and it is not more than 5 percent of his total income.[4]

In Massachusetts a legislator's proprietary interest, and those of his immediate family, should total less than 10 percent and be fully disclosed. The contract must also be made through competitive bidding. In Suffolk County (New York) a remote interest is under 5 percent.

Several other aspects of contracts seem worth considering. One is the matter of size of contract; matters under $50, for instance, are exempted in Ohio. Another concerns contracting with *associates* of the legislator, not only his immediate family (spouse and children) but also brothers and sisters—and clients, tenants, and customers. As others have pointed out, there are frequently cases in which the legislator had nothing to do with giving the contract, but a client, ignorant of the mysteries of state government, might think that he did and feel obligated.

Even the safeguard of competitive bidding has its pitfalls. After a contract is signed there are often a number of discretionary aspects during actual fulfillment of it in which a legislator's influence can be important—quality inspection, delivery schedules, and so forth.

Disclosure is, of course, one of the most useful devices in preventive ethics. One method of using it, in the matter of contracts, is mandatory disclosure of interest, through compensation or ownership, which in turn is placed on file with the regulatory or contracting agencies involved.

[4] For useful summaries of a number of state laws, see the Wisconsin Legislative Council's "Preliminary Staff Report on Conflicts of Interest of State Legislators," November 21, 1966; and the Legislative Reference Bureau's "Comparative Study of State Codes of Ethics," March 4, 1968.

Eagleton favors some flexibility in this area. In *municipal* codes of ethics this matter is particularly difficult to handle. Many city councilmen in small municipalities do business with the city. It would be impractical to forbid them to continue. Thus, only a disclosure of interest is normally required.

Similarly, there are situations in which the legislator's company is the *only* source of supply; or in which it is a practical impossibility for the legislator to divest himself of his interest. On the other hand, a flat ban on doing business in sensitive areas (racetracks, insurance for the state) seems eminently worthwhile. For other forms of business certain other protections would seem desirable: competitive bidding, and disclosure of interest filed with regulatory or contracting agencies.

We have discussed representation before state agencies and contracts with the state. There are, of course, other irregular means of securing special privileges but we have reserved these for discussion under conflict of interest.

In summary, then, Eagleton recommends that:

(169) *A prohibition on a legislator's use of his official position "to obtain special privileges" be adopted.*

(170) *When representing themselves or clients before state agencies:*

  (a) *legislators not appear for compensation before state agencies subject to review by committees of which the legislator is a member;*

  (b) *legislators be prohibited from seeking franchises or licenses in short supply;*

  (c) *all requests from legislators to agencies (other than those seeking general information above) be made a matter of public record.*

(171) *Whenever state contracts are involved*:

   (a) *legislators, their families, and business associates avoid contracting with the state on any matters where their interest is substantial as defined by the Joint Legislative Ethics Committee*;

   (b) *public notice and competitive bidding apply in all circumstances where a legislator has an interest*;

   (c) *disclosure be made to the legislature and regulatory agencies of a legislator's interest in firms contracting with the state, providing that the interest and the size of the contract are both above certain minimums.*

USE OF INSIDE INFORMATION

There was a time when using inside information was one of the prerequisites of power. Tammany bosses bought property they knew would soon be needed by New York City, sold it for outrageous profits, and called it honest graft. Wall Street insiders, at least until recently, have played the stock market to their own advantage, with the average investor often footing the bill. Now, as the Securities and Exchange Commission has held, it is time to "eliminate the idea that the use of inside information for personal advantage was a normal emolument of corporate office."

Section 3 (C) of the proposed bill states that a legislator or employee "shall not disclose confidential information obtained through his official position nor use such information for the personal gain or benefit of himself or others."

Both of these prohibitions seem to us self-evident. The crucial test of whether there has been any irregularity is whether the same information is available to other citizens in the same circumstances. Confidential information is the property of the government, not of the individual. In wartime, its use could involve national security. In peacetime, its use for private gain is a breach of a public trust.

United States Senator Clifford Case of New Jersey has recently asked that the profit be taken out of such breaches of trust by making the trustee (public official, legislator) account for every penny he makes. Civil suits against office-holders can be brought by legal representatives of various levels of government. Senator Case believes private citizens can bring such suits as well.

Eagleton therefore recommends that:

(172) *The proposed prohibition on a legislator's use of confidential information for gain be adopted.*

INSIDE LOBBYING

Section 3 (D) of the proposed bill provides that a legislator or legislative employee "shall not accept employment nor engage in any business or activity when a principal duty therefore is to promote or influence legislation."

A legislator has convictions and he should attempt to persuade his colleagues of their merit. He is also free to join an organization, or work for a company, with legislative interests. But he should not be paid to lobby while at the same time serving as a member of the legislature.

What of his business firm? Should it be paid to lobby—even if other members of the firm did the lobbying, and the member did not share in the fee? Illinois has recommended full disclosure in this regard, and we believe it would be a useful refinement to Wisconsin's already comprehensive lobbying laws: to identify, in the registration of lobbyists, those who are affiliated in business with legislators.

Some governmental units prohibit lobbying activities for a period of time after a member leaves the legislature. This was discussed by the Benson Subcommittee but no action was taken. It does not appear to be a problem in light of present lobbying laws. Figures for the period 1949 to 1955 showed that less than 10 percent of all registered lobbyists were former legislators.[5]

Eagleton recommends that:

(173) *No legislator or legislative employee accept employment where a principal duty is to promote legislation.*

(174) *All lobbyists affiliated in business with legislators be forced to disclose this affiliation as part of their registration.*

A JOINT LEGISLATIVE ETHICS COMMITTEE (JLEC)

The heart of the Benson Subcommittee's proposal is, of course, the establishment of the Joint Committee (JLEC) to carry out its mandate. Its proposed duties have been described in the section above on the Subcommittee's bill. But the proposed makeup of the joint committee was subject to further discussion with Senator Warren's Subcommittee dealing with committee structure, which suggested that members should be the same as those on the Legislative Council Board, plus the two assistant minority leaders, to give each party equal strength. All members of the Board would thus be ex-officio members of the JLEC.

Eagleton approves the co-opting of the legislature's leaders for this difficult and politically sensitive task. No legislative function would be more important in the event of a charge against a member. We believe, however, that it would be

[5] Leon Epstein, *Politics in Wisconsin* (Madison: University of Wisconsin Press, 1958), p. 195.

preferable to have: (1) an odd number of members on the Committee and (2) public members.

Public members, we believe, are particularly important. One of the purposes of an ethics code is to maintain public confidence in the legislature. To do so we must remove all suspicion that it is a "club" where members judge themselves. If meetings are closed and there are few public hearings, this becomes even more important. Nothing would hurt the legislature's reputation more, or destroy the effectiveness of the entire ethics effort faster, than a public outcry of "whitewash." This could happen, regardless of whether the charges were true, if meetings were held behind closed doors with only legislators present.

There are precedents for going outside the legislature. In criminal actions, it is the executive branch that prosecutes a legislator, and the case is tried in the judicial branch.

Ethics committees are composed solely of legislators in California, Illinois, Minnesota, and New Jersey. Only New York, Washington, and Louisiana, to our knowledge, have public members as well. But commissions in Illinois and elsewhere have consistently recommended this safeguard. Most members of the JLEC, we believe, would welcome the advice of others in these matters.

How many public members? Eagleton would suggest three. They should, of course, be individuals of outstanding character and integrity chosen for the contribution they can make. The attorney general, the dean of the University's law school, and the governor might each appoint one. It would be important to have an odd number of members. With its public members, the JLEC would be set up as an advisory committee to the Legislative Council Board. This is appropriate—the JLEC is an advisory committee. Its powers would derive from the Board.

Eagleton therefore recommends that:

(175) *A joint Legislative Ethics Committee (JLEC) be established as an advisory committee to the Legislative Council Board (LCB);*

(176) *The JLEC be composed of an expanded LCB, serving ex officio, plus three public members appointed by eminent officials outside the legislature.*

Procedures

The Benson Subcommittee's draft proposal called for using the rules of criminal evidence in all committee proceedings; it asked that any complaint be sent by registered mail to the respondent prior to being filed with the committee, and specified that no investigations, hearings, or records thereof be public except by request of the respondent.

Eagleton agrees with the Subcommittee that all possible precautions should be taken to protect the rights of those charged with unethical conduct—particularly in a situation where the charge alone is often tantamount to conviction. But it questions the methods used.

Asking a complainant to notify the respondent before filing with the JLEC will undoubtedly discourage complaints from being made. Having complaints submitted in writing to the JLEC should be sufficient. The respondent would then be notified in writing. Nothing would be disclosed to the public.

Should the JLEC be bound to the rules of criminal evidence? Every safeguard should be taken to protect innocent persons with the fullest possible measure of due process, including representation by counsel, and the right to present witnesses and cross examine. But it does not seem necessary to restrict the powers of the JLEC in advance. The JLEC's latitude should be co-terminous with confidence placed in it, and it should not be given less investigatory power than other committees of the legislature.[6]

> Those reports, of course, are hearsay and cannot be considered as evidence to prove the truth or falsity of the charge. If a hearing should be ordered, only legally competent evidence would be admissable. However, in ruling upon this motion [to quash the complaint], we are not concerned with the truth or falsity of the charges, but only with the legal sufficiency of the presentation thereof.
>
> The provision of the law relating to complaints does not specify that the charges must be based on the personal knowledge of the complainant. If complaints could be filed based only on the personal knowledge of the Complainant, it would be virtually impossible for a legally sufficient complaint to be filed under the Code of Ethics. It would be very unlikely for any one other than a party to a violation of the Code of Ethics ever to know personally all of the facts comprising the violation.
>
> The Elector Complainant under the Code of Ethics occupies substantially the same position as does the Prosecutor or Grand Jury with respect to criminal prosecutions. The function of those officials is to present charges based upon information obtained. We see no reason to impose a more stringent requirement. . . .
>
> It is true that the law requires that the complainant must be willing to appear before the Board to testify in support of his complaint. This does not imply that he must necessarily have personal knowledge of all or any of the facts upon which his complaint is based. The reasonable meaning and purpose of that requirement is that if the complainant does know any facts, he must be willing to testify to them, and otherwise must be available and willing to declare under oath the source of the information upon which his complaint is based.

On closing all meetings to the public, the question has been asked whether the United States Senate would have censured

---

[6] Eagleton's position is supported by a finding on Complaint No. 1, issued by the Louisiana Board of Ethics for State Elected Officials on September 11, 1968, commenting on a series of newspaper articles submitted to them as a complaint.

Senator Joseph McCarthy or Senator Thomas Dodd if the proceedings had been closed. The answer, of course, is that many committee meetings in both those cases were secret. Certainly all initial investigation and preliminary hearings should be handled in the same way in the JLEC. Again, it would seem wise to leave the decision on public hearings to the JLEC. Its members are, after all, among the most eminent men in the state. Sometimes a public hearing, scheduled at the JLEC's option, will do more to clear the air than keeping the matter bottled up. After all, nothing in the bill will keep the complainant from talking to the press if he so desires.

The JLEC should also have the power to initiate complaints and to take strong action against unauthorized disclosure of information. It might also be able to act for the filing of reckless and irresponsible complaints. In Illinois criminal penalties were proposed for both.

One of the most valuable functions of an ethics board lies in providing advisory opinions on matters that have reached the stage of charge and countercharge in the press. The Borough President of Manhattan, in New York City, and the Attorney General of Louisiana have, in the past, both asked their respective ethics boards to investigate conflict-of-interest charges made against them. In both instances investigations were made and factual statements issued that cleared the air and served the cause of justice.

The findings, of course, were interpretations of the code of ethics that had been adopted—not subjective judgments. In time, such rulings build up into a body of opinion covering conduct in all kinds of situations. The New York City Board of Ethics has handed down more than one hundred opinions, which are collected and published ten at a time.[7] The American Bar Association, the National Education Association,

[7] We are indebted to Mr. S. Stanley Kreutzer, Counsel to the Board, for a number of facts in this portion of the study.

and other voluntary groups have followed the same practice with their codes.[8]

Many of the JLEC's interpretations of the Wisconsin code will, of course, result in passage of joint resolutions on ethics —a supplement of the code that would be veto-proof and perhaps somewhat easier to adopt and change than the statutory code itself.

As previously mentioned, the Benson Subcommittee has already drafted two "interpretive principles" which "are to be adhered to by the [JLEC] in administering the code." One of these, similar to the California law, exempts from the ethics code a legislator's acceptance of "compensation, free meals, and reimbursement of travel expenses in the course of fulfilling any speaking engagement, or . . . for published works." It then requires a public statement be filed by the legislator "within thirty days of said receipt with the clerk of his own house."

The Attorney General, in his testimony, felt this provision to be "entirely too broad" for it permits acceptance of "compensation of any kind and for any reason" and in effect provides a "bath of immunity from the code."

Eagleton is confident that the Benson Subcommittee members would agree to tightening the proposal. We would suggest that compensation should be "reasonable" [9] and that such compensation and reimbursement for speeches be provided only when the legislator is outside his own district.

Because advisory opinions represent a continuing body of interpretation, some continuity in the membership and staff

[8] It is interesting to note that the codes of the American Bar Association, the Motion Picture Association, and several other groups are enforceable even though voluntary.

[9] On published works, one is reminded of the director of the Division of Antibiotics of the United States Food and Drug Administration who accepted $287,000 as royalties for his writings over an eight-year period. His pay was tied directly to subsequent reprint sales and advertising volume.

of the JLEC is important. The appointment of public members, and the use of the Secretary of the Legislature, provide this opportunity. Finally the JLEC should issue reports, with recommendations, on at least an annual basis.

Eagleton therefore recommends that:

(177) *Complainants be required only to file complaints in writing with the JLEC.*

(178) *The JLEC be empowered to:*

(a) *adopt its own rules of evidence;*

(b) *decide when meetings or hearings should be open and when and in what manner reports and findings should be made public;*

(c) *initiate its own complaints; and*

(d) *recommend penalties for unauthorized disclosure of committee information.*

(179) *The JLEC should recommend additions to the joint rules that clarify and interpret the code of ethics.*

(180) *The JLEC should issue advisory opinions, with the identity of individuals protected; collect them for subsequent publication; and issue an annual report on its activities.*

Codes of Ethics

The report of the Illinois Conflict of Interest Laws Commission suggests three codes: (1) rules of conduct for legislators (similar to Section 3 of the proposed Wisconsin bill which is reviewed above); (2) ethical principles for legislators; and (3) ethical principles for special interest groups and close economic associates of legislators.

The first code would be enforceable by the legislature, probably through censure. The second, ethical principles, would set guidelines for conduct in situations where a member's conscience would be the chief means of enforcement. (The member's voluntary disqualification of himself in a conflict situation would be an example.) The third and final code would provide guidelines for the other members of a legislator's law firm or other business affiliation.

The last two codes would not be enforceable. But the JLEC could develop these principles of conduct, carry out investigations of alleged violations, and issue findings of fact and recommendations to the legislature, the bar association, and to prosecutors as needed.

What additions are needed in the code?

One matter that occasionally turns up in the press involves supplemental compensation for legislators from private sources and privately financed expense funds.

> Legislators should not have their official salary supplemented by private parties although, of course, [they] should be allowed . . . compensation for private employments. A . . . more difficult problem arises (from) . . . a fund for official expenses . . . supplied by private contributors.[10]

This problem has occurred primarily at the national level. When it does occur in the state it creates a very poor impression. The best solution, of course, is to provide sufficient services to legislators to make this unnecessary. Illinois and Louisiana have both prohibited such supplemental funds in their statutes.

Another provision that might be considered by the JLEC is a general ban on "conduct unbecoming a legislator." As Professor Sacks has pointed out, this is a catchall provision, sub-

10 From a paper by Howard R. Sacks, Dean, University of Connecticut Law School, delivered at the Eagleton Seminar, August 1, 1968.

ject to abuse by an enforcing authority, and perhaps best left to a code of "ethical principles." But potentially it could be a help in reaching unpredictable abuses of trust. Again, Illinois, after long study, has included such a provision in its code.

An area requiring rulings by the JLEC will perhaps be the conflict of interest involved in voting. Twelve states have constitutional provisions requiring that a legislator with a personal interest in any measure disclose that fact and refrain from voting on it.

The Benson Subcommittee felt that a legislator should be excused from voting only when his interest was substantial. A farmer would not be excused on an agricultural bill, but would be on a claims bill benefiting him or his firm. "Substantial interest" is left for JLEC to define.

In many states, abstaining from voting reduces the necessary majority of the members required for passage of a bill. For that reason it is granted only in clear-cut situations. California handles it by requiring the member's disclosure of interest, but allowing him to state that he is able to cast a "fair and objective vote."

On the matter of "disclosure" of legislators' interests, many witnesses at the hearings took issue with the Benson Subcommittee. Their point: to control conflict of interest it is important that a statement of a legislator's interests (equities and income) be publicly known.

This issue is perennial in the United States Congress, and an important one in any ethics discussion.[11] If legislator A owns stock in or handles legal work for the X Y Z bank, this will explain his vote on a branch banking bill, and the possible conflict of his private interests with a public trust. Disclosure provides the public with knowledge of his possible bias,

[11] It is also part of a much wider and more complex subject of increasing importance: the invasion of privacy in an electronic age.

and perhaps acts as a deterrent to members inclined to vote their private interests.[12] It may also facilitate enforcement of the "conflict" sections of the proposed code of ethics, and reduce rumor and suspicion about a man's interests.

Full disclosure can, however, create hardship. It can influence a man against serving in the legislature. It can put him at a business disadvantage vis-à-vis his customers or competitors. It can be an invasion of privacy.

Eagleton feels, nevertheless, that a *limited disclosure* plan would have benefit. This can take several forms. One device is the filing of a sealed envelope, containing copies of income tax and other disclosure data, in a trusted depository. The envelope can be removed only by majority vote of JLEC and official notice to the member. It can be opened only in executive session.

Another form of limited disclosure would require a listing of all holdings over $5,000 (including stock options) of the member and his spouse and children among state-regulated companies; a listing of all clients for whom services were supplied totaling more than, say, $1,000 annually; and a listing of all offices, directorships, and salaried employments (amount of compensation not included). Such a listing would be required from each legislator by January 15 each year. Under this plan a man's income and wealth are not made public. But the *sources* of private interest are disclosed.

Such a plan would not satisfy the proponents of full disclosure in the United States Congress, where membership is a full-time, relatively highly paid job.[13] But it has proved to be

[12] But campaign use, by local opponents, alleging conflict of interest have rarely been effective without a clear-cut violation of some legal provision. In fact, such allegations often boomerang on the candidate making the charge.

[13] And where 20 percent of the members of the United States Senate are millionaires.

relatively painless and therefore acceptable to the citizen-members of a state legislature. New York has a modified version of this plan.

What penalties should be provided in the proposed law? Criminal statutes on bribery and corrupt practices, of course, reach the most flagrant violations of law. The purpose of an ethics code is to provide a means of combating less flagrant and borderline abuses, particularly in the difficult field of conflict of interest. If, indeed, the state were to depend on criminal statutes alone, very little would perhaps ever be done. Judges and prosecutors hesitate to apply such harsh sanctions on many of the lesser, and more common, irregularities that occur.

In California the Joint Legislative Ethics Committee reports its findings of fact to the house of membership, the attorney general, and the concerned district attorney. Violators are guilty of a misdemeanor, as they are in various other states. Illinois, Louisiana, New Jersey, and New York apply fines ranging from $500 to $5,000. All states, regardless of whether the language appears in their law, refer cases to the member's house for a possible vote of censure, removal from office, or even referral of the case to an appropriate prosecutor.

One of the important continuing functions of the JLEC would be the dissemination of the ethics code (and principles, if adopted). The chief value of the code, after all, is its potential as a deterrent. Lobbyists and associates of legislators and the public should be apprised of its contents, too.

In New York, each legislator, at the time of signing his disclosure forms, signs an acknowledgment that he has read an official booklet on the code. A "creed," based on the ethics and ethical principles codes and outlining the obligations of public service, might be attractively prepared, framed, and hung in various places in the capitol.[14] Orientation programs surely provide an excellent opportunity to make both legislators and staff aware of the public trust they share.

In summary, then, Eagleton recommends that:

(181) *The JLEC consider*

    (a) *formulating additional guideline codes on ethical principles for legislators and ethical principles for special interest groups and close economic associates of legislators;*

    (b) *a prohibition on supplemental compensation and privately financed expense funds for legislators;*

    (c) *a prohibition on "conduct unbecoming a legislator";*

    (d) *a prohibition on a member voting in cases of "substantial" interest.*

(182) *The Code be amended to provide for a plan of limited disclosure of assets, income, and business interests.*

(183) *The JLEC undertake a continuing program of education on the ethics code among members and staff of the legislature, lobbyists, and the public at large.*

[14] For a fine example, see International City Managers Association, *A Suggested Code of Ethics for Municipal Officials* (Chicago, 1962), p. 32.

CHAPTER IX.

SUMMARY OF RECOMMENDATIONS

In this chapter all recommendations made and explained in detail in the body of the report are repeated. They are numbered and listed in the order in which they appeared in the text.

To improve the legislative committee system, Eagleton recommends that:

(1) The Legislative Council, as presently constituted, be abolished, and the functions of Council committees be taken over by parallel standing committees which operate jointly during interim periods;

(2) A ten-member Legislative Council Board be created, composed of the speaker of the Assembly, the president pro tempore of the Senate, the Senate majority leader, the Senate minority leader, the Assembly majority leader, the Assembly minority leader, the Senate assistant majority leader, the Assembly assistant majority leader, the Senate assistant minority leader, and the Assembly assistant minority leader;

(3) The Legislative Council Board be responsible for the supervision of joint legislative services, the coordination of studies and investigations of joint legislative committees, and the development every two years of a long-range plan for the legislature which will spell out specific priorities for the legislature during that period;

(4) It be the responsibility of the Assembly and Senate Operations Boards to coordinate the activities of the standing committees of each house;

(5) Each joint committee present separate budgets for its regular expenses and for special study, expenses to be approved by the Legislative Council Board, and each standing committee follow the same procedure in its relationship with the house Operations Board to whom it reports;

(6) Each standing committee be required to go before the Operations Board of its house for allocations of staff, monies, and the necessary jurisdiction required for each new study. When a joint committee, operating mainly in interim, between sessions, undertakes a study, it should be up to the Legislative Council Board to supply these resources. In order to coordinate staff resources between the two houses, each house's Operations Board should act in its capacity as a subcommittee of the Legislative Council Board;

(7) Each standing committee supply to its Operations Board a report every month of its activity and planned agenda. Interim committees should do the same with respect to the Legislative Council Board;

(8) The Legislative Council Board be responsible for appointing a five-member advisory committee for each legislative committee, to serve during the term of the legislature;

(9) Advisory committees to interim committees also serve as advisory committees to component Assembly and Senate committees;

(10) Legislative members not formally be members of the advisory committee itself, since it is assumed that the members of the committee and the advisory committee will work with the legislative members throughout the life of the advisory committee;

(11) Advisory groups be permitted to vote on whether or not to recommend a proposal to their parent committees, but have no power to vote with legislative committee members on whether or not to introduce bills to the legislature;

(12) An administrative subcommittee be organized for every standing and interim committee;

(13) The administrative subcommittee plan, schedule, and facilitate the work load of joint and standing committees; select and request staff in conjunction with the Legislative Council Board; and be responsible for the appointment of subcommittees, and in the case of minority members, the views of the ranking minority member should be weighed heavily;

(14) Each of the standing committees in the two houses be encouraged to establish subcommittees, which would be responsible for subject areas selected by the administrative subcommittee of the full committee;

(15) The chairman of the full committee be an ex officio member of all subcommittees;

(16) Subcommittees be authorized, with the approval of the administrative subcommittee, to hold hearings and write reports for the consideration of the full committee;

(17) Because of the demands which will be made on the subcommittee chairman, no person serving as a subcommittee chairman be assigned to more than one subcommittee;

(18) There be established eleven standing committees in the Assembly and seven standing committees in the Senate;

(19) Major legislation, affecting a particular program, be sent by the presiding officers in each house, first to the legislative committee, under whose jurisdiction the legislation properly falls and then, if necessary, to the Finance Committee; each piece of legislation be accompanied by a recommendation of the standing committee to which it was first referred; and the Finance Committee take the recommendation of the substantive committee into consideration;

(20) In the Assembly there be established, in addition to the Operations Board, standing committees on: (1) Finance; (2) Governmental and Military Affairs; (3) Judiciary; (4) Commerce; (5) Transportation; (6) Agriculture and Consumer Services; (7) Natural Resources; (8) Health and Social Services; (9) Human Resources; and (10) Education; and in the Senate there be established, in addition to the Operations Board, standing committees on: (1) Finance; (2) Judiciary, Governmental, and Military Affairs; (3) Commerce and Transportation; (4) Agriculture, Consumer Services, and Natural Resources; (5) Health and Social Services; and (6) Education and Human Resources;

(21) A subcommittee of the Assembly Governmental and Military Affairs Committee, known as the Governmental Subcommittee, be established, and that members of this subcommittee be among the legislative members of the newly named Commission on Intergovernmental Relations;

(22) A second subcommittee of the full Governmental and Military Affairs Committee be established. We recommend that it be known as the Military Affairs Subcommittee. It will be the responsibility of this committee to oversee the Departments of Military Affairs and Veterans' Affairs. This subcommittee shall be responsible for legislation relating to national guard units, air defense, state armories, operation of veteran homes, housing loans to veterans, rehabilitation loans to veterans, education grants to veterans, and advisor service to veterans;

(23) The establishment of subcommittees of the Assembly Judiciary Committee on the courts and on law enforcement;

(24) There be two subcommittees of the Senate Committee on Judiciary, Governmental, and Military Affairs—one known as the Judiciary Subcommittee and one known as the Governmental and Military Affairs Subcommittee;

(25) The Assembly Committee on Commerce be divided into two subcommittees: one on insurance, banking, and business and the other on labor;

(26) The Assembly Committee on Transportation be divided into two subcommittees: one on highway and motor vehicles and the other on public transportation, which will include other modes of transportation outside of motor vehicles;

(27) The Senate Committee on Commerce and Transportation establish two subcommittees: one on transportation and the other on commerce;

(28) There be two subcommittees of the Assembly Committee on Agriculture and Consumer Services: the Agriculture Subcommittee and the Consumer Affairs Subcommittee;

(29) The establishment of two subcommittees of the full Assembly Committee on National Resources: one dealing with conservation and the other with natural resources;

(30) The Senate Committee on Agriculture, Consumer Services, and Natural Resources be divided into three subcommittees: Agriculture, Consumer Services, and Natural Resources;

(31) The Assembly and Senate Committees on Health and Social Services be divided into three subcommittees: Health, Mental Health, and Social Services;

(32) The Assembly Committee on Human Resources be divided into a Subcommittee on Labor which would have jurisdiction over matters related to industrial safety, building plan review, workmen's compensation, apprenticeship program, fair-labor standards, employment service, and unemployment compensation; and a Subcommittee on Human Relations dealing with problems of equal opportunities and human rights throughout the state structure;

(33) The Assembly Committee on Education be divided into a Subcommittee on Higher Education and a Subcommittee on Elementary, Secondary, and Special Education;

(34) The Senate Committee on Education and Human Resources be divided into two subcommittees: one on education and one on human resources;

(35) The Assembly Operations Board consist of the speaker, the majority and minority leaders, and the assistant leaders of both parties; and the Senate Operations Board consist of the president pro tempore, the majority and minority leaders, and the assistant leaders of both parties;

(36) As a leadership committee, the Assembly Operations Board should assume the functions of the committees on contingent expenditures, engrossed bills, enrolled bills, printing, revision, rules, and third reading;

(37) As soon as the budget document has been distributed, each standing committee of the legislature review that part of the executive budget document that affects the area of state government for which it is responsible, and a written committee report, based on this program review, be made to the Joint Committee on Finance and to the legislature no later than thirty days after the receipt of the budget document;

(38) The Joint Committee on Finance not consider any changes in the executive budget until receipt of the program report from the standing committee responsible for the areas of state government that the change affects or until thirty days after the receipt of the executive budget document;

(39) All bills introduced in either house of the legislature for the appropriation of money, providing for revenue, or relating to taxation, which have a full biennial impact in excess of $25,000 be referred to the Joint Committee on Finance before being passed;

(40) Standing committees utilize the services of the Legislative Fiscal Bureau, both when considering the budget and when working in areas related to new legislation;

41) Representatives of the Joint Committee on Finance and the substantive committees with responsibilities for different sections of the budget be permitted and encouraged to attend the governor's budgetary hearings;

(42) The Joint Committee on Finance invite each relevant committee to the joint budget hearings when a department's budget, which has previously been considered by the standing committee, is discussed by the Joint Committee on Finance;

(43) The Joint Committee on Finance appoint subject area subcommittees for the purpose of studying the reports of the standing committees of both houses which have considered particular sections of the budget;

(44) Four subcommittees of the Joint Committee on Finance be established. These subcommittees on education, health and social services, governmental affairs, and a general subcommittee (catchall) should be established to achieve integration between all standing committees and the Joint Committee on Finance;

(45) Legislation with a fiscal note of less than $25,000 need not be referred to the Joint Committee on Finance;

(46) The statutes authorizing each of the statutory committees be carefully reviewed, and where it is possible to include the statutory committees in the standing-joint committee structure, this should be done;

(47) The staff of the Joint Survey Committee on Tax Exemptions continue to operate as it has up until this time, minus the legislative members of the committee, and the staff

be under the general supervision of the administrator of services;

(48) The staff of the Joint Survey Committee on Retirement Systems continue to function and report to the administrator of services, but no legislative members be on the committee;

(49) In order to broaden the Building Commission's responsibility to the legislature and better integrate it into the budgetary process, the State Building Commission retain its powers, but become advisory to the Joint Committee on Finance;

(50) The Board on Government Operations be abolished and the Joint Committee on Finance assume the Board's operational responsibilities;

(51) The Council for Home and Family retain its present form and become an advisory committee to the Joint Committee on Health and Social Services, and with the approval of the latter committee, reports of the Council for Home and Family be sent to the Judiciary, Governmental, and Military Affairs Committee for consideration;

(52) A separate Joint Committee on Judiciary, Governmental, and Military Affairs coordinate grant-in-aid programs and supervise the legislature's office in Washington, D.C.;

(53) The name of the Committee on Interstate Cooperation be changed to Intergovernmental Relations Commission and that the duties of the Commission be expanded to include state-local and inter-local relations. The Intergovernmental

Relations Commission should consist of the governor's council on intergovernmental relations and the advisory committee on intergovernmental relations of the Joint Committee on Judiciary, Governmental, and Military Affairs. This advisory committee shall serve as an integrating mechanism for the entire legislature;

(54) The Menominee Indian Study Committee continue as an advisory committee to the Joint Committee on Judiciary, Governmental, and Military Affairs and, specifically, the Subcommittee on Governmental Affairs;

(55) The Committee to Visit State Properties be abolished;

(56) The Commission on Uniform State Laws continue functioning in its present form, although in an advisory capacity to the Joint Committee on Judiciary, Governmental, and Military Affairs;

(57) Departments, at the first available time in the session, make presentation of their policy goals to the appropriate standing committees of the legislature, and that standing committees make every effort to inform themselves in a comprehensive manner about the several programs operated by the departments and agencies (when possible, this should be done in joint meetings of corresponding committees of both houses);

(58) The departments, officers, and employees of Wisconsin state government, and the governing bodies of the political subdivisions of this state, assist legislative committees in the completion of their tasks; provide legislative commit-

tees with ready access to any books, records, or other information relating to such tasks; and upon request by a legislative committee, and within the limits of existing appropriations, supply such specialized staff assistance as a legislative committee may require;

(59) Each standing committee of the legislature review all administrative rules for the area of state government that is the responsibility of that standing committee;

(60) Wherever possible, legislators should serve on only one committee and in no case should serve on more than two committees;

(61) In the Senate, the number of members on each committee be determined by the appointing authority, but be not less than three nor more than nine;

(62) In the Assembly, the number of members be determined by the appointing authority, but should be not less than five nor more than thirteen;

(63) Each committee reflect, as closely as possible, and with fractions resolved in favor of the majority party, the political composition of the house in which it is located, but each member serve on at least one committee;

(64) The Senate chairman will preside in meetings of joint committees, but members of the committee, as a committee, will vote as individuals;

(65) The minority members of each committee be selected by the minority leadership of each house;

(66) Where possible, each committee have a constant meeting room and these rooms adjoin the offices of the committee chairman;

(67) The members of a committee initial a notification slip at the time notice of a hearing or meeting is received and that such notification slips be returned to the committee chairman;

(68) Committees and subcommittees travel as much as necessary and hold hearings in different parts of the state;

(69) Whenever possible, committees hold hearings on related bills;

(70) When a public hearing is scheduled, legislative representatives submit their testimony, in writing, to the chairman of the committee, as far in advance as possible; copies be distributed to all committee members; and oral remarks to the committee be in the nature of a summary, not lasting longer than five minutes;

(71) Public hearings be scheduled in the afternoon, whenever possible;

(72) Committee members may question witnesses only when they have been recognized by the chairman for that purpose and only for a five-minute period, a time which can be extended only with unanimous consent of members present;

(73) Questioning of witnesses at full and subcommittee hearings be initiated by the chairman, and opportunities be alternated between majority and minority members;

(74) The administrative subcommittee set a definite period of time for hearings on each bill;

(75) Whenever possible, a verbatim or summary transcript of remarks at a hearing be kept;

(76) After a hearing on a bill is completed, each legislator be provided with a brief committee report deposited in his bill folder relating to each bill, which includes a list of those persons or organizations who appeared either in favor of or against a bill;

(77) The same set of committee rules be used for each standing and joint committee. These rules can be found on m.s. pages 3 to 66 of our report;

(78) All proposals should be considered as soon as possible, and the chairman of each committee should regularly report to the speaker and the president pro tempore of the Senate the number of proposals in the possession of his committee;

(79) Each committee report present major issues related to a bill with arguments both pro and con synopsized by the committee staff for the benefit of the members; in unusual circumstances relating to a piece of legislation in which a committee has devoted a large amount of time and energy, an oral report be made to the entire house, meeting as The Committee of the Whole, by the standing committee; and every bill submitted by a legislative committee (both standing and joint) have a negative or positive report attached to it by the committee;

(80) All proposals, in the form of bills, resolutions, petitions, and motions, which are referred to a committee, be acted upon as soon as practicable;

(81) Bills be arranged in committee journals, by subject, for reference by future legislators who may wish to consult a committee journal from a previous year;

(82) Each joint committee which conducts an interim study be required to prepare an in-depth report dealing with the committee's findings and recommendations, including suggested legislation, and these reports be submitted to the legislature at the start of each new legislative session;

(83) Staff be assigned to standing committees by the administrator of services, and this staff work with a combined joint committee operating in the interim;

(84) When staff, either permanent or temporary, is supplied by the Division of Services from a research pool, such personnel be assigned to a committee only upon approval of the administrative subcommittee of the committee;

(85) The Judiciary, Education, and Health and Social Services Committee in both houses be staffed on a full-time basis;

(86) Quality control over committee staff be the function of the administrator of services;

(87) In addition to the orientation session for new legislators, the secretary of the legislature hold an orientation session with each committee and its newly provided staff and

explain all the ways in which staff may be used and the resources open to the committee and staff in the legislature;

(88) A legislative handbook be prepared by the secretary of the legislature, incorporating, among other things, an inventory of legislative services and setting forth committee procedures;

(89) The administrative subcommittee be responsible for staff assignment and no committee staff member be used for any task other than the work of the committee;

(90) In cases where outside consultants are deemed necessary, a committee chairman request from either the Legislative Council Board, in the case of the joint committees, or the Assembly or Senate Operations Boards, in the case of standing committees, such authorization to employ these consultants.

To improve legislative sessions and scheduling, Eagleton recommends that:

(91) The Wisconsin legislature authorize annual sessions, the length of which will be determined by the legislature;

(92) For the present, Wisconsin continue with a biennial budget, which permits the legislature, at its discretion, to make modifications and revisions in the second year;

(93) Shortly after the election of the legislature, caucuses of both houses should meet and informally organize, so that on the first Monday in January they are ready to formalize the election of leadership;

(94) Committee chairmen and committees be decided upon and the staff of the legislative services division meet with the newly designated standing committees and begin orientation sessions;

(95) The legislature make more frequent use of the rule allowing organization of the full houses into Committees of the Whole, to hear explanations by standing committees of particularly controversial or technical legislation;

(96) Air conditioning be installed in the capitol building;

(97) Moving what previously constituted the Third Order of Business to the Fourteenth Order of Business in the new schedule. Inasmuch as amendments are automatically recorded in the journals, it is not necessary to "read them." This change is reflected in the new schedule. Under the new "Orders of Business" both houses will operate under similar procedures. In addition, bills relating to similar subject matter should be considered together;

(98) Only one person, the chief record clerk, be designated responsible for receiving amendments;

(99) Special orders be taken in sequence and receive priority over regular Orders of Business on the calendar;

(100) The rules on "Previous Question" and "Committees of Conference," be changed to read as on pages 89 to 91;

(101) The Wisconsin legislature make greater use of the existing procedure and make it more understandable by renaming the "special calendars" consent calendars;

(102) Legislative salaries be raised to $12,000 per year for rank-and-file legislators; $17,000 per year for the president pro tempore of the Senate and the speaker of the Assembly; $16,000 per year for the majority and minority leaders of the Senate; $15,000 per year for the co-chairmen and ranking minority members of the Joint Committee on Finance and assistant floor leaders; and $14,000 per year for chairmen of the party caucuses;

(103) The present per diem allowance of $15 for residence in Madison during legislative sessions be increased to $25. On the basis of rates in adequate hotels and motels in Wisconsin and on the basis of food prices which legislators must pay in even moderately priced restaurants, where they dine with their colleagues and constituents, $25 per day is not at all unreasonable;

(104) This rate of reimbursement apply for all interim and joint committee meetings;

(105) The Legislative Compensation Council be abolished or, at the very least, the legislature rather than the governor be responsible for appointments of the Council's members.

To improve legislative services Eagleton recommends that:

(106) All joint legislative services staff be organized into a single Department of the Legislature and brought under the control of a single Legislative Council Board;

(107) The Legislative Council Board (LCB); (1) determine the type and extent of tasks assigned to the Department

of the Legislature, approve its budget, issue reports and make a continuing study of possible improvements in the legislative structure, procedures, and services; (2) be empowered to conduct demonstration projects and hire outside consultants; and (3) be deemed a continuing body to keep its policies and programs in effect until change;

(108) The Legislative Council Board report annually to the legislature on the problems and progress of the legislature and particularly on the role of legislative service agencies;

(109) As "chief of staff" to the Legislative Council Board, the secretary of the legislature be provided with sufficient assistance to:

(a) serve as secretary to the Board in ethics cases:

(b) serve as secretary to the Board for its meetings;

(c) develop plans for the continuous improvement of the legislature;

(d) coordinate, with the Board's approval, the operations of legislative committees;

(e) serve as chief architect of a public relations program to bring the legislature to the people;

(f) supervise a Washington office for the legislature; and

(g) plan and conduct orientation schools for new legislators;

(110) In carrying out the Legislative Council Board's policies, the administrator of services exercise administrative control over the bureaus and review their work, but without interfering with the essential independence of their findings;

(111) An experienced assistant, with clerical staff, be provided to the administrator of services to handle payrolls, expense vouchers, and reports for the entire legislature, and an assistant to the administrator be provided to specialize in personnel in all its aspects, including recruitment, training, job classifications, and the other duties of a personnel manager;

(112) All services, facilities, and equipment for the legislature—other than those specifically attached to the chief clerks and sergeant-at-arms—be brought under a single Division of Services, and that within the Division of Services there be six major bureaus, each headed by a director, for Audit Fiscal, Legal, Library and Reference, Policy Research, and Statutory Revision;

(113) Within this Division of Services the administrator of services be empowered, with the consent of the bureau directors involved, to shift personnel to meet developing needs;

(114) Senate and Assembly divisions be established under the Senate and Assembly Operations Boards, and these divisions be composed of a Clerical Bureau and a Sergeant-at-Arms Bureau;

(115) The chief clerk of each house serve as the administrator of his respective division, an assistant chief clerk and the sergeant head their respective bureaus within that division; and these officials be nominated for their posts by their respective Boards and elected by their houses on the basis of competence to serve for the full biennium;

(116) The Classified Service include all personnel in the Division of Services, including the bureau directors, who should be appointed by the Legislative Council Board;

(117) Unclassified positions in the legislature include the secretary of the legislature and the administrator of services, the chief clerk and sergeant-at-arms of each house, the caucus analysts, assistants to legislative leaders, and the special professional, technical, or investigative experts that serve when authorized by the Legislative Council Board;

(118) In the Senate and Assembly, staffing patterns be established, by resolution early in the session, setting the number, and type and total cost of positions that are: (1) unclassified and (2) limited-term employees, and within those patterns the chief clerks, as administrators, have the authority to hire and dismiss staff, subject to possible review by their Operations Board;

(119) The administrator of services, as personnel coordinator for the Division of Services and the entire legislature, recommend position and pay classifications to the Senate and Assembly divisions; administer necessary qualifying examinations for them; assist them in recruiting their help; and work with the service agencies of other states to establish meaningful classifications, training, and experience requirements for all staff positions;

(120) Supervisors should have positive control over personnel through the granting of merit increases, promotions, training, and compensatory time off; and negative control, when needed, through reprimand, demotion, and dismissal;

(121) Appropriate training manuals for staff should be prepared by the administrator of services as part of his training program for personnel;

(122) Attempts be made to reduce overloads on the bill-drafting staff during the session by experimenting in the following ways:

    (a) dropping the fifty-first day cutoff date on the introduction of bills; or

    (b) requiring committee approval for the introduction of bills after the cutoff date; and

    (c) encouraging members to give bill drafters enough time, and reminding members of the wasted effort involved in unnecessary drafts;

(123) Bill analyses be continued and strengthened, and extended to cover: (a) a review of those analyses done outside the legislature and (b) engrossed bills and joint resolutions that contain substantial amendment;

(124) The responsibility for rendering legal opinions to the legislature be formally transferred from the attorney general to the Legal Bureau, without the legislature surrendering its right to secure additional opinions from the attorney general;

(125) The Legal Bureau provide legal counsel to standing committees in their consideration of bills, and in reviewing the rules and regulations of administrative agencies;

(126) Have primary responsibility in representing the legislature in court proceedings;

(127) Provide informal legal advice to legislators on constituents' complaints involving government agencies;

(128) The Legal Bureau should be formally required to provide parliamentarians for each house, and assist the chief clerks in recompiling rules and precedents;

(129) As a means of preserving rare documents, the legislature continue to provide funds for the microfilming of selected materials;

(130) The Reference Library Bureau be staffed to meet the increased demand on its reference service; continue, as in the past, the preparation of briefs and informational bulletins as a practical means of informing the legislature on current problems; assume the functions of indexing the bills for both houses; and provide a full-time editor for the *Blue Book*;

(131) The Legislative Research Bureau be adequately equipped to supply staff to standing and joint committees from its pool of experienced personnel;

(132) Assignment of professional staff to committees be with the approval of the Legislative Council Board and the standing or joint committees involved;

(133) Preparation of in-depth research on pending or proposed measures be continued for committees and members;

(134) Summaries and digests of committee hearings be prepared as part of the permanent record of the legislature;

(135) The rules of the Senate and Assembly prohibit amendment of correction bills from the floor; correction bills continue to be clearly distinguished from revision bills; and

both correction and revision bills be considered as early in the session as possible;

(136) The Fiscal Bureau be set up as an independent agency within the Division of Services;

(137) All estimates of quarterly allotments submitted by state agencies to the budget director of the administration also be submitted to the secretary of the Joint Committee on Finance (Director of Fiscal Bureau);

(138) The secretary of the Joint Committee on Finance review all estimates and advise the co-chairman of the Joint Committee on Finance, if he has reason to question, whether legislative intent has been properly interpreted, or if he has reason to believe the allotment is more than is needed to carry out the intent of the legislature;

(139) The Fiscal Bureau assist the Joint Committee on Finance in establishing the sequence and timing of subjects taken up at hearings on the budget;

(140) After enactment of the budget, the Joint Committee on Finance provide a summary projecting and describing its impact on the state;

(141) The Fiscal Bureau be able to request special audits by the Audit Bureau with the approval of the Joint Committee on Finance and the Legislative Council Board;

(142) The Fiscal Bureau, with the approval of the Joint Committee on Finance and the Legislative Council Board, be authorized to hire outside consultants as needs arise;

(143) The role of administering, expediting, and 'policing' the preparation of fiscal notes be transferred from the Department of Administration to the Fiscal Bureau; or

(144) At the option of the presiding officer, a member be able to have a fiscal note analyzed by the Fiscal Bureau and printed and distributed in the same manner as an amendment to a bill;

(145) Where amendments have apparently increased or decreased state revenue, appropriations, or fiscal liability, the engrossed bill be required to carry a fiscal note similar to an original bill;

(146) Fiscal notes include estimates of fiscal impact on the next biennium wherever appropriate and possible;

(147) State agencies attach worksheets to fiscal notes showing the calculations used to formulate final figures;

(148) The Audit Bureau:

    (a) conduct audits on a two-year, rather than a three-year, cycle;

    (b) be provided funds for performance auditing staff even beyond its budget request for the next biennium;

    (c) report annually on its operations;

    (d) be empowered to use outside accounting firms with the approval of the Joint Committee on Finance and the Legislative Council Board;

(149) The Joint Committee on Finance assume "sponsorship" of the Audit Bureau's work and:

> (a) provide periodic comment on audit reports and make recommendations thereon to the legislature;
>
> (b) report on the status of the auditor's recommendations;
>
> (c) collaborate with and keep the Audit Bureau fully informed of all its actions;

(150) The responsibility for developing performance standards be part of the planning and budgeting function of the operating agencies, with the assistance of the Bureau of Budget and Management;

(151) As a first step toward performance auditing the Audit Bureau should:

> (a) audit an increasing number of management controls;
>
> (b) begin assembling figures on basic maintenance costs;
>
> (c) appoint specialists for data processing;
>
> (d) encourage internal audits;

(152) An Audit Advisory Committee be established to advise the auditor on problems and standards for audits of state agencies and to comment constructively on the work of the Audit Bureau;

(153) For each party caucus staffs from the Senate and Assembly be merged at least on an experimental basis, to provide greater efficiency;

(154) A director of caucus staff be appointed by his party's members on the Legislative Council Board;

(155) The director, in turn, appoint the rest of the caucus staff with the consent of his party members on the Legislative Council Board;

(156) The director of the Research Bureau, or his deputy, be made general director of the intern program, be given the time and support to make the program work, and be available to interns and their immediate supervisors each day;

(157) An orientation and rotation program be worked out to train interns at the beginning of their employment;

(158) Training of interns be continued on the job with the help of their immediate (staff) supervisors, seminars, rotation of their work as desired, and counseling by the director of interns;

(159) Interns be given a title (research aide, e.g.) other than intern when they assume a regular assignment;

(160) An orientation conference for new (and old) members be held as soon as practicable after election day, with an additional session in early January if desired, together with subsequent evening meetings;

(161) The conference cover how to operate a legislator's office, how to use the legislative services available, how to keep one's constituents informed, and provide background information on substantive issues; one segment of the conference be used to discuss legislative ethics; field trips emphasize

visits to hospitals, penitentiaries, slum areas, and other locations that have not normally been seen by new legislators; a "buddy system" be tried to assist new men, particularly on problems of procedure on the floor; orientation manuals be prepared for use during the conference and later; evening seminars on major social problems be considered in cooperation with the University of Wisconsin; and food, lodging, and transportation be provided all legislators for the meetings;

(162) Both houses have a verbatim transcript of proceedings; daily proof sheets be available for validation the next day if possible; and the entire record be indexed and bound at the end of each session;

(163) Minutes be prepared for all standing and joint standing committee meetings.

To improve Legislative ethics, Eagleton recommends that:

(164) The proposed code of prohibition on acceptance of any "gift, favor, or service" be adopted;

(165) The bribery law be strengthened through enactment of a bill eliminating "corrupt intent" or "guilty mind" as a necessary condition for finding violation;

(166) The present lobbying law's ban on even small gifts be maintained without change;

(167) The proposed code be amended to prohibit "soliciting" as well as "accepting" gifts, favors, or services after the fact, or to influence subsequent acts;

(168) The prohibition on "favors" include restrictions on the granting of economic opportunities as well as excessive compensation to legislators and employees;

(169) A prohibition on a legislator's use of his official position "to obtain special privileges" be adopted;

(170) When representing themselves or clients before state agencies:

    (a) legislators not appear for compensation before state agencies subject to review by committees of which the legislator is a member;

    (b) legislators be prohibited from seeking franchises or licenses in short supply;

    (c) all requests from legislators to agencies (other than those seeking general information above) be made a matter of public record;

(171) Whenever state contracts are involved:

    (a) legislators, their families, and business associates avoid contracting with the state on any matters where their interest was substantial as defined by the Joint Legislative Ethics Committee;

    (b) public notice and competitive bidding apply in all circumstances where a legislator has an interest;

    (c) disclosure be made to the legislature and regulatory agencies of a legislator's interest in firms contracting with the state, providing that the interest and the size of the contract are both above certain minimums;

(172) The proposed prohibition on a legislator's use of confidential information for gain be adopted;

(173) No legislator or legislative employee accept employment where a principal duty is to promote legislation;

(174) All lobbyists affiliated in business with legislators be forced to disclose this affiliation as part of their registration;

(175) A Joint Legislative Ethics Committee (JLEC) be established as an advisory committee to the Legislative Council Board (LCB);

(176) The JLEC be composed of an expanded LCB, serving ex officio, plus three public members appointed by eminent officials outside the legislature;

(177) Complainants be required only to file complaints in writing with the JLEC;

(178) The JLEC be empowered to:

    (a) adopt its own rules of evidence;

    (b) decide when meetings or hearings should be open and when and in what manner reports and findings should be made public;

    (c) initiate its own complaints;

    (d) recommend penalties for unauthorized disclosure of committee information;

(179) The JLEC should recommend additions to the joint rules that clarify and interpret the code of ethics;

(180) The JLEC should issue advisory opinions, with the identity of individuals protected; collect them for subsequent publication; and issue an annual report on its activities;

(181) The JLEC consider:

    (a) formulating additional guideline codes on ethical principles for legislators and ethical principles for special interest groups and close economic associates of legislators;

    (b) a prohibition on supplemental compensation and privately financed expense funds for legislators;

    (c) a prohibition on "conduct unbecoming a legislator";

    (d) a prohibition on a member voting in cases of "substantial" interest;

(182) The Code be amended to provide for a plan of limited disclosure of assets, income, and business interests;

(183) The JLEC undertake a continuing program of education on the ethics code among members and staff of the legislature, lobbyists, and the public at large.